Sarah's Choice
1828–1832

Ramsay MacMullen

Sarah's Choice
1828–1832

Windfall Software

Also by Ramsay MacMullen

Sisters of the Brush: Their Family, Art, Life and Letters 1797–1833

MacMullen first pages   2001/1/17 10:03   v6.0a   p. ii

Windfall Software

Sarah's Choice

1828–1832

Ramsay MacMullen

PastTimes Press 2001

MacMullen first pages 2001/1/17 10:03 v6.0a p. iii   Windfall Software

Design & composition: Windfall Software, using ZzTEX.

Publisher's Cataloging-in-Publication
  (Provided by Quality Books, Inc.)

MacMullen, Ramsay, 1928–
    Sarah's choice, 1828–1832 / Ramsay MacMullen. — 1st
ed.
    p. cm.
    Includes bibliographical references and index.
    ISBN 0-9658780-1-5
    1. Woolsey, Sarah Dwight, 1828–1832—Correspondence.
2. Women intellectuals—New York—Biography. 3. Women
intellectuals—New York—History—19th century. 4. New
York (State)—Intellectual life—19th century.
5. United States—Intellectual life—1783–1865. 6. United
States—Civilization—1783–1865. 7. New York (N.Y.)—
Intellectual life—19th century. I. Title.
F123.M33 2001   974.7'03

                                      QBI00-902045

Published by PastTimes Press, 25 Temple Court, New Haven, Connecticut.

Printed in the United States of America.

Contents

v

Figures

MacMullen first pages   2001/1/17 10:03   v6.0a   p. vii   Windfall Software

Preface

*A*ffective history requires an unusual kind of source-material. It must show the *force* of feelings that invest events and situations. Sources able to convey that to a reader are hard to find. One may, as Dr. Johnson tells us, "turn over half a library to make one book"—one may check the inventory of many hundreds of collections of family correspondence, and read many thousands of letters in many research centers.[1] But the fifty-odd letters that form the throbbing heart of this book reward the search.

The most casual readers of the story here may find pleasure in being touched, as I hope; they may satisfy their curiosity about so great a city as New York, seen here in its adolescence; or they may enjoy the challenge of trying to understand two lovers' relationship, its language, and the reception it received. The whole indeed may be read as a short novel, oddly similar to Henry James' *Washington Square (The Heiress)*.

But historians, too, may profit quite as much from a reading of exactly this sort, to open up the deepest levels of causation.

To explain: it is not only such persons as Savonarola or Tyndale, Julia Ward Howe or William Lloyd Garrison, that some strong feeling sets at odds with established values around them. We are used to seeing history made by such conflicts; but the past can be explained through the conflicts of quite unheroic persons, too—just such as Sarah Dwight Woolsey and her Hunn Carrington Beach, with her father in the wings playing an ultimately decisive role. Individually these three have no importance; there is nothing about them on a grand scale; but the needs for which they are ready to risk a great deal of personal happiness—needs, therefore, evidently felt to the heart, and the focus of the pages that follow—were widely shared in their society, centered in quite everyday concerns: *how to respond to the attractions of European culture, how to choose a partner for life, how the generations should relate to each other, how eccentricities should be*

MacMullen first pages 2001/1/17 10:03 v6.0a   p. ix

Windfall Software

disciplined. For the very reason that such choices were everyday, and the protagonists quite ordinary people, together they hold historical interest, quite as much as the interest to be found in some important individual. By definition, what is ordinary repeats itself innumerably. It forms, as it expresses, an entire society.

The affect surrounding the choices in these pages appears with unusual clarity, a fact giving the correspondence an unusual value. For surely actions that any historian would like to understand, whether they are repeated and ordinary or are rather significant, singly, are not wholly determined on a rational calculation of material benefit. Surely not— wholly or even at all. They are rather urged by indignation, loyalty, hope, belligerence, pity, an appetite for love or approval, for influence over others or for adventure.[2] If their expression is blocked, if conflict appears, then the force of this urge may appear, too.

We know this well, simply by looking within ourselves. Yet commonly with the records that an historian handles no similar in-feeling is possible. Participants only appear *doing* something, without explanation; they are inarticulate, they are hardly in the habit of analyzing and candidly writing down what moves them; or if they do offer some explanation, it will be long on the rational side, short on the emotional.

The record, then, to be whole and true must be filled out; and this, we ordinarily do by asking, What emotions would be at work in ourselves if we were to be seen behaving as those people did in the past? Tolstoy or Solzhenitsyn, reaching back some generations to exactly the same sources that historians have always had on their desks before them, of 1812 or 1914, may be allowed such a train of thought, or of imagining. They can tell us what moved the participants; and we believe them. We are satisfied, because we are made by their art to feel, that they are right; and we offer no resistance. They are novelists. Novelists may attribute feelings to their characters *ad lib*.[3]

Historians, on the other hand, can rarely venture beyond brief bare assertions: "there was widespread dismay," "the king's decision provoked a strong reaction," "anger on the Left carried all before it." Thus far they may go only by inference from what appears in the record as observed fact—visible action.

If they insist on their interpretation, it must be quantified: so many men volunteering for the front, proving the national will; so many fortunes lost in war, showing the pain of it; or, in peace, so many emigrants venturing abroad, showing dissatisfactions, or belonging to an average congregation in one sect or another, or subscribing to this or that newspaper or novel; or so many years of penal servitude assigned to a given crime, implying the perceived gravity of it; and so forth. Social-scientific in appearance, even such totals calibrate only the surface of the past, no more than that. Only science in the laboratory really looks beneath, *quantitatively*, at eye-blink, blood-pressure, or focus-group responses among persons chosen for special study. Historians have no laboratory. The past is not that, no part of it is. At the root of things they want to understand, the causes that they suppose—"indignation, loyalty, belligerence," in the catalogue I offered a page earlier, or communal routines and values—cannot be further evaluated. They can at best be inferred and then named.

Unless—unless sources can be found that analyze or candidly confess to motive, all feelings included. Such are the letters informing us of Sarah's choice. Like a novel, they are full of expressive language, begging to be read with the same sensibilities that *The Heiress* or any work of fiction invites, so as to produce a vicarious experience of the three protagonists' various thoughts and impulses. To evaluate and describe them as history seems almost to require not the historian's but the novelist's art.[4]

Focus on only a trio of people is not too narrow to be of use. It rather allows clarity and detail to the point of demonstration. The choices examined in these pages must differ according to time and place, age, sex, class, or religion. The participants are after all not living on a desert island, acting out mere biological urges. They are the product of a community, they respond to it. So, for example, in the study of courtship or the family, the collecting of information from all over some vast region, indiscriminately and without context, can help in our understanding hardly at all. It can distinguish America from Borneo, no more than that.[5] Fortunately for the editor of Sarah's letters to Carrington, they are surrounded by a thousand others of the family's papers, crisscrossing the inner and outer circles of their acquaintance, defining life and values. They are to be combined with hundreds more in the Way-Champlain correspondence from the same time and place, thousands of pages of Joseph Scoville's reminiscences, likewise of New York and of about the same social strata, and John Pintard's journal kept for his daughter and sent her in installments as letters.[6] It is therefore possible to picture the actors within a certain quite wide and very influential community, to which they respond and of which they are all three representative.

In short, letters and the sources around them offer something close to those social-scientific focus groups of semi-quantifying demonstration. But they may offer an interesting story, too.

On the following page, I offer a view of the various *dramatis personae*—the more important individuals in bold letters. My object is, first, to place them in their interconnections; but some readers will only be put off by the tangled web. It serves, however, a second purpose: it brings out at a glance the highly compressed and cohesive character of the world in which the story is set.

As my third chapter will show, there was a great concentration of commercial influence here, not by chance but by the nature of relationships. Or consider the concentration in the realm of higher education: besides William Samuel Johnson the elder (1727–1819), like his father in turn a president of Columbia, there are three other college presidents shown here and still another off-stage (a son of Jonathan Edwards; see below, chapter 3 at nn. 1 and 3). Whatever the young republic may have been in other regions or spheres, at least Sarah's world was no free-wheeling meritocracy. Decisions here, Sarah's choice among them, were made with due regard for who was who, a quite oppressive regard for relationships that both secured and confined.

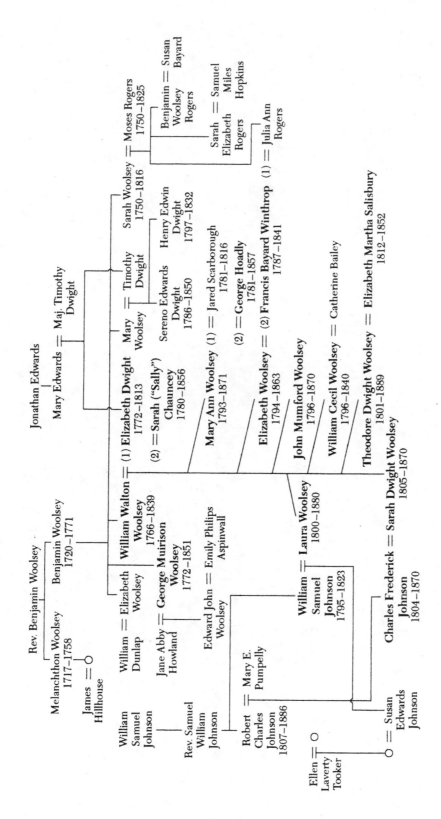

Sarah's Choice
1828–1832

Sarah's First Choice

unn Carrington Beach, calling himself Carrington, was Sarah's first choice—she, Sarah Dwight Woolsey (1805–70) of New York. They met most likely at the church they both attended, the Fifth Avenue Presbyterian as it was later called, toward the beginning of 1828. At any rate, by September when the earliest of her surviving letters to him was written, she could speak of an acquaintance that had promised "intimacy" between them from at least the spring of the year.

He was not an obvious young man for her to fix on. As both his parents were dead, and he an unknown to the city without any line of occupation that might have introduced him to her father or brothers, he had nothing but himself to recommend him. That proved, however, enough for all.

He had come from upstate New York, Utica, halfway between Schenectady and Lake Ontario—had started out as a clerk there in a private firm, moved on to a local bank, and thence to New York.[1] In New York by the end of 1827 he had been taken on as a partner in their auction-house

1

by Sarah's brother William and George Ward. The house had its offices at the corner of Pearl and Pine Streets. Ward had the most business experience but William's name led off because that was, through his father, so well known and would help to attract customers and credit. As to Beach, he was of the right political party as his partners were not, to get a license as an auctioneer. Every house needed one, just as a brokerage must have its own member of the stock exchange.[2]

The firm's location was prime: surrounded on the other three corners by three other auction houses, not offering competition to *Woolsey Ward & Beach* so much as concentrating the market into the most vibrant point of commerce to be found in all the city, perhaps in the entire country. Here could be found the people who handled cargoes of ships putting in to the city, the people who found wholesalers and retailers to bid for those cargoes and who acted in concert with anyone willing to advance money to a bidder—middlemen playing an absolutely essential role in the economy.

Membership in such a firm gave Beach that natural entrée to society, indeed at an enviable level, which he had lacked on his first arrival a year or two earlier. And everyone liked him, inside and beyond the Woolsey family. Remarks to that effect were eagerly noted by Sarah and passed on to him in her letters. Her brother Theodore Dwight Woolsey (1801–89), severe and cerebral but fair-minded, at a moment when he might have been expected to sum up Beach's character in a hostile or at least a grudging manner, instead challenged anything of that sort: "I consider Mr. B. to be a very amiable and kind man with respectable sense and such a one as would make a better husband than 3/4 of the men you see in the world."[3]

There were plenty of agreeable young men of business moving about in the Woolsey's world, rich and polished as it was. What set Beach apart from them all was his having spent some substantial period in Paris in 1825.[4] As will appear in the next chapter, he knew French well enough to read its literature for pleasure; knew some Spanish and Italian, too—else why would Sarah address remarks to him in those languages?—and on his return from abroad was sufficiently colored by his experience, or pleased about it, to be accused of Frenchified manners. In time they wore off.[5]

Just how he decided on a Paris sojourn in the first place and how he could afford it (apparently enjoying no very great wealth) doesn't appear in the record. It seems an odd thing for him to have done with what money he had; but it put him in the forefront of a movement of considerable importance to the cultural history of the young republic. Where, earlier, there had been only the rare adventurer imitating the Grand Tour, now from the twenties of the nineteenth century a sharply increasing flow of Americans directed their curiosity across the Atlantic, some like Theodore for specific purposes of study, a larger number for no single set purpose at all.

Theodore had once intended to prepare himself for a career in the church, and was in fact ordained, after graduation from Yale and further work at the Princeton Theological Seminary. Being interested about his studies, however, or rather, being extremely good at them and in fact much better at learning than at maintaining so deep and high a piety as he thought he should, he chose for a while to defer an active ministry. Off he went, then, to the home of theology, ancient Greek, and textual criticism, Germany, in the spring of 1827. He stayed for many academic terms, adding travel in Switzerland, Italy, France, the Netherlands, and Britain, till his return home in the fall of 1830. By then he was reasonably at home in the modern foreign languages, too.

To explain such pilgrimages as his, the names that are most often mentioned are Mme. de Staël, first, because of her much-read and early-Englished book "On Germany" (1814), copiously excerpted by a New York periodical of that year and well calculated to open people's eyes to the intellectual riches in the country she describes; then, George Ticknor who spent 1815–17 there and returned to teach very influentially at Harvard; next, perhaps, Edward Robinson in Europe in 1826–30 and thereafter in the Andover and Union Theological Seminaries as a professor of theology.[6] Robinson in Halle became acquainted with Theodore, they corresponded, passed around the names of other Americans in other nearby universities;[7] at the same time, Theodore's uncle Henry Edwin Dwight was winding up his long residence in Europe, German universities included (1823–28), and preparing his notes for what became his *Travels in the North of Germany* (1829).[8] The Woolsey family followed and discussed the reception of this book, about which Theodore's father was rather defensive: it might be taken, though quite wrongly, as not sufficiently orthodox in its religious views.[9]

The relevance of all this to Sarah's romance, let it be clear, lies in the opening of her mind to things beyond the ordinary purview of herself and her close circle, brought home to her by someone she specially listened to; for she and Theodore enjoyed a specially affectionate relationship. She "idolized" him as a teenager, and a decade later could write, "I believe Theodore you understand me better than most people do, and you know that I love you better than almost anyone else."[10] In the intervening years, in the family correspondence, he had addressed a great many letters to her from his European days, letters of course shared with his parents and siblings but meant especially for her eyes. He was continually sending books home in foreign languages, too, which she could then get at in his library; and the talk around the dinner table noted this, and approved and validated all of his opening of his mind, and by implication, hers as well, to the European world.

Theodore's career choice had at first been made in the religiously fervent days of the earlier 1820s, a second Awakening, to which he and his closest friends responded eagerly.[11] In due course, a decade later, his fiancée would write to him in the same strain, sure of the reception of her ardor; and the Woolsey parents were of the same mind if more measured: Mr. Woolsey very active in lay activities, as will appear later, and Mrs. Woolsey a great one for long sermons twice a day, however taxing to her health; their son William Cecil (1796–1840) was strong for the church; Sarah, too, like the rest of her family.[12] "Dr. [James M.] Matthews," she writes to Theodore concerning their friend and minister, "has another daughter. I have lately attended his little class which I find very interesting as inducing me to study the scriptures more attentively than I have ever done before. I think it is much to be lamented that children acquire habits of reading the bible much too carelessly. I am sure many parts with which I have always been familiar from childhood pass through my mind without conveying any meaning."

This piety, however, which took her brother to Germany, along with other seminary graduates of the 1820s, was in herself much less pressing and of course could issue in no academic degree or ecclesiastical career. She took her bible classes, she spent her Sundays in a religiously respectful way, she certainly approved of Theodore's theological studies abroad; but for herself, the attractions of European culture were much less focused— in fact quite unconnected with her faith. They were rather all over the map, so far as she could, bit by bit, come to understand it.

In this way she joined a far wider movement of the New to the Old World—joined, if only intellectually; for her travels were to be very long deferred. It carried her luckier friends and others like them in great numbers across the Atlantic. They visited France and Italy and Britain, occasionally Spain and other parts: a handful at a time in the mid-1820s, soon in scores and scores. Philip Hone was an early one, a millionaire enjoying retirement in his forties, Mr. Woolsey's associate in various city ventures, doing the Grand Tour with his family. In Mr. Woolsey's Friendly Club were three other veterans of the experience, perhaps the best known, Washington Irving and James Fenimore Cooper who wrote home about it in letters or essays; also Samuel Miller. Eventually (1832) Emerson went abroad, with many others by that time.[13] The revolution in Paris in 1830 was much reported, if only because of Lafayette's role in it; that of 1848, by Emerson and others. But that takes the story past Sarah's.

It's to be noted that among the early travelers bent only on pleasure were Sereno Dwight, uncle on her mother's side, and Nathaniel Chauncey, uncle on her step-mother's side, of whom the latter was a quite generous correspondent in the 'twenties, and often a visitor in the house for long stays after his return. A friendly, chatty, kind man with ample means to do almost anything he pleased except work. Further, too, her aunt and uncle George Woolsey in Italy for economy's sake, from 1829, but in touch with the New York relatives; Theodore's father-in-law-to-be, Josiah Salisbury in his younger days; in the later 'twenties, Charles Frederick Johnson, cousin to Sarah's brother-in-law William Samuel Johnson; and any number of her friends: an uncle of Theodore's bride, and the Sheldons, Van Ness, Howlands, Benjamin Curtis, and so on.[14] Theodore in Rome described to his family the American community celebrating Washington's birthday there in 1830, and his friend Yates the year before had found "a great many Americans in Italy; indeed a great many more than I wanted. There is nothing more unpleasant to me in travelling than being obliged to move in a flock." An ageless complaint.

How gladly would Sarah have been a member of that flock! When Theodore mentioned perhaps visiting Italy, "I could hardly help a selfish feeling of regret that you had changed your mind." With him, she could have at least seen it vicariously.[15] Europe sounded so exciting, its scenes so inspiring or curious, its ornaments and manners so superior, in certain respects—so, returning voyagers told everyone who would listen. They had, by their voyages, indeed taken on that superiority themselves and themselves become enviable. They all came from among the well-to-do, they were all to some degree or to a great degree prominent in the city and naturally talked about, their ways were closely watched and remarked on.

They could speak in tongues: uncle Henry Dwight to Theodore in a single letter writing in Italian, then French, then German, and signing himself "Henrich, cugino caro;" on which behavior, imitating his bits of foreign languages dropped into conversation, Sarah smiles: "Henry Dwight goes on like mad about that subject," his search for a woman eligible for his hand. "He cannot say two words without 'revenant aux moutons,' matrimony & the loss of hair are his topics."[16] His pleasure in his accomplishment was quite innocent, not a means of mounting above others, innocent like Mrs. Sedgwick's or Susan Cooper's dropping quite needless French phrases into their letters home from Paris, where the latter and the Fenimore Coopers were resident, and where, for example, they could visit the celebrated Mrs. Opie "sans cérémonie." The city held such luminaries of literature, or it had once been their home: from Racine to Krüdener. It was of course the home of French theater, too, of which, over the course of Sarah's early years, William Dunlap adapted ten scripts for the American stage.[17]

But those without the fashionable command of more than English were not likely to see its display as innocent. The novelists of the time are the best indicators of the fact. When they want to present a character of irritating conceit, someone anxious to climb in the world or obnoxiously already at the top, they give that person a sprinkling or a flood of French phrases in conversation, whether the scene is English (Bulwer Lytton's *Pelham* will do) or, more to the point, New York.[18] Mrs. Sedgwick, setting the example in her best-sellers, felt it natural or necessary to drop in French words and phrases. In her *Clarence* alone she uses some scores of them for artistic purposes in scenes depicting show-offs and phonies. She was peculiarly able to teach: a woman authoritatively representative of *haut ton*, as she would have said, making clear that one should know French, and correctly, and how could one be known to know it except by using it a bit? but one must not use it too much; and Italian and Latin were wonderful as extras, but might best be translated.[19]

Foreign visitors to the city noticed a preoccupation with fashionable clothing, for the most part meaning Parisian, among women who could afford to discriminate.[20] The shops were filled with such imported luxuries, as a glance at the advertisements in any newspaper will show. No doubt all these gave some foundation to a curiosity about European civilization which might be expressed in language-learning. Languages, however, as they did not come easily, remained a mark of the privileged. They could be acquired on the spot, overseas, as Theodore chose to do; or in the very popular *Norman Leslie*, the hero's development is completed by a long period in Italy, there to pick up French and German as well as the language of the country.[21] Yet the ordinary way to acquire French was to find one's self a tutor among the immigrant population. He (I find no mention of women) would come to one's house and give lessons. A famous one was credited with the instruction of many thousands of pupils between 1827 and 1836.[22] That was how girls received such education; and the young of the other sex could attend *l'Ecole économique* from the early 1800s, and universities at a later date—later than Sarah's adolescence and her early womanhood.[23] She herself no doubt, like her older sister, had started French instruction at home while still a girl.[24]

How she added to those beginnings from her later teens on appears in her letters to Theodore and her uncle Nathaniel Chauncey abroad. She doesn't mention any teachers, then, in the winter of 1823–24, but had evidently made progress in Italian sufficient to enjoy the poets most in favor, and was ploughing through *Don Quixote*.[25] The following winter she began on French; for "the acquisition of languages is my favourite pursuit and I mean the most useful tongues in Europe shall be familiar to me."[26] By the spring of 1826 she was quoting French proverbs and writing whatever she had to say with some degree of confidence, if not a high degree of correctness; by the winter of 1826, was able to speak, indeed was singled out at a party as perhaps the only guest who could speak, in his own language to a visiting Frenchman.[27] She kept up reading in all three languages. But her studies had tapered off by the spring of 1830 and she was discouraged.[28]

She could always use French to her brother John, who evidently would understand it; and so too would her uncle Nathaniel; but for a real fellow in her efforts she could count only on Theodore. He of course was out of the country until the fall of 1830, and, when he returned, busy on various affairs of his own life. Sarah's pertinacity seems all the more to her credit for having been so little supported by anyone around her. More or less on her own she had come to know Cervantes and other Spanish authors,[29] Dante and especially Tasso among various Italian poets, with minor prose works thrown in,[30] and a good number of the most approved French authors: Saint Pierre's *Paul et Virginie* both in its original language and Spanish, Voltaire, Bossuet, playwrights; novels like Mme de Krüdener's *Valérie* (1803).[31] In the literature of her own language, her tastes were wide and rather predictable: *Robinson Crusoe* remembered from childhood, Scott, Boswell, Byron, Wordsworth, Emerson, Lady Mary Montague, various works of history and biography, sermons, novelists: several Bulwer Lytton novels, Mrs. Sedgwick, Mrs. Sigourney, Fenimore Cooper, and others. She made good use of a local subscribers' library.[32]

The Woolseys were by no means illiterate. Sarah's older sister Laura read novels, their mother confessed to "not holding the pen of a ready writer" but liked to be read to, and her husband read when he had time, often in religious publications.[33] Reading aloud at home was the most common way in which literature was passed on to the rising generation, more so than in schools, and there are many mentions and scenes of the time to illustrate the habit. Some may be found in popular novels: lovers read to each other.[34] It was by her family's habit that a mind such as Sarah's would have received its initial stimulation.

She had opinions. Fifteen years old, and already expressing them, when a book irritated her![35] She continued to hold them and to develop them with more critical insight. In due course, the names Schiller and Schlegel turn up in her letters to Theodore (it is he to whom almost all her mentions of her reading are addressed, he doubtless who had suggested these names to her).[36] An older brother who read literature for his post-graduate degree and then for his living, as a teacher at Yale in the early 1820s and then from 1831 on as a professor of Greek, proved a wonderful sounding-board, a source of advice on what next to read and what to think, if Sarah's own very independent mind sometimes hesitated.[37] He himself wrote and, under a pen-name, even published poetry, as so many enthusiasts did in those days, or wished they could do, in New York periodicals; and she too wrote poetry, specimens of which appear in her letters to him and in the next chapter, offered to her Carrington Beach.[38]

Alone among the various arts and accomplishments that young women might claim, the writing of poetry survives in the record. We cannot hear the singing in people's homes or in the city's amusement parks; performances of what passed for serious music are all lost, too, though their quality may be guessed from the popularity of the composer most favored, Ignaz Josef Pleyel. Whatever the style of lectures at the Athenaeum, those that Sarah listened to cannot be recovered. Only her versification remains, in some two hundred lines scattered among her letters (nos. 6f., 35, and 57). They have no great merit. Readers in the next chapter may therefore skip over them with understandable impatience. Yet, as their author says, they do offer a way of knowing her. They show something of her views about a wife's role and extend a promise of warm affection and duteous submission. One poem in the sixth letter tells a tale of dramatic grief, and demonstrates great sensibility if not literary powers.

Still twenty, she wrote to the agreeable uncle Nathaniel in Paris, "J'ai lu dernièrement quelques scènes des tragédies de Racine, avec bien de plaisir. Je lis à présent la philosophie de l'âme par Stewart, parceque je pense que je suis trop gaie, et c'est pourquoi je me suis mets à la philosophie morale et si ceci ne suffriroit pas, j'essayerai ce que peut faire les mathématiques. Je ne doute pas de parvenir à ce bût, au moins quand je serais vieille." The effusion is genuinely funny, a glimpse of wry humor in a family not given to much laughter (Theodore hopeless in that regard, her father occasionally able to laugh, but only at, not with, whatever seemed amusing—not a "gai" household).[39] It is pleasant to gain a little sense of the edge of her mind, as it may be called: the sharp edge.[40]

She attended lectures at the city's Athenaeum and could have heard, in a typical monthly series, Bryant on poetry, Samuel F. B. Morse on painting, the splendid Columbia Professor of Moral Philosophy John McVickar on "Beauty," John Hone on "Commerce," and the Reverend Dr. James M. Mathews, her own family's minister, discussing whatever struck his fancy under the title "Anniversary Discourse." Several of the lecturers were members with her father in the Friendly Club. She also attended lectures at the National Academy of Art, with a practicum attached; looked at the paintings in an exhibition; attended the opera (*Der Freyschuetz*), though she lacked at home the music that her friends often enjoyed. Young women of privilege commonly got some; but it was generally not an art for men, and her father arranged no lessons for her.[41]

Sarah gave no indication of special talents; but what her situation offered she generally took advantage of, to make herself what we may call a cultivated human being. She had a thirst for it. In the language of the time, however, what she had made of herself was that dubious thing, a *bas-bleu*, an intellectual female. She was already recognizable as bookish when she was sixteen, "an empress of literature." As a young woman, in her very disclaimers—sincere enough and indeed sad enough—she gave proof of her unusual enlightenment: "I always feel," she wrote to her uncle Nathaniel, "such a sense of my own limited sources of information that I am sure I can impart nothing adequate to what I receive, and sometimes I feel that the very few informed men I see must converse with me as you would talk to a little child whom you have discovered to be tolerably hopeful and wish to improve."[42] She went on, "These feelings however . . . do not prevent my enjoying highly the conversation of such gentlemen as your friend," a man fresh back from Europe. Travellers like this she was likely to enjoy especially. Conjecture turned them into beaux.[43]

She judged other people a little too uncompromisingly (her sister-in-law was amiable, "mais ce n'est pas un esprit fort," as she could say privately to Theodore). She was, however, aware of the risk in such judgements and worried about "that nonsensical story of my talents & acquirements which

Fig. 1

made [Martha Salisbury's] cousin say she felt afraid of me."[44] The recipient of the confession was Theodore, and Martha was his fiancée, evidently put off by Sarah and ready to snub her.

A few years earlier, Sarah's elder sister Laura had described her to Theodore with faint praise: "Sarah's manners have much improved since you went away [to Europe in 1827]. She is gradually getting rid of angular awkwardness & converses with more than common facility."[45] No passage in the correspondence allows us to get closer than this to a portrait of our subject. Yet it fits very well with the other hints and glimpses just given, of a girl and then of a woman too clever, too well read, too spirited in conversation. And plain? Did she resemble, perhaps, not the handsome Laura but the formidable Theodore (fig. 1)? If she had been blessed with good looks, at some point there would be some mention for us to notice; daughter of an extremely rich man, she was never beset by suitors.

Describing a relative, old John Pintard wrote in 1816, she "is a lady of great intellectual accomplishments, but I do not think in any degree obtrusive as is too often charged against ladies of superior acquirements. This may arise from the envy of their inferiors."[46] They should rather be welcomed to relieve "the general insipidity of fashionable society," declares a woman of that world in one of Mrs. Sedgwick's novels, "if the persons who constitute it were generally infected with Miss Mayo's zeal for mental accomplishments; but then, one does so shrink from the danger of being called a blue, when one sees, as in Miss Mayo's case, that even youth, beauty, and fashion, cannot save one from the odious appellation." When the heroine, Gertrude Clarence, forcefully disagrees, "'Lord!' said John Smith to Major Daisy, in a sort of parenthetical whisper, 'is Miss Clarence a blue? I never heard her talk about books.'" The subject is further hashed out, to the benefit of the gentle reader who might feel in need of support against the prejudices of the social world. It recurs in other scenes of fiction. Difficult it was to please, certainly, for the likes of Sarah. Her tastes set her apart, no doubt uncomfortably, from the rest of her sex in the upper class, among whom "all are occupied in les details de ménage and nursing children," and "devote almost their whole life to the management of their household and the education of their children." Such were the impressions of their visitors of the same class from abroad, not altogether different from Sarah's own verdict on "those temperate zones, the literary circles (s'il y en a un) of our metropolis."[47]

The division between the sexes of the New York upper class, encouraging in women a manageable ignorance and docility, left men in charge of higher civilization; and those so inclined gave it such time as they could spare. Some with a college education had taken advantage of the privilege. George Templeton Strong, thanks to his diary, comes naturally to mind as an example such as few youngsters can have been. His father (Mr. Woolsey's acquaintance and Greenwich Street neighbor) had given him a strong start at home. At Columbia, especially thanks to the Philolexian Society, the boy found a few friends like himself. But such were rare. Many leading men among the commercial classes were rather self-made. Mr. Woolsey had finished his schooling in his earliest teens. Later, he and his lordly friend James Kent belonged not only to the Friendly Club with its roster of much admired writers and artists, but served as vice presidents of the Athenaeum. It is hard to know just what this meant. They with their families paid tribute to enterprises of this sort. Some read quite widely. Kent admired Friedrich Klopstock's verse.[48] Philip Hone, of a great merchant family, in his diary commented on a recent publication of Bryant's poetry with real feeling and critical sense; John Pintard in 1818 reported to his daughter, "we are instituting a literary club" of a dozen members to meet on Saturday evenings; and in the Bread and Cheese Club that Fenimore Cooper had founded six years later, Hone and Gulian C. Verplanck, of another great merchant family, were members from the start.[49]

Their interest was genuine, undeniably; their favor most important; but their numbers few. What is much more easily discovered in contemporary reports of the city was rather the blinkered money-grubbing of the leading citizens (male), bent only on their business. "The men," meaning those prominent enough to be noticed by the discriminating traveller, "are all merchants; and commerce, although it fills the purse, clogs the brain. Beyond their counting-houses they possess not a single idea;" "the first society of New York . . . is composed of tradesmen . . . All who have made a voyage to Europe, try to ape the exclusive manners of which they have been the victims on the other side of the Atlantic; affect to value everything foreign . . . But apart from this society is that formed by the merchants, shipowners, lawyers, physicians, and magistrates of the city. This is truly American: they do not amuse themselves by apeing European manners; among them, conversation is solid and instructive, and turns upon business and the politics of the day."[50]

A word further on such views as these most commonly prevailing among the elite: hostile to trans-Atlantic airs acquired in London particularly, hostile to those idiots who had there learnt contempt for their own country and its ways; easily put off by imported elegance in the drawing room. Imagine, as does Timothy Dwight in the 1820s, the man "of flesh and blood; who intends to live by business . . . He has hitherto spent his life, perhaps, in acting vigorously in the counting-room, contending strenuously at the bar, or pursuing with diligence some other business"—how should he meet the demands of a too-delicate society? The challenge is directed particularly against manners drawn from fashionable fiction,

filled as it is with ornamental conversation and ceremony.[51] The ladies
loved this and hoped to get it from their gentlemen. Dwight finds words
for the irritation felt by these latter, generally untravelled and not very
broadly educated, against some imagined rival, "some man of art and mis-
chief," as he puts it—the very type to shine in that society in which women
made the rules; and another critic, too, the Bostonian Samuel Knapp in
1818, deplores young women's addiction to trashy stories and, as a result,
"that *penchant* of our (= we males') fair co-ordinates, that gives to fops
and coxcombs their undeserved influence." Yet on the other hand, a more
thoughtful observer John Pintard sees two sides to the matter. Or perhaps
times had changed. Comparing those in 1830 with those around 1815, he
accepts today's well established tastes, and asks,

> Pray, are not females of the present day indebted to their constant
> novel reading for their colloquial and epistolary powers? The novels
> of the modern school are generally elegant narratives and free from
> stiffness and affectation. In your time [that of his eldest daughter
> in her youth], we were not deluged with these effusions from the
> press as at present. Walter Scott has given an elevation to this class
> of writers. "What makes young ladies [like his youngest daughter,
> today] express themselves so much better than young men?" was
> a question I put to a flippant young dandy not long ago. "Because
> they are eternally talking and reading novels." There is much truth
> in this sarcastic reply, and it is fortunate when *belles* can take their
> own parts and shine well in conversation.[52]

At the heart of this brief exchange was the broader question, so often
discussed then and since, How did, or how should America look at Europe?
"I have heard of the corruption of Europe, and the total departure from
natural sentiment and moral rectitude which characterizes the great body
of refined society in that quarter of the world," wrote Fenimore Cooper in
1831. He was a man by no means ill-informed, one would have thought;
but similar impressions prevailed among others both earlier and later
whose writings were much read (the theology taught in Germany being a
scandal to itself).[53] They were naturally to be found among the Woolseys:
Theodore's mother worrying about him in "a foreign and corrupt country,"

Paris (where he indeed went to see the guillotine at work, "which was a kind of holiday"); others in the family registering their low expectations of life abroad occasionally confirmed by the horrid truth before their eyes, when they got to Paris or Germany or Italy: nakedness in paintings and statuary displayed before ladies, and widespread disregard of the Sabbath.[54] Such was the civilization hidden behind curtseys and bows and elegant speeches, making European elegance itself, suspect.

Sarah's and Carrington Beach's enjoyment of the novel *Pelham* (1828) makes real the manners so distrusted by the merchant class. Apparently the two did not give much or any time to the mass-market romances, so generally condemned by the better-educated and especially the clergy.[55] Bulwer Lytton's work was much more sophisticated. Excessively so. In what might be called a vaguely picaresque Bildungsroman, the hero who gives his name to this novel, fresh out of Cambridge, grows bored with titled ladies "discussing persons and things, poetry and china, French plays and music." He will treat himself, or rather, his father will provide "his blessing, and a check on his banker," for a stay in Paris. It should be fun. That is his intent. He decides to present himself there from the start as exquisitely stylish, witty, and polished, an invented character "because nothing appeared more likely to be remarkable among men, and therefore pleasing to women, than an egregious coxcomb." It is a role recalling that of Disraeli's Vivian Grey (1826). Pelham mingles in the best company, among the duchesse This and the baron That, "excessively enamoured of oyster paté and Lord Byron's *Corsair*." But he tires of it. In due course he returns to England, where his character evolves into something more serious. "I became more thoughtful and solidly ambitious."[56]

The English chapters include passages of literary criticism, giving the author a chance to present his ideas about some better known poets and such recent writers as Mrs. Hemans and Byron. For example, in remarks by Pelham's friend: "'It would be interesting enough,' observed Vincent, 'to trace the origin of this melancholy mania. People are wrong to attribute it to poor Lord Byron—it certainly came from Germany; perhaps Werter was the first hero of the school." And a modern critic points out the influence of Werther on Bulwer Lytton's first novel, the epistolary *Falkland* (1827): both have as heroes "delicate, charming young men of artistic

*He took her miniature from his bosom, he held it up, and earnestly
viewed it by the moon's pale ray.*

Fig. 2

temperament, intense imagination and a passion for glory [who] believe
passionately in the vast superiority of feeling and 'the heart' to reason."[57]

   Sarah and Carrington read together also the epistolary novel, *Valérie*,
whose hero Gustave carries about with him and contemplates ecstatically a
miniature of his love, painted by no less an artist than Angelica Kaufmann.
He recalls the moonlit act of the hero Alonzo in a tale of that name vastly
popular in the 1820s, illustrated by a woodcut (fig. 2). Valérie is shown by
Kaufmann in a twilit scene with the sea and an abbey in the background,
her head inclined in a sad gesture. At another moment, when she sings, the
tears well up and invade her song, she throws herself in a chair to weep.
Well may she "reproach herself for her excessive sensibility," while a critic

may rightly describe Gustave, too, as "d'une volonté d'aimer pour aimer, d'une énergie de sentiment telle qu'en vivre serait la trahir." He is like Carrington caught in a love that can never be realized.[58]

Disraeli of *Vivian Grey* and Bulwer Lytton in real life, by their ostentatious dandyism, exemplified their heroes—as, in a very discreet way, so too did Sarah and Carrington; or at least, as the next chapter will show, they not only savored and talked about *Pelham* but in some degree acted it out; and in regard to *Valérie*, aside from such details as a miniature portrait, a lock of hair, and so forth, they may even be said to have lived an epistolary novel. Being kept apart, they had no choice but to write, during most of the period of their engagement. The impact of art on life is certainly detectable.

It is detectable through the word *sensibility*, *sensibilité*; and another word, *melancholy*; and a cluster, *delicacy*, *sensitivity*, *sentiment* recalling Sterne and the popularity his works enjoyed in the period here studied— "the pathetic story of Maria," which the proper heroine in later novels cannot read aloud without a rush of sobs.[59] I illustrate the point with an echo in art of the time (fig. 3). But there was a contrary view of this just as there was of excessive polish and dandyism—condemnation of "the false delicacy and mock sensibility of a thorough novel-reader."[60] The various expressions of feeling about feeling, the written commentary on what was more consciously called *romantic*, indicate to the listener today a sharp polarity: a time of change of manners and tastes in society, some people being very strongly attracted, some equally repelled. It was hardly possible to live among the educated without responding at least inwardly to one side or the other.

How one might be repelled, and express one's distrust through one's actions, will appear in the third chapter, where the views of Sarah's father are examined. It is enough at this point only to recall the passages already used in both text and notes, with all their strong language, "odious," "disgust," and so on.

As to the attraction of the romantic, apart from the sales-figures for fiction of that sort, there is the pilgrimage to its home in Europe undertaken, though not only for this reason, by more and more Americans. That too can be roughly quantified. It constituted a significant movement.

Fig. 3

And then there is Sarah's choice, illustrative. It presents itself with its attendant affect, its curiosity and enthusiasm and devotion.

Really, when the inclination of her mind is understood—however imperfectly—it appears quite foreordained that only Carrington Beach or someone like him, some rare one, would answer her needs and longings. It was so, despite the opposition she could predict and sense around her; and once he was chosen, she could hardly let him go.

Sarah's Letters

I t is time, now, to turn to what I termed in the Preface "the throbbing heart" of this book: letters, the principal writers of which have been adquately introduced, Sarah Woolsey and (much less) Carrington Beach. As the correspondence goes on over the years in desultory fashion, a sort of story-line will be seen to emerge, with some gradually clearing character development of the two lovers; and a third person, Sarah's father, will emerge as well. Until his part in that story becomes prominent, however, I make no attempt to explain him, leaving explanation rather to my final chapter. Puzzling references I explain so far as I can, wherever they occur, but I try to keep editorial intrusion to a minimum. In that way the nature of the whole document, not a word left out or changed, can best appear.

The letters survive in a very convenient form: copied into an originally blank notebook now included among the Woolsey family papers. The pages were numbered in the corner. On the title page was printed,

A COMMON PLACE BOOK upon the Plan Recommended and
Practised by John Locke, Esq., New York, No. 10 Wall-Street, 1814

This object Carrington must have bought in preparation for his European
trip, explaining the entries on the first thirty-two pages: neat jottings to
make a sort of encyclopedia article titled *America* followed by *La Mar-
seillaise*. Then comes a blank page, and, copied out much later in an
exceptionally careful, middle-sized hand, a set of letters. Each one is given
a number. Excepting only two, the first fifty-seven are Sarah's to Carrington. They begin in the middle of things, when it had become necessary
for the two to write rather than speak to each other. They are followed by
others between Carrington and members of the Woolsey family.

The originals do not survive, nor is there any saying when they were destroyed. Unexplained and quite puzzling is the fact of the copies surviving.
It is clear from chance evidence in the family correspondence that parts
of it have disappeared which should have had as good a chance of being
kept as all the rest; but there was some weeding out of letters by a family
member; and if so, then the preservation of this letter-book quite mysti-
fies me. It shows a passage in the Woolsey history that is at least subject to
misinterpretation, or on the edge of discreditable. Or did it not seem so,
perhaps?

In any case, here it is, beginning out of the blue:

Sarah

No. 1 [page 36]   New york September 20. 1828

I have a painful task to perform which delay will only make more
so. After you left me yesterday, Mama said to me that my Father
had requested her to say that my intimacy with you would be very
displeasing to him. I spoke to her of my high opinion of you, and
then openly to my Father. I told him what passed last spring, and
that since then I had seen more of you, and liked you much, and I
wished you might at least have a trial.

I said all I could, his answer was a decided negative, without assigning a reason.

I need not express my friendship nor my deep sorrow that your happiness should be wrecked thro' my means. You understand me. I would only add what is best to be done. We cannot meet as we have done yet I would wish you to visit us occasionally, trust to my self command to make your visit less awkward. You know that no one but my parents think you have aimed at more than my friendship, so I hope that you will continue your intercourse and attentions to all my friends you have become acquainted with, and if as you have flattered me by saying you have received any opinions or motives from me which have [page 37] done you good, let me have the happiness to think them still in force, that I may not have been wholly a curse to you. I dare not hold out any hope for the future, but this course is the best for you, and do for my sake be as good and happy as you can farewell.

Carrington evidently responded to Sarah's news with defiance, or at least with a proposal that he should meet and reason with her father. She judged this useless.

Sarah

2   September 22. 1828

I fear from what you said to day that you flatter yourself, and cannot bear that you should be exposed to farther mortification through my means. My Father repeated after I wrote you his sentiments, that he wished everything to be at an end between us. I told him I should do as he pleased, which you know is my duty. I therefore fear that you will obtain nothing from the course you proposed but an opportunity to justify yourself respecting any unworthy motives, which I earnestly wish you to do, but think you may do it better after more reflection than now. I did not understand whether your confidence in W[illia]m extended to your own feelings or not. My brothers are both my best friends,[1] and you may I am sure rely on them in all things for advice and sympathy. I said nothing to them because it was <u>your</u> secret.

Sunday evening

Sarah

3 [page 38]   September 26. 1828

I am desirous of seeing you before I go to Phil[adelphi]a and do not know what day I shall go. Will you come and see me to day or Monday. I believe you are engaged to-morrow.

Yours   S.

Sarah

4.   December 24[th] 1828

I am going to the bible class in the lecture room next our Church [on Garden Street], to day at 12 o'clock, and shall remain there till 1 o'clk or half past one, and then go to my sister's [Catherine, sister-in-law]. Will you mon bon ami call there then? She will not be at home probably, but inquire for me. I would rather ask your arm from Garden Street to her house [on Pine Street], but am uncertain as to the precise time. We meet so seldom, and never when any but ordinary conversation is possible, and I have just now so many things à vous dire, that I am constrained to this démarche, although it must be confessed not quite in unison with the usual rules of your friend   S

In the letter that follows, two words should be noted: "friend," which the usage of the time could apply to a dearly loved person, one's own closest relative, father or the like; and "perfect confidence" or trusting openness, the offer of which was, too, a usage of the time expected between lovers.[2] It had not been so in the previous generation.

Sarah

5   January 1st 1829 4 o.c. P. M.

I return you the note which you gave me, and regret that Margaret's [Aspinwall's] kind heart should be disturbed as I know it must have been. She has been worried at the fear of giving you pain [page 39] and making you think ill of me and mine. The last I trust nothing but my own act can do, and hope that you have not been pained by such a rumour which has not probably reached many ears, and is the natural consequence of the restraint thrown over our intercourse after it had been more free. I <u>need</u> not satisfy on this point, but still I like perfect confidence in all things so much that I will add that I never mentioned the circumstances which gave you pain last spring except to my parents at the time I told you of it, just before I went to Phil[adelphi]a. I told W[illia]m Johnson of Papa's objections to you, and requested him to extend his friendship to you at that time, but at that moment whether my confidence in him was more full or not, I utterly forget, for I was agitated and hurried.

Do not be pained that such a thing should be said, do me the favour to believe that if fate is not very much against us both the world will one day have a proof that I am not <u>very</u> <u>much</u> determined against you. I may be obliged to go out tomorrow at half past 12 o.c. If I do and am alone I will walk through Greenwich Street, and if I have the pleasure of seeing you, you will tell me the "many things" to which you alluded this morning. One thing more in case I should not see you, I am very frequently enquired of whether the report of an [page 40] engagement between us is true. I say not, but that we are the best of friends. Is this wrong? What can I say? The tie though indirect and unacknowledged is binding on feeling and principle, and I hope makes you easy, may I not say happy? I beg you to destroy this, and let no witness remain to the circumstances to which it alludes and believe me yours.

Sarah

At the end of the following, after the poetry, Sarah asks for "a simple ring" in exchange for the one she gave Carrington, explaining it in terms of "Pelham." The person in question is the hero of Bulwer Lytton's novel, the perfect judge of good style; and the exchange of rings was a convention of love well understood, of course, and illustrated in a French play that Sarah and Carrington shared together, *La somnambule*.[3]

The lovers (to use an old-fashioned term for convenience) are seen sometimes acting out what they had read. Life imitates art, as art, life. In the previous chapter as again in the next, comparisons are drawn between what the participants in this present drama say or do, and what anyone today can find in browsing through the fiction of their time; and there is a passage worth quoting from a modern commentator:

> One way to conceive of the influence of fiction is to recognize that people thought of their own lives as stories, following narrative lines like the ones they so frequently read. They intermingled literature and life. Diarists, letter writers, and memoir writers, in describing their experiences, lapsed into prose that seemed to be taken from books. They would sketch scenes that could easily have taken place in stories.[4]

Imitation was all the easier for our two since, in the real relationship, the exchange of letters played so very important a part, or was indeed, for weeks or months together, all that it consisted of; and for their model, they had such a work as Mme de Krüdener's *Valérie*—Sarah had met the Baron, and recalls one of the novel's details, below—where the narrative flows entirely through the medium of letters. So it does, too, in Bulwer Lytton's first novel, *Falkland* (1827), which they would know, and in stretches of Mrs. Sedgwick's works, and much of the fiction of the preceding twenty years that they were likely to have picked up.[5] There too (hardly in her early schooling) Sarah would have learnt that high tone in which she chooses to express herself. "Pray, are not the Females of the present day indebted to their constant novel reading for their coloquial and epistolary powers?" asks a father of daughters, John Pintard, in 1830.[6] The question was quoted in my first chapter.

Sarah

6   January 11th 1829 10 o.c.

To my friend and cousin Mary Denison,[7] on her marriage New
Haven October 4th 1825

Mary! To-morrow eve will seal thy fate,
And when yon moon shall rise 'twill smile on thee
A happy bride, drest in thy bridal gear
And the white chaplet which adorns thy brow
Will not be paler than thy maiden cheek
Nor purer than thy heart. 'Twill not be fear,
Nor sorrow, that will chase the rose away—
For thou art happy—'tis that nameless feeling
Which dwells in woman's heart too deep for words
And turns her trembling thoughts upon herself
As all unworthy—and on <u>him</u>, her lord
Her chosen one, her trusted guardian here,
Her helper and her all on Life's rough way,
Her fellow traveller to Heaven's gates—
As one whose love will be her home of rest
[page 41] And tho' her soul is confidence, yet asks
If it <u>indeed</u> be true that all his love
Is fixed on her alone? yet mingles pride
That woman's weakness can subdue man's strength
With youthful hope and maiden bashfulness.
There will be many who will watch thee then
And none with coldness, but among the rest
There will be one perchance will shed no tear
While others weep at parting—while <u>they</u> raise
Their high congratulations <u>I</u>'ll not dare
To say God bless thee, nor to wish thee joy
But I will turn aside and muse on all
The happy hours that we have spent together
When night's dark curtain fell around our couch

And we have wak'd as girls are wont to do
And talked of all the past, of all our plans,
Our summer's sorrows light as summer clouds
For soon we clos'd our eyes and I have slept
Full many a night with thy dear arm around me
And wak'd to see thee still, and share with thee
My daily pleasures and my daily toil.
A long farewell now waits us, thou will go
To thy new home, and form new ties, new friends
Will love thee tenderly, the past will fade—
But well I know, no other friend will be
To thee and me, what we have ever been
To one another—but my pen must stay
And I will wish thee all the bliss on earth
That mortal here can feel, when thou shalt rise
[page 42] To heaven's high courts, a disembodyed soul
Be thine in Christ more perfect happiness
Than mortal ever felt.

Oh that my weary soul could spring
   Away above this mortal scene,
And hover with elastic wing
   O'er those who lov'd in life had been.
Each dear companion would I seek
   At midnight hour and linger near,
No warning word my voice should speak
   But gently whisper notes of cheer.

I would not tell that friends betray
   That love even in its birth is cold—
I would not chill young fancy's play
   Nor clip her soaring wings of gold.
I would not tell that smiles are fair
   But smooth and false as summer's sea

I would not tell what women are
  Nor publish man's inconstancy.

I would not tell that rich looks fade,
  And bright eyes wither in their gleam,
I would not tell that Death has laid
  His fingers on their brilliant beam
I would not tell the young heart's glow
  Which bound a patriot's debt to pay
That soon its pulses chill—Oh no!
  Let them be happy while they may.

[page 43] But I would fly where truth has stray'd
  And found on earth her tranquil nest,
And I would bid the doubting maid
  Upon her lover's faith to rest.
When friendship's pure, I'd fan the flame
  When love is warm I'd bid it turn
To that bright world from whence it came
  And there for endless ages burn.

April 1826

The circumstances mentioned in this copy of Verses are true,
and happened to a Mrs Bailey sister in law to Mrs Post

She stood upon the broken shore,
And turn'd her dark eyes on the wave,
That eye with tears was moisten'd o'er
Yet hope her smile of promise gave

She could not see that sea of gold,
She only heard its billows beat,
The feathery mist beneath her roll'd
And lay in surges at her feet.

Yet still she sought to pierce the gloom
And prayed that Heaven might gracious be,
And shelter from a wat'ry tomb
Her life's best joy—now on the sea

Hark! the loud cannon near her roll'd
At once the misty veil ascends
[page 44] A gallant ship the waves uphold.
The silvery spray her white sail bends

And soon it reach'd the rocky shore
To land, one eager form has sprung
She saw a well known face, once more
Upon her husband's neck she clung.

She felt again his raptur'd kiss
His tear has fall'n on her cheek
She heard him breathe in notes of bliss
"My wife", 'twas all his lips could speak.

Too soon the days have pass'd away,
Too soon the parting hour has come
When he to foreign lands must stray
Far distant from his happy home.

He left her, whispering hope and cheer
And said not long his voyage should be,
That's soon his signal she should hear
From wat'ry echoes o'er the sea

And when the genial spring once more
To the bare woods their covering gave,
Again she linger'd on the shore
Again she watch'd the breaking wave

A dark spot rises on the deep
Which nought but love's keen eye could mark
[page 45] Near it came—her pulses leap
It is her husband's gallant bark

She watch'd it stem the billow proud
And nearer now the shore it makes,
She listen'd for the signal loud.
No sound the boding silence breaks.

No well known face with greeting warm,

A stranger slow to meet her came.
They bore her husband's lifeless form
They bore to her a widow's name

I have copied these "halting sonnets of my own poor brain" for you mon ami, and that they are not legibly or elegantly done, my apology must be that I am not well and very tired, yet I have done it with much pleasure because I know that it would give you some, not that I think them of any intrinsic value, yet as <u>mine</u> they are valuable I am sure in your sight, and I am glad of any opportunity to give you a further insight in my tastes pursuits &c and to secure to myself your sympathy in them. I selected them out of "a heap" as the Georgians say and the said "heap" I will amuse you with, quand le bon temps viendra good night

Yours Sarah

[page 46] Did you understand what I said to you as we parted? It was that you would give me the very ditto of the simple ring which, if you follow Pelham's rules, is such an one as a gentleman may keep. I have worn it many years but will wear its substitute with much more pleasure. Am I not a strange bold girl to do this? I think so.

10. o.c. Sunday evening

Sarah

7   January 23.1829

Mama's friend Miss Sebor[8] and Miss Aspinwall[9] pass the day with us, to day, and Mama asked their respective sisters to meet them in the evening. So mon ami will you defer your visit that when it is paid I may not be obliged to talk to other people? I send you les vers, in place of seeing me you must read them and find all the faults in them you can, and tell me of them to see how amiably I can control the asperity of an author. Adios amigo mio que el cielo tu guarde

pari mi.[10]   S.

P. S.

I send the paper merely as a cover for my communications. Do
not forget to return it to me. You gave it me, did you not?

[page 47] If with the crowd who strive for gold
And labor on from day to day—
If with their busy ranks I hold
The even tenor of my way—
'Tis with the hope thou will partake
The wealth I hoarded for thy sake.

If I with eager gaze explore
The path where knowledge points the way,
Or with rapt senses linger o'er
The immortal poets' charmed lay,
Ah then thy tones I seem to hear
Which start with me the unbidden tear.

When on the Historian's varied page
The record of the past I trace,
When noble themes my mind engage
The heroes of an anoint race,
Oh then I long with thee to hold
Sweet converse on the days of old.

If I am sometimes found among
The votaries of fashion's shrine,
Believe me love, amid the throng
I seek no other form than thine.
I mingle in the mazy dance
To touch thine hand, to meet thy glance.

I wake and with the morning ray
Thine image rises to my sight,
[page 48] It cheers my lonely hour by day
And when amid the shades of night
I close my eyes, my waking theme
Is still the burthen of my dream.

When twilight throws her mellow dyes
When silence reigns, nor breath nor sound
Disturb the visions which arise—
Each sense in fairy raptures drown'd—
Then dearest thou art with me there,
To share my "castles in the air".

While with no friends no kindred blest
Throughout this weary world I roam,
Alone unsolaced and unblest,
The image of a peaceful home
Where thou with me in love shall dwell,
Comes o'er my soul—a soothing spell.

Yes dearest in this constant heart
Thou art of every pulse the spring,
And tho' condemn'd awhile to part,
Thought flies to thee on rapid wing.
While by thy side, while absent far,
Thou ever art my guiding star.

(The above Eight stanzas are intended to embody many of my sentiments expressed to their Author in more humble prose)

Sarah's reference to ill-health is one of many in the family correspondence, beginning in her early twenties, and raises questions about her affair: did she so often feel unwell because that was how her mother handled life and set the example—which involves pure speculation about an older woman constantly half-well, half-sick? Or as a psychosomatic result of her own distressing situation at home, and with Carrington, and among her friends, whom she could not be candid with? Or was the cause purely physical, of a nature beyond speculation?[11] In any case, when it was cause for remark that she "had not had one fainting fit this summer" of 1827, there was something wrong. She was herself the one who retails some of her symptoms, later, which she obviously ascribed to tuberculosis. There was so much of this about, her anxiety was understandable. To Carrington she could be frank about not feeling well, perhaps, because it was permitted to young ladies: pallor, swoons, all, making them "interesting" in the language of sentimental fiction.[12]

Toward the end of the letter, as often when conventions or taboos or manners got in the way of plain speaking, she turns to French, to assure him that, if their union is forever forbidden, and if he for his part "still retains the memory of my love, remember all that I have said to you, gaze on my ring, remind yourself, so long as I have not reclaimed that proof of my love, that my heart is ever yours."

Here, too, she introduces a theme of many letters to come: the absolute necessity that Carrington make money, enough to answer to her father's definition of a suitable suitor. Yet he must do so "free from blame," suggesting that what eventually got *Woolsey, Ward & Beach* into trouble had begun to attract comment.

And she proposes the trial of his powers to win her, meaning, to win over her father, as a test of his devotion, along lines common in romances and in their reflection in real life, which letter-manuals catered to. The lover must be sent away for a time, he must prove himself in the world, and so forth. Only in this way can he be confirmed.[13]

Sarah

8 [page 49]   Tuesday morning January 27. 1829

I did expect to hear from you this evening and then to have told you what was necessary, but as I have given up going out this week on the plea of ill health, I must write. On Sunday my Father spoke of you after coming home from Church, and ended by saying that you should never be anything to him without dissolving all connection between him and the person [Sarah herself] who should form one with you. At that moment some one came in and I said no more. I told my mother yesterday that I must sacrifice my happiness to prejudice, and this morning she has been talking with me on the subject, and giving me Papa's wishes. They are in unison with his declaration, and leave no hope. He says that if I choose to marry you, it must be without hope of his consent. This I know your feelings revolt at as much as mine. Alas for us both, we are doom'd to unhappiness, for what I told you the last time we met at my sister's must ever be true on my part. But for you who have no home or friends, if you can ever be happy, think not of the heart which you have gained, and the hope which is taken from you, if you [page 50] can be ever happy with another, think not of me, and I will try to be glad that you are happy and forget the past. Si ceci n'arrive pas, si vous conservez toujours le souvenir de mon amour, rappelez tout ce que je vous ai dit, regardez mon anneau et souvenez-vous lorsque je ne vous ôte cette épreuve de mon amour, mon coeur est encore le votre. We shall not often meet now. You must not distinguish me by your attentions. I shall never be able to see you here without so many painful thoughts that it is best that we should not meet except when you come to see some one who may be here, or when we meet by accident. Come still to our Pew, but do not join me, any such thing would irritate my Father. And my dear C, will you not so far regard my peace of mind as to persevere most unremittingly in your business and in improvement, and in your conduct. I beg you, be not only free from blame, but free from any thing that looks like it. Especially form your character as a man of business, and know that the only mitigation I can feel is, that you are properly valued and appreciated. You will do all this for the sake of one [page 51] who is suffering much for you, and you will not say anything to any body about me. Let the remembrance of the past be sacred to both, and kept in our heart of hearts, but never spoken of to the world. And now mon ami I have only to say God bless you and keep you and make you every thing I fondly hope you are and will be, and once more, tho' it seem unfair, I beg you to shun every thing which may make your conduct suspected, even tho' it should spring from good feeling. My last injunction is, act as if our mutual happiness hung upon your winning a good name, though alas, that happiness is destroyed

Yours. S.

Let no eye ever see this letter. My Father and Mother have both said that except on this subject, they wish to be friends to you.

Yours à jamais
S.

Sarah

9   Wednesday P. M. Jan[uar]y 28.1829

My friend to whom both you and I my dear C, owe so much for her friendship and sympathy gave me your letter this morning.

I am happier for it though I knew all [page 52] your feelings before—yet I am happier for the expression of them. We are indeed to be pitied, yet for you I can bear any thing, and would rather share your sorrows than be happy without you. You seemed hurt that I mentioned that you might be happy with another. I wrote from the impulse of the moment I hardly know what and only admitted that sentiment when I contrasted my situation with friends and home with your lonely one and felt that you were most to be pitied. But cher ami neither your imagination nor wishes can paint my attachment more fervid than it is. This unhappy circumstance removes all disguise, and I feel it no departure from feminine delicacy to say so, conscious that my heart is in the safe keeping of an honorable and upright man. Therefore I dare to say that the idea of losing your affection or of giving my own to any other, is indescribably painful and as far as my heart is concerned will never be done. I cannot see you at present, I am not fit for an interview, nor would it do on other accounts. Be satisfied that I understand you and all you feel, but not to meet en particulier is a sacrifice [page 53] which we must make to duty, so painful my dear C, that I am sure you will not render it more so by your entreaties. We shall meet however some time or other, accident will bring us together, then we must behave as well as we can, and I am sure we need now no assurances of our mutual affection more than what a kind look can always convey. I believe if it were not that you are connected in their minds with me, my parents would like you. I heard of my Father's saying that he did not think you a business man. This I know time will prove to be a mistake, but take care of your health. You must not answer this—keep it as un gage d'amour avec "le chere anneau", and while each preserves these testimonies of affection, let there be no doubt to intrude or disturb.

We must be separated, but not disunited. May God bless you my dear friend, and preserve you from any bitter or repining feelings, and may your future conduct prove you all that fondly believes your S.

I have forgotten to say that you are more than pardoned for your communication to Miss A[spinwall]. You will not think my restrictions proceed from any motive but a sense of duty. How gladly would I do all that could gratify you if I could.

Toward the end of the following letter, Sarah again refers in French to "the dear ring," to place its echoes among the lines of *La somnambule*. She adds reference to "your beloved image," the miniature portrait that she carries (below, in the forty-third letter, cf. chapter 1, fig. 2). "The poor Valérie," whose portrait her Gustave carried, is explained in my first chapter through Mme de Krüdener's novel.

And she concludes in Spanish, "Again, I tell you, I am yours for ever." In that language, she has mastered the second person singular; not in French (where her preference for the second person plural in lovers' dialogue would sound singular indeed, today; but it was more common long ago).

Sarah

10 [page 54]   Friday February 6th 1829

Your letter my dear friend was in some, nay in all points very gratifying. I regret that W[illia]m should have hurt your feelings, and am obliged to you for your forbearance. He probably said it merely, that he thought it best even by a bitter remedy to cure you. If he speaks to me, my answer will be what yourself would suppose and suggest. Now I will tell you what my wishes are, and you will I know yield to them tacitly. You know I cannot act against my Father's wishes, but I am desirous that for so great a stake as happiness every effort should be made. For one year let us meet only as we meet others—there must be nothing concealed, nothing clandestine, no peculiar attention on your part, and nothing more than friendliness on mine. That period will try whether the prediction is true—it is needless for me to assert or profess here, what you already know.

Then at the end of that time, more known and established as you will be, go to my Father, tell him that you had gained my affections, but in conformity to his will, we have for a twelve month, scarcely met and only casually, that our feelings remain [page 55] the same, and your character being proved, that you hope for his consent, that your happiness and mine depend on it. If he refuse what can I do for you, but live single, and regret our unhappy fate. If he do <u>not</u> refuse, and may God grant you success, then your sweet picture may be realized, and I need not add to all your "wishes and imagination" can paint. We have at least a year of <u>hope</u>. Will you do this? I know you will. Be entirely silent respecting me to any member of my family. W[illia]m has not said any thing to me on this subject, nor is it probable the measures you speak of will be taken. During this time, this year, I shall not go in general society, and shall, you may be sure, be careful that nothing may cause uneasiness to you. But we will abide by this plan, and I will not even have the miniature I told you I would keep. If at the end of that time we are separated, then "laissez moi votre image", that I may not be like the pauvre Valérie, Good-bye. I can only add in my haste and cold how truly je suis la votre à jamais.

S.

On thinking over my letter I think I have not given my reasons for my plan, they [page 56] are that a continuance of intercourse would not only irritate my Father, and while you do not visit here, or only visit formally and seldom, it is not delicate or respectable to appear to the rest of the world on more familiar terms, and also the period of our acquaintance being short, after the lapse of a year, time will have added his seal to our hearts' impulses.

I am sure W[illia]m will never interfere in Mr Johnson's reception of whom he pleases in his house, and as to your fear that he may induce my Father to forbid my speaking to you, my dear friend there is a limit to every thing, and no power on earth shall induce me to treat him whose affection is my honor and happiness otherwise than in a friendly manner.

I am sure of your concurrence in my wishes from the uniform regard you have shown to my feelings. Do not answer this. Otra vez te diré que soy la tuya

para siempre

S.

Sarah

11

Thursday february 12. 1829

Mama told me that she had a conversation with William (he has not spoken to me) in which he seemed hurt that you [page 57] spoke so plainly of my affection, as he thought boastingly, and he felt it was not delicate even to him, and also he understood what you said about persevering as if you meant to expose me to great difficulty by continuing your attention in the face of every body, not as indulging one little hope for better days. He thought this was selfish. I told Mama that he had entirely mistaken your feelings, that if there was any blame it was to me and not to you my dear friend. I write against my own restriction to beg you to say nothing of me or of my feelings to W[illia]m, but to take some opportunity when you are calm and collected, to speak in such a manner of your feelings that he may appreciate the delicacy and generosity of your attachment which I feel such confidence in. W[illia]m thought you were bitter towards my Father. In this too you can undeceive him. I charge you mon ami, by all that I have suffered for you, to speak when you are cool and to avoid on all occasions any difference with W[illia]m.

He was only mistaken. Perhaps you can incidentally say what your feelings are better than formally, when you may both have your feelings excited. Perhaps I am selfish in proposing a protracted term of suspense [page 58] which may be longer, much longer, than the period I mentioned. If you were like other people I should tell you to try to forget me, as the least painful course, but you know what is best for your own happiness—that is all my care now, for my own is so uncertain as not to deserve any concern, yet it is in part secured while I hope you are proving your character for virtue and respectability to the world—that hope I claim as a reward for all I have suffered.

You need never feel any doubt as to me while I keep the "cher anneau". Once more I charge you, if you can need such a charge to be very careful to speak to W[illia]m in such a way as shall not arouse his extreme sensitiveness as to his sister, and at the same time make him understand that the generous feeling you once expressed to me, "that while my Father thought ill of you, it was right in him to act as he did, it was your part to prove him to be in a mistake respecting you".

Nothing you ever said, not even your warmest expressions of affection gave me more pleasure than this sentiment so honorable to you. Now farewell, you will not blame my jealous care of your reputation in the eyes of my mother and [page 59] brother, and I repeat it. W[illia]m was only in a mistake which seemed to surprise him as to your feelings. May God bless you, and make you happy, whatever becomes of your friend

S.

After an interval of only three days, Sarah adds what she calls "a little note" to clarify what she had said before. At the beginning she refers to letters which are best explained as his European ones, written home, which he then had returned to him as a form of journal (below, L-b 62).

Sarah

12   February 15. 1829.

I was almost hurt that you should think of exculpating yourself to me, who never blamed you my dear friend. The letters amused me much while by my poor mother's sick bed. I have been amused by thinking of their contents, tho' the traces of sadness in them make me more than ever sorry that your path is not joyous. I write these few words to say that I hope the impression on Mama's mind [is] not so unfavorable as you fear, for she said yesterday she was very glad

Laura could show you kindness and would gladly do it herself if it would not be misunderstood. As to W[illia]m I rely on your promise to be not warm in what you say. When you tell him you expect nothing from me while my Father's mind is unchanged, that your conduct to me is distantly respectful, but on that little hope depends your happiness and that is your all, can he, can any one blame you for retaining it? Not I at least, who share and have authorized it. This is what in Spain is called a <u>cartita</u>, Adios.

Sarah

13 [page 60]   February 25th. 1829

I will ask Miss Silliman[14] to give you this letter which she will do as an article of yours I have in my possession asking no questions. I spent a very pleasant day yesterday with Miss E[mily] Aspinwall,[15] but have so severe a cold I feel stupid as possible to-day. Against my injunctions which we both so ill observe respecting no "concealed communications", I enclose these few lines for there is one thing I want to add to all my requests, which would tire any patience but yours. I recollect you told me the last time I had any conversation with you, that you saw it would not do for you to have any intercourse with my Father, only to meet his advances. I suppose in business there are occasions when you and he meet, and I have feared that your feelings of delicacy might cause a distance on your part that might give the idea of resentful feelings which I know you do not entertain. You may be sure I do not <u>blame</u> you for the line of enquiry which I received with pleasure but mon ami, had we been more careful I do believe we might have prevented the expressions of disapprobation which have separated us for so long a period, and during this anxious period you may [61] well imagine I am anxious to shun any farther expressions of the same nature, so very painful to me. I wish at least to preserve undisturbed and in silence the only spark of hope I have, so you must be very careful for my sake not to conduct [yourself] towards me in such a manner as shall excite any more painful remarks. You will receive this chez Madame M. where we once passed an evening together. "Te souvient il encore de cette soirée"? Je sais que tu t'en souviendras mille fois pendant la soirée. Addio mio caro amico. This is the last time I will transgress in this way. Addio allora, and may you share in all the blessings which fall to the lot of tua amica

　　　　　　　　　　S.

Sarah

14　　　　　　　　　　　　March 11th 1829 10 o.c. P. M.
　　　　　　　　　　　　　　　　　　Wednesday

　　I am afraid my dear friend that you thought there was froideur [chilliness] in my manner this morning, and if I have hurt your feelings which I should so much lament, let this acknowledgement be my entire excuse in your eyes. You remember you told me you would "follow my injunctions", and one of them was that accident only should bring us together. A departure from [page 62] this would be a want of sincerity towards my friends and would lessen my self respect, qualities which as my friend and (what word shall I use, guide?) you are interested in preserving in their perfection. Besides could you know the entire despondency I feel often which only my confidence in your affection can alleviate, you would never add to my unhappiness that of having to refuse the slightest request from you.

　　I have just come from Miss Coit's[16] where I spent the evening with Miss Silliman, Miss E. Aspinwall and her cousin. Miss A spoke of you "con alabanzas" [with praise], and what do you think particularly pleased me? She said "when she first knew you, you had a french manner which you had entirely lost". Miss Silliman has gone to Mrs McGregor's, will you not call on her before she leaves town again? I will try to send you your european letters with this [above, L-b 59], and you can better than I give them to Miss A[spinwall], if you choose. I did not, for there were many allusions to former feelings which I thought possibly you may have forgotten and not wish to expose. I had a great wish to act the swindler with respect to them, but honesty prevailed and les voici. Do you know I have a [page 63] wonderful curiosity to see and know your Utica and Albany friends. Mr. Bloodgood particularly.[17] If I can go to see my cousins the Hopkins[18] as I sometimes think of, tell him to come and see me. I shall like him even if he is de glace [chilly]—and now I will say good-night with an apology for my cold fingers and the consequent bad writing. <u>They</u>, at least are de glace, but so is not

Your affectionate

S.

Whenever I do see you again, you can tell me if W[illia]m Johnson has ever said any thing to you respecting nos affaires. He and my sister always seem very kind to you. Are they not so?

Sarah

15   April 1st 1829

I will enclose the letter of my friend of which I have spoken, but had it not with me when I chanced to see you. These few lines are to make you amends for bidding you good-bye as I do when we meet. In your last note you told me you "were glad I had told Mrs Berger the story", I never spoke to her myself on the subject, nor could have done so, but she had often rallied me sur votre sujet, so I asked Sarah to explain the reason of [page 64] the seeming inconsistency in our conduct to each other, and ask her to say nothing about it. Not long since I was walking with [sister] Laura, and I told her that I was very glad she could pay you those friendly attentions which are so valuable to a gentleman without a family circle, and I believed you felt them very much from her, that in consequence of Papa's disapproval of your attentions to me, you no longer visited us. She said "that was no reason why she should not be kind to you, that you always seemed to feel as a friend there, and she was much gratified by it", and more to the same import. The other night as you were sitting at the table and W[illia]m asked you for your watch, there was something so affectionate in his manner that it delighted

me. He loves frankness and openness and all honorable qualities so
much that I am sure you and himself may be very good friends. I
was much obliged to you for offering your arm to Mrs H[odge][19]
as we came home, instead of to me. On monday I went to see Mrs
Hodge. George Pumpelly[20] was with me and we had a long talk
about Willis. I told George what I thought of his change of manner
and tastes &c, and he could not but agree with me perfectly, but
added that "to him his friends had from [page 65] the beginning
persevered in the same heart and manner, and of course he was
bound not to desert him". George is to join Mr Kent's office[21] for
the summer. I hope you will know him. He has the faults of a very
young man, who has been rather superior to those around him, but
his heart is admirable, and I have a great reliance on his friendship.
You will like I think, and I hope you will take an opportunity to form
his acquaintance. I have extended these lines into a real letter, so
I may as well complete what I should say if I could speak freely.
You told me not to despond. Mon cher ami how can I help it? It
is not that I do not confide in you and rely on you. You will do
every thing I know in your power that uprightness of conduct and
correctness of deportment (on which last very much depends) can
do, but success in this world is not so certainly the meed of those
whom (humanly speaking) deserve it by their exertions as to divest
me of a trembling, feverish, and sometimes irritable anxiety. Besides
my health is so indifferent that it cannot but affect my spirits even
if there were no other cause. Mais trève à ce sujet la [enough of
that]. I have read two of the volumes of Scribe's plays, and find them
all amusing. I liked particularly, "l'intérieur [page 66] de l'étude",
et "La Somna[m]bule" more than the others. They have not the
delicate sentiments of "Valérie" nor indeed has any other french
comedy I have ever seen. Female character is never what it might
be. If they are represented as spirituelle, it is always finess and trick
and adroitness in which the esprit consists, and there is always a
want of that something which is better understood than expressed,
which constitutes the beauty of a female character, and which the
Poet compares to the tremulous dew of the violet, and the soft blue
of the grape. Now is not that last sentence sentimental enough for a

person with blue eyes and long ringlets and an italian name? Good-bye, plût au ciel que vous soyez heureux [may Heaven grant you happiness]

Your affectionate

S.

Sarah next writes at a time of visits from various Philadelphians, gathered for the wedding of her friend Mary Binney, for whom she was a bridesmaid. She had visited that other city in the previous autumn.

Sarah

16   April 19. 1829

I am in hopes of seeing you one Wednesday, the last day of my class meetings.[22] so will trespass so far as to tell you I received your note, and regret much the traces of sadness I could discover. Do not I beseech you be too much cast down, [page 67] call to mind all you have often said to raise my spirits, and let your own arguments convince yourself. You would say I am sure that it is better as we are, than as we were at this time last year, but I will say no more on this. I was almost disposed to scold you for sending your letter to my friend for she is too kind to be troubled with our affairs, so you must not give her another missive and you know you ought not to write any, mais parlons d'autres choses [let's change the subject]. I do not like Mr Peugnet[23] at all. He is a solemn coxcomb, and I thought you knew it before. I am sure I have laughed at him in your presence often. I am glad you find Mr. Dwight[24] agreeable, he is a particular friend and one of my nearest relations, being cousin on both Father's and Mother's side. Do you know George Pompelly? I hope you will notice him if occasion offers, he has some faults, but many virtues, and one which is of weight in the eyes of mon meilleur ami. He is a very warm friend of mine. I supposed that business prevented your being at Mrs Van Beuren's[25] & presume that you are happier for occupation, yet must wish that the leisure hour will come ere long to your relief. Have you any [page 68] time for reading? I hope so, you know I want you to improve and keep up knowledge and taste in the literary line. I cannot, indeed I cannot acknowledge for you the kindness of Mr and Mr[s?] J. You will do it by your actions far more eloquently than I could by words, for I should lose my composure. I am glad you like Ms Wallace's[26] letter, by "the seal" she meant to answer a question of mine, "whether the seal of the letter (brighter hours will come) was not meant for me in particular". Now as to "Charles Ingersol and Gilpin", they are both young men of distinction in the beau-monde of Phil[adelphi]a, the latter a friend of Miss W's I am only slightly acquainted with, the other was one of Mr Cadwallader's[27] groomsmen, and is a very odd amusing personage, a great favorite in Phil[adelphi]a but entre nous, more agreeable than estimable. James Bayard is cousin to Doctor Hodge, an excellent young man, for whom I have a high regard, and to whom I am much indebted for great kindness in all my visits to Phil[adelphi]a, and in peculiar for his gentlemanly attentions to Susan and myself on our voyage home. "And surtout <u>the</u> Colonel" is cousin to my friend's husband, was [page 69] my groomsman, and was in duty bound very civil to me, perhaps more than duty would exact, and just enough as he chose to laugh about his own innermost danger as he called it, to make other people laugh too, and his friends who are empressés to marry him to somebody, fixed on me as the mistress of a fine place somewhere near Trenton on the Delaware, which calls him Master, but as his impression was not too deep to be made a matter of jest on his own part, it gave me no great elation and I found him a well informed and perfectly well bred man, agreeable of course tho' a little old bachelorish, and spoiled a little by being "stretched on the rack of a <u>too</u> easy chair". So much for the Colonel whom if I have never mentioned, it is because when we do happen to have a moment's conversation there are subjects so much nearer us that others are forgotten. I thought mon bon ami very amiable to bear little Sue's[28] uneasiness to-day when she was leaning on you so long. She seems to be fond of you. I hope you will call this week to see Catherine and Mrs W[oolsey]. Very likely W[illia]m has not invited you, [page 70] but you know he is inattentive and queer, and as you have visited her it seems due. If you were here Carrington I should have a better pen, and have written better, but as it is c'est à vous. Good night,

Yours
S.

Sarah

17   Wednesday 10 o.c.   May 10. 1829

I think it probable that we may meet to-morrow evening and my dear friend must excuse me if I write a line of expostulation.

The last time I saw you our conversation left a very painful impression on my mind. You said you did not doubt me, and yet the observations of Mr J[ohnson] and Miss A[spinwall] evidently had affected you. Let me tell you the causes you have to doubt me. I plead [=pled] with my Father and Mother, and expressed my sentiments towards you in opposition to my kind Father's, and even when I knew from his character that nothing would change him, unless he saw <u>that</u> in you, which would alter his opinion. I never said I could change my sentiments. I only said I would act according to my Father's injunctions. Since that time my conduct has been unvarying [page 71] to you, and against the strict line of duty I have allowed you to hope, I have given up society in general for your sake, and certainly never expressed any thing but reliance on your affection, and is it kind or generous in you when we meet so seldom, while there is such room for present unhappiness and the future presents so little hope, is it kind my dear friend to add another drop of bitterness by speaking of doubts and requiring assurances?

Believe me I know and appreciate the affection that prompted them, and my heart would anticipate all you would say in excuse, but remember my dear C. that unhappy circumstances have mingled much sorrow with our feelings for each other, that my health is such as often to make my spirits (never the most sanguine) very low, that I cannot but look on the probability of a change of opinion in my Father as very slight—think of this and you will acknowledge that

I need from you support and encouragement, and cannot bear a
hint such as those which have wounded me. If I have hurt you in
thus writing forgive me I beseech you. I heard nothing said of your
visit. I do not know whether Papa knew it, but presume he did. It is
not an experiment which it would be prudent to repeat soon again.
However, now the [page 72] pleasant weather has come, I am in
hopes we shall at least hear of each other's welfare more frequently.
Are you on good terms with W[illia]m? I hope so—for my sake keep
so, for you know that much would naturally depend on that with
Papa. You must not think me ungrateful for your affection and the
constant exertions you make for my sake, I assure you, not such is
the truth, but in saying what I have, I wished to set before you the
causes you have for trusting your affectionate

                                          S

Tuesday evening.

    I changed my plan and dined with my Sister yesterday, so I had
not my note with me, and I did not regret it, because I feared it
was not written as kindly as it should be, but mon ami, after all this
expostulation accept the assurance that I do not regret any thing I
have done and felt for you. If we are ever in happier circumstances,
all these clouds which trouble us will "melt in thin air". How much
I wanted to talk to you last night, mais trop du monde [too much
company present]. Mr Sheldon[29] said to me once, "you are absent",
so I rallied my thoughts. Oh I had forgotten that I am provoked
that [page 73] you did not come across Wall Street, and speak to me
yesterday morning. I thought you looked troubled when I saw you.
Do tell me why. Buena noche, amigo mio

Sarah

18   Wednesday evening May 13. 1829

    With body and mind equally fatigued I seat myself to give my
dearest friend the reasons I promised to-day. We have had company
at tea, Laura's Visitors, Mrs Philips and Miss [Sarah] Aspinwall,[30]

and feeling unequal to any thing I have been trying to entertain them. Two things have pleased me to-day, first that Miss [Margaret] McWhorter praised you so kindly, and secondly, that in a delightfully sociable visit to Mrs Rogers[31] in her bedroom this afternoon she spoke of you as liking you very much, and said she already felt more acquainted with you than with most of the household. She leaves town to-morrow but will return in ten days when I hope your acquaintance will be improved. You will find her accomplished and she owes it to herself almost entirely that she has a considerable knowledge of the modern languages and exquisite skill in painting, that is, in the minor works of the art. She has employed her talents [page 74] in teaching Mrs John Winthrop's (her sister's) children which is more to her credit than the most brilliant success. Thank you for taking my expostulation so kindly, and my dear friend if my manner should sometimes be less cordial towards you than you are pleased it should be, or if I should be not quite reasonable, do lay it to the account of these disagreeable circumstances which give me an awkward constrained bearing to you that I am always sorry for and will endeavour to throw off.

As to W[illia]m I know your feelings have been tried, but you will for my sake do all you can. He cannot indeed invite you to our house. Papa would not allow it, nor my dear friend do I wish it, while I cannot meet you as my feelings prompt, it is excessively painful to meet you in presence of those who would observe the conduct of both. I do not know that I can hardly make you comprehend all my difficulties. The reason I spoke of to-day as influencing John is this. He knows, if I am seen or known to be with you, that it would expose me to Papa's displeasure—he would think that I was openly authorising a line of conduct in you, in direct opposition to his will, or that you were very presuming. Both of these I would avoid. Papa told me that day he spoke so [page 75] severely of you that one or the other must be true. John thinks if he can prevent by being with me any appearance of more than common intercourse between us, that it will save me from Papa's displeasure, and I have no doubt it would. My dear C, you will for my sake use the same forbearance you have used, and trust me if you hope for better days that it is the only way. I know how hard it is, I know and feel that our attachment instead of bringing you happiness has been a source of abundant mortification and vexation to you. I know that you toil for my sake without sympathy, but mon cher ami do not think you are alone. Believe in all your efforts, and all those moments "when there is no one to say you have done well", that my thoughts and wishes are ever with you, and if it be ever my lot to devote myself to your happiness, you shall find a reward in the devoted affection of your nearest friend for all and tenfold more than you have borne for her. I shall say too much and yet I am not afraid to speak openly to you of my affection. It is one light shade at least in our dark prospect that its very obscurity makes me dare to tell you what perhaps a feeling of timidity [page 76] would cause me to hide, if our way were smoother and brighter. The reason I was so anxious to speak one word to you in Wall Street was that I had before met Papa and W[illia]m going home. I assure you I shall always know and appreciate the motives of your conduct on any such occasion. I cannot tell you how worried I am of company and even of everybody, and to-morrow we have company to dinner. If I could only shut myself up awhile I should be so much more comfortable. Yesterday after my walk when I felt so unhappy and tired and sick I tried to read a letter from Theodore, and I could not, I ran up stairs and threw myself on the bed thinking to recover alone but they would come and bring me restoratives and for a short time I lost my self command entirely. I would not go to Saratoga and be obliged "to fool it up to the top of my bent", for the world. It would be so disagreeable to receive attentions from the gentlemen I should meet. You can understand me in this mon ami. I must bid you good night, it is very late, and I will close this long letter and put your note which lies open before me under cover with the others from you, with an endorsement which would make you look [page 77] grave—it is a request to my Mother on the envellope to return the enclosed papers to you unopened in case of my death, then tied appropriately with a black ribbon.

To-day's packet brings to the Ralston's the news of the death of a favorite brother in Paris.[32] What a stroke! He died in a fit.

Good night, and may God bless you. Believe of my heart every thing that your own wishes prompt. When I once confessed to you the share you have en mi corazon [in my heart] it implied steadfastness, fidelity, and above all perfect sincerity, and until that declaration you may rest assured that it is in the full measure of all those qualities that I am <u>yours</u>

S.

Not from Sarah but included by Carrington as an item in her correspondence, because no doubt she meant it to lead to their meeting, we have the following, from her friend Miss Aspinwall:

19   Wednesday evening May 27. 1829

Mrs Berger requests the favor of your company to dine tomorrow at 4 o'clock. We expect only Baron Krudener, Miss Van Ness[33] and another lady. Perhaps it will be expedient not to mention at the Store [i.e., to his business partner, William] that you design us the pleasure of your company

Your cousin in anticipation
S[arah] A. Aspinwall

20 [page 78]   June 1st 1829

I forgot to give you the watch case. I did not understand making it and am ashamed of it, but will give it you and hope to learn better for another

21   Friday evening June 19. 1829

I regretted very much mon cher ami that I could not accompany you and my friend this afternoon, but Mama did not think it best, and faithful to my prescribed line of conduct I would not do it without her knowledge or against her will. I regretted it the more as you looked sad (not to say a little provoked). My dear C. cannot have entertained this last feeling long against his fellow sufferer. I have felt very much out of spirits lately, since the return of my Parents our separation has weighed on me more and seemed more complete. I must tell you that while walking with Mr Curtis[34] the other day he began to speak of you, and told me his belief of something like the true state of feeling between us. At last he urged me so earnestly to tell him and in a way that made me feel as if he might have some strong reason, that I gave him to understand that there [page 79] was more than a mere friendship between us, but we were interrupted, this afternoon I have again commenced, again with interruptions, my story. He seemed to feel very much, and wished he might be of service. I could not of course speak so openly and composedly as if he were one of my own sex nor indeed as I mean to do. I would willingly have shunned the subject, but could hardly do it and preserve truth without being utterly uncivil in my reply, besides, I thought he had better believe the story and you would not disapprove. What a long statement of a simple affair. I see by the papers that death has deprived you of one of your few friends in Mr Lathrop,[35] and felt for the shock it must be to you. Now my dear C, good bye. I must close with a renewed request to you to be very prudent towards me now, and hope that time may remove the need of this caution and at least that we may deserve if we do not win that happiness   La tuya

S.

I will not complete my thoughts and close my eyes without the assurances of my entire affection which is all I can do for your happiness, even when I constantly feel that you suffer much uneasiness à cause de moi, but that is something, is it not dear C? Duorme bien, y que tus sueños sean dichasesimas [sleep well, and may your dreams be the happiest]

Sometimes a reader suspects that Sarah communicates in a foreign language less for the sheer pleasure of it, or to show off, than to protect its contents—which, however, is innocent enough: "Greetings, my friend.

I'm sending you my pencil-case, which you can return when you come to get the news at my sister's, before you leave. My thanks to you for this and all the other times that you've shown such kindness to your fine and devoted friend."

[signature: Sarah]

22 [page 80]   July 6th 1829

Buenos dias amigo mio. Te envio mi lapicero que puedes traerme cuando vengas para noticias à mi hermana, ante de tu partida

Te doy gracias para esta y todas ostras acasiones en quales has mostrido tanta benevolencia hácia tu fina y aficionada amiga—

S

[signature: Sarah]

23

Si j'avais songé à vous voir aujourdhui j'aurais porté mon cher anneau [if I had thought I'd see you today, I would have worn my dear ring]

[signature: Sarah]

24   July 10. 1829

You were so kind as to offer to make enquiries about the Lowndes[36] party for me. If you succeed, will you call for me at Mrs Johnson's in the afternoon and accompany me in a visit to them?—(Do not give yourself any trouble if it is a warm day.)

Again in the following, as in other letters past and to come, Mr. Woolsey is seen communicating his ideas and wishes to Sarah regarding Carrington through his wife, a choice of conduct which is characteristic of the family: very reluctant to show feelings. Woolsey is so especially, witness his letters to his children. One of them is quoted at length in the next chapter. Theodore at a later point must reassure his fiancée that she is after all acceptable to the family, as he himself knows her to be. He can tell, "though indeed they are not much given to making assurances."[37]

It remains plain, at least to Sarah, that her father can never be reconciled to her engagement until Carrington is making more money.

Sarah

25   Tuesday 10 A. M. July 21. 1829

I wrote you my dear C, a note which I requested W[illia]m J[ohnson]. to deliver but as he seemed [page 81] to think it might involve him in our affairs in a way that was improper in his situation in our family, I took it again and must welcome your arrival with uncomfortable intelligence. My Father was in Town a day during last week and said he did not wish me to go to the springs with W[illia]m. I thought he might speak in consequence of your being there, so I wrote to Mama that you would leave there, on hearing of my plans, and that your own were to be in Albany before or soon after my arrival. She answered me that Papa wished me to give it up, as he did not like us to meet, and that your conduct had been incorrect with regard to this and displeased him. I wrote to him again expressing my wonder at that, and my own opinion, as also fully speaking of my feelings to you. Since her return she has again spoken of it, and said she was sorry to write as she did but Papa wished it. He has not spoken to me and I hope in mercy he will not, but his manner was colder than usual, and he evidently was irritated, but as [they] are and will be a few days absent, and I shall soon go to Connecticut, I trust it will pass away. But my dear C. [page 82] there is one thing you must promise me if you love me, and value my health which sinks under my unhappy feelings and my comfort which this late evidence of Papa's continued disapproval has broken up. You must not take any pains to seek my society. Our hearts are united by a tie too strong for any thing but unfaithfulness and unworthiness on your part to dissolve, but my dear friend we must be apart until we can be on such terms as we could wish.

We have drawn this proof of disapproval on ourselves by imprudence. I told you it would be so, but you did not agree with me. You see I am right and the full expression of my attachment did no good. I am determined while I think of you as I do now, that nothing shall ever drive you from my heart, but I am equally determined that we shall not meet except accidentally, and I have such confidence in your regard for my peace, that I know you will help me to shun another expression of Papa's displeasure which would be a final one. My sister [-in-law] Catherine spoke of you to me, and I spoke to her of our attachment. She said she had often feared W[illia]m had hurt my feelings, and had [page 83] spoken to him of his want of civility to you on some occasions. When we meet again my dearest friend, or rather when we are in the same City, you will be in the midst of business, and I trust in the earnest pursuit of that, will find some pleasure, at least in the idea that you are doing all that in you lies to remove the obstacles that are between us. What my feelings are on leaving Town and my constant state of spirits I dare not tell you—they might gratify you, but you are generous enough to regret my unhappiness even when it flatters you. But my health is far from good. I hope to be soothed somewhat in Connecticut. Here I have been in a constant state of fever and excitement of mind. Farewell my dear friend. Be only what I fondly hope, and may the future give you only so much good as wishes and prays

Your
S.

Sarah

26   Monday 10 o'clock P. M.
                                          June 23. 1829

I return you the french manuel, which as it was not yours ought to have been returned long ago, and while expressing my thanks must also express my fears that the [page 84] manner of my expostulation hurt your feelings. If so, "mon ami que tout soit oublié" [may it all be forgotten, my friend]. I am never so much troubled as to observe after all my unvarying "walks and conversations" towards you a symptom of distrust on your part, but trève à ce sujet la. I ask it as a peculiar favor that you will destroy my note, but <u>remember all</u> <u>my</u> injunctions.

I well remember the passage touching the anneau. She [the somnambulist] says in her sleep, "Otez le de mon doigt, je n'aurai jamais la force de vous le donner", or something like it [take it from my finger, I shall never have the strength to give it to you]. I wish I had marked all the passages that pleased me, that you might enjoy them with me. This afternoon I went with Mrs Sheldon to Coney Island. I rode with Miss Sebor, the children and Mr F[rederic]k Sheldon. On the way Miss Sebor told me that Mrs Sheldon wished me in returning to take her place with son beau frère H. T. S. in his gig, and added, "I hope you will not object". I replied that I hoped she thought me too much of a lady to object to any arrangement of Mrs S's forming. So when we stopt he asked me formally to "do him the honor". I thought of your quotation "jusqu'à l'etiquette qui conspire contre moi" [to the full extent of those good manners that are my enemy]. But as the best was to be made of it I resigned myself to an unavoidable but [page 85] disagreeable necessity. I always had a particular aversion and disapproval of <u>Gig rides</u>, but I must say Mr Sheldon was very gentlemanly and pleasant, and let me hold the reins for about eight miles, till we came to the "haunts of men" again.

Did you know <u>driving</u> was one of my accomplishments. W[illia]m Johnson taught me at Stratford in "days of lang syne".[38] We reached home at 7 o'clock, and I feel wonderfully better for the air and exercise, but am very tired, so as I have said what I wished to say, I will close my eyes only begging you si tu me amas, no otra vez que soy—y seré para siempre tu fiel y aficionada [if you love me as I am—and will be always yours faithfully and affectionately]

Sarah

H. C. Beach

27   Saturday evening, Aug. 22. 1829

To Miss Sarah Aspinwall

I found par hazard among my books the four volumes of plays accompanying this and thought that some of them might amuse you. I was told by a gentleman to-day that the french company would play but five nights more.

I wish I felt at liberty to reply to the affectionate notice of myself in Sarah's letter [page 86] but may I ask you to say when you next write her, that I begin to be <u>very</u> <u>actively</u> engaged in business, that I go to the french play now and then, that I am glad she reads french with Mr Colomb, that I hope she likes Miss Schroeder, and that it gives me the greatest pleasure to hear her health is improving. May I ask you to say all this, and by way of postscript un petit mot sur la durée de sa visite [just a word on the length of her visit].

Now if you will not be offended at so much trouble, I shall be assured I may consider you my friend as I am

Very truly yours

H. C. B.

Sarah reverts in her next to the problems of her friend, the love-lorn Curtis—"How are things for you? Going well, I hope" "Not very . . ."—who naturally has the sympathy of someone love-lorn herself.

And she does, for a change, remember to *tutoyer* Carrington.

Sarah

28   Sunday September 20th 1829

I have been reading two volumes of plays of yours my dear C, and Miss A[spinwall] is to lend me two more. I have been amused with them, but they are not so refined and so much like one feels as Scribe's. I found nothing to <u>mark</u>. I have read [Bulwer Lytton's]

Devereux and noticed as you did the scene where Isara and Morton are separated.

The book did not please me quite as much as I expected, but it displays great talent. I like the french picture of love, but not quite [page 87] so well as the devoted wife in the "Disowned". <u>We</u> do not think such strength of feeling beyond nature, do <u>you</u> dear C. <u>I</u> do not and from my heart assure you that from the day I told you, "I would try to love you", till now I have never wavered one instant. All my happiness now is in the confidence I have in your affection which I do not allow a thought to profane—and in the picture I sometimes draw to myself of "une charmante vie journalière", when my constant and dearest cares will be directed where it will then be both my duty and inclination to bestow them. Oh if you only <u>knew</u> me, you would never again speak of coldness, but believe that if my manner to you is ever tinged with froideur, it is because a different conduct would meet censure and make my life very uncomfortable. Did you meet my Father the morning you came for the keys? He came in a moment after you had left the house, and seeing the letter asked who brought it. I told him that you did and came for the keys.

He said nothing but looked not pleased, and this morning as I came in Church motioned me to sit by <u>him</u>. I took my own seat however, not apprehending pollution from your neighborhood. It seems ridiculous [page 88] but I beg that you will sit at a distance from me hereafter. They all know my feelings, that is some comfort to me, because it seems more candid on my part. I must tran[s]fer to you Mrs Schoeder's[39] thanks for the prompt execution of her commands as you sent the bundle so kindly. She wrote me quite a letter and thanked me for mine, adding, "it would have been welcome with another page". Pretty, was it not? I almost forgot that I wanted to ask a favor of you which you will of course take no pains about if impracticable or improper. A most excellent woman, a poor widow with a very large family who was formerly our laundress, and now sews for my brother [-in-law] occasionally, has a daughter bred to the trade of a Tailoress. You know that a great proportion of the work of the great shops is given to women, and Mr Johnson recommended her to his Tailor St. John who employs her, but not sufficiently, as she has a Sister who can help her. Could you recommend her to the inimitable Mr Wheeler? If you could it would be a great charity. Her name is Helen Beatty. I do not think mine would shine as her underwriter in this affair because I have not the honor to write myself Madame, but Laura [Johnson] has [page 89] the dignity of a married woman, so take hers. I repeat it, do not trouble yourself about this if difficult, or if you do not like to. I know you love to do good if possible. The story of Miss Van Ness' rejection is false as I know from what Mr Curtis told me last summer. The other day I said to him when some one was by, "comment vont vos affaires?—Heureusement j'espère", "Pas trop" repondit-il, and looked rather troubled, but I believe, or rather I <u>guess</u> that he begins to think some other person might suit him as well. Forgive my pencil for my ink is too pale for any thing. Toujours à toi

ton amie

S

Sarah

29   Thursday P. M.   Oct. 22. 1829

My friend Sarah [Aspinwall] just left here and at parting asked me if I received a Note she left for me yesterday, and told me where to find it, in my work table where it had been lying perdue for twenty four hours. This must excuse me in your eyes mon cher ami for a tardy answer. I thank you for mentioning what you did, but I repeat I will have no [page 90] interference in this matter from those who have no right. I have chosen my own part in life and have no wish to alter it. On the contrary, attended as our affection has been with many trying circumstances and melancholy moments (if not despairing ones) there is that in [it] which is dearer to me than any thing else the world can offer. "I would not leave thee on a mossy bank, to meet a rival on a throne". But professions are always useless and empty. My conduct I hope and trust dear, will set your heart at rest, it is too good a heart to be uneasy.

We were not invited to Mrs J. Stone's. It was a small supper. Were you there?

To night there is a party at Mrs Donaldson's for the Collins'. I declined going there, but am obliged malgré moi to go to Mrs Kent's to-morrow. Perhaps we shall meet there, and if we do I shall not regret going. I was to have made a party for Mrs Collins to-morrow, but she was previously engaged. I did not regret it for I thought Mama would <u>perhaps</u> not invite you, and if that was the case it would have been very painful to me. I should have requested it. While speaking of our engagements I told her I [page 91] never desired to go to a party again. She said to me, "I hate to have you feel as if your happiness was so entirely blighted as you seem to". I told her I could not help that, I tried to do my duty. She replied, "that my treatment of my parents was lovely but she could see that my interest in other things was gone. Let me ask you one question said she, though you may think it a strange one. Would you if your Father did consent at once marry Mr B.? Do you think you know enough of him? I told her I felt that I did, though an immediate marriage might not be prudent. She said nothing more, but some kind things to soothe me, for my feelings were much excited. I do not know why, but I felt a <u>little</u> more inclined to hope after that conversation, for I thought if she had not some idea that Papa would one day consent she would have spoken differently. I shall try to send you your pencil case with this.

Mr Curtis goes to Europe on the 1st. I presume he means to prosecute his suit, and Mr [Nathaniel] Chauncey and I, think he is a fool if he does not.

I have not yet seen Miss Schroeder but hope to to-morrow. I must close [page 92] this. Have no uneasiness ever about me my dearest friend, but believe that our circumstances are so constantly in my thoughts that I am prepared for every emergency—except a favorable change. That would overcome me

> ever yours
> Sarah

Sarah

30   December 1st 1829

You were not here on Saturday nor at Church yesterday, and I fear you are ill my dear friend, especially as I recollect your complaining some days ago.

This idea makes me very unhappy. You will not think my curiosity <u>very</u> <u>silly</u>, will you? I dreamed that you had a consumption and the Physician said could never recover! Laura and myself paid our compliments to Mrs Duvivier this morning. I enclose this with some letters from my friend Mrs Kinloch, whom you may have heard me speak of. She is daughter of Mr Lowndes of Charleston and a very lovely being. I met with the letters the other day in turning over my year's collection, and reserved them as I thought they might interest you.

Ever your,

Sarah

Sarah

31 [page 93]   December 3d 1829

I had no time this morning to show you the imprudence of your accompanying me to church, and you were hurt and I was distressed by it. And yet mon ami why should you be hurt when you must be aware that it is my affection which prompts my caution.

I am always in fear of some imprudence drawing upon us such an expression of disapprobation from my Father as would be final. If that must be our fate I hope at least that it will not be given till you feel it best (or you would say till I do) to apply to him. Oh my dear friend if I could describe to you the sadness of heart with which I write now, and which so often oppresses me, but why should you know it? May you be able to hope with more sanguine feelings than

I do. I must reluctantly request you not to call here next week. When I said so I thought it of little consequence as no one was at home but myself, but I thought it most proper to mention your visit to Mama. On my telling her that you enquired for her she said "Mr B. does not like me and I cannot help it". I [page 94] told her I thought, nay was sure, you did. She replied ["]you would be the last one to know it; he attributes to me much that has passed; it is natural enough that he should, but entirely erroneous". I begged her to tell me the reason she had for saying so, for knowing by experience that the best of friends are careless of what is entrusted to them, I feared that you had unguardedly spoken of her to that effect to some one, but she said perhaps she was mistaken, so I presume it was mere conjecture, and was rejoiced to think it so, for you have always felt and spoken so generously about my family's objections as to make [me] confide in your heart and disposition ten fold.

Did I tell you that Mr Johnson [father-in-law of Sarah's sister Laura] of Stratford wrote to Robert Ch[arle]s[40] that it was the united wish of their whole family that you should join their Christmas party. I was much pleased. They like you, and you have only to be attentive to Mrs G, quiet about the house for Frances' sake, and not promote drinking to please the old gentleman to be vastly popular with all. I hope you will enjoy yourself there. You will there and at all times if the wishes and prayers are of any avail from your affectionate

S.

Sarah

32 [page 95]   Sunday evening 7, o'clk Dec° 6. 1929

I am suffering from a sick head ache just now, yet as I have the prospect of some time to myself, I must devote it as I would freely every thing that is mine to you. Your letter gave me great pleasure. I thank you "de corazon" [from the heart] as the Spaniards say for feeling as you do to me and mine, but though I have no idea of ever relinquishing my title of "dearest", you must [not] say "your only friend". How many more than two years ago. Mrs Rogers speaks

of you in a way to insure <u>my</u> gratitude. She said "I wish I could
do something for him. I wonder if he does not often [want] some
little service performed". Perhaps some time you may find occasion
to express to Mama your confidence in her goodness. I am sure it
would be well taken. Your feelings as to the regard of an elder female
are from the natural and unsullied feelings which have always been
very pleasing to me in you since our first acquaintance, and make
me feel as if my happiness would be secure in your keeping. I did
not mean what I said about Stratford as <u>hints</u>. I told Catherine [page
96] the other night that I was hurt that W[illia]m never mentioned
your being ill to me. The other day Mrs Bailey [William's mother-
in-law] asked Catherine when I was by, where Mrs Johnson bought
something she had. Catherine said it came from Mr W's. William
said, "she employs Mr Beach, not me, to shop for her". Margaret
answered sur le champ [on the instant], "That is because he is the
most obliging I guess". I told Mama of it when I returned, and she
laughed and said it was true, and spoke of Laura's regard for you,
but from her answer I thought she wished to end the conversation.
Do I not tire you by writing all such bagatelles? But as I cannot
talk to you just now I must write conversation tho' my letters dance
before my eyes. I would by no means you should relinquish visiting
here mon ami, only "act your judgment" about it, and be prudent.
I would rather not know when you mean to come, and shall always
if Mama is not present speak of it to her. If we could feel about the
difficulties which are around us, in the same manner that we should
regard the loss of friends or fortune, as if it were a trial from our
Heavenly Father, how much softer our feelings would be? Let us
regard it [page 97] in this way, and you who have been so much
without friends and deprived of your earthly Parents, have great
reason to trust in the orphan's God. You ask me what I mean by
"final disapprobation". The only reasons given by my Father were
such as certainly leave room for a further trial on your part, else I
should have despaired at first, but as he did not think you a business
man &c, you certainly have a fair opening for an application to him
when time has proved that. Time also will convince of the strength
and durability of my affection. I have therefore entertained hopes

which must be crushed if he should refuse his consent after these proofs of desert on your part, and constancy on both. My affection is yours forever, unless what it is idle to suppose you should throw it away, and my only wish in this world is to supply to you all that you have ever felt the want of in your isolated situation. I <u>will</u> hope in the bottom of my heart till I am obliged to open my eyes to the certainty that hope is vain. Try for my sake to be as well and contented as you can now mon cher ami, en attendant every happiness which can be the gift of a heart [page 98] devoted to you. But my head will ache terribly and so farewell my dearest friend. I wish I could <u>say</u> God bless you. Give Mrs K[inloch]'s letters to Miss Aspinwall when you no longer want them, perhaps she may like to read them. I need hardly repeat to you that happen what may, my treatment of you must always be what my heart dictates, for I do not concern myself "infringing the duty I owe my Parents" in so doing.

Again farewell

The interesting gossip, as some would see it, that attached the two lovers to each other against Woolsey's will moved on naturally to the conjecture that they were seeing each other secretly, thanks to sly tricks and deceits practiced by Sarah—and all that is to be guessed from what she says toward the latter part of the following.

33   February 25. 1830

I am obliged to pass a few minutes in idleness and my thoughts when not actively employed cannot admit any other object than that to which they are always inclined to turn. Our last interview gave me great pleasure on some accounts. I am rejoiced that Mr W[ard] is going out of your concern and delighted that you and W[illia]m have settled your continuance "à l'amiable".

I know you will for my sake do everything to make him like you and appreciate you and I look forward sanguinely to a greater degree of friendship and cordiality between you. I wish business opened brighter [page 99] this season, mais esperence ou plutot esperons [but, hope! or rather, let's hope so]. To look at the other side of the picture the idea of my Father's avoiding you in the Exchange, and not speaking in Church makes me very sad. You are right in not coming longer to our pew but I hope you will get a seat in our Church. Few things would give me so much pleasure, but if you do not wish to do it, I hope you will act as you think best, without recollecting that I have expressed such a wish.

I have "tante e tante cose" to say to you. Before you think anything about the application to my Father I have a million things to say, even the "five hours" would not exhaust my volubility. One thing which I forgot to tell you at your last visit was that some things I have heard said about our affairs which you must excuse me from repeating have wounded my feelings so much as to cause in part the depression which you chided. I have determined never to allow you to walk with me unless in company with a third person. You must not blame me my dearest friend.

I would sacrifice life, health, anything for you, but I cannot put my delicacy in the lips of idle and illnatured people by any act of my own. Do not speak of this [page 100] to me, for we shall not agree, but if you could know how much I have been hurt frequently by the observations and enquiries of others, you would not combat this feeling. When I am the subject of conversation between yourself and my Father, you must tell him that you wished to speak to him on the subject a year ago, but I would not permit it. If there be any blame I wish it to fall on me, not on you. My sister is going to Mrs Howland's[41] I believe. I have the impression that you have never visited her in town, and of course do not belong to the number of her five hundred friends. If so, come and see Laura's dress

Sarah

34   March 16. 1830

I believe my dear C, that it is about a year since the satisfaction of an uninterrupted conversation fell to our lot, and it is folly to expect that pleasure at present. So I am reduced to the necessity of employing my pen in what I could so much more clearly explain myself viva voce. The conversation I mentioned to you this morning began on my side. While I was sick I lay revolving your frequent requests to [page 101] speak openly with Mama and determined to comply with them. I asked her if Papa's feelings were the same as a year ago, and told her that all that time you wished very much to speak to him on the subject, but I thought it not best, that you felt that he was right in acting as he did as long as his opinion of you was unfavorable and your proper course was to remove his prejudices by your conduct, that you had always felt the highest respect and esteem for my Parents, and having no friend to look up to, was peculiarly desirous to secure their friendship, that however differently she might have believed these were your feelings, and if you had ever express'd yourself in any other manner it must have been in a moment of excitement, that you had learned at the time that Papa's objection was founded on his not believing you to possess stability of character, and his not giving you credit as a man of business, that these were things which time would prove, and I was desirous of knowing if Papa's objections were yet in full force and if an application to him now would be proper on your part. What I said further in your favor dear C, your own heart may suggest.

She told me that she not believe that Papa [page 102] would persist in his objection, but that at present business was not prosperous, and though she knew nothing of your circumstances she presumed from your having always depended on yourself, that they were entirely dependant on the business of each year, that though she knew me capable of any sacrifice, still from the entire ease with which I had been surrounded it would be imprudent in us as it would be in any one to begin life without being more advanced (Forgive all this business talk which I believe I do not express intelligibly). She did not think that an application to Papa would be worth while now for these reasons. He would consider giving his sanction to an engagement between us imprudent in him in the present state of business. My principal object in speaking to her was to save you the mortification of speaking to him if he was

unfavorable still. She said she believed that Papa and herself had seen
you in an unfortunate light in the beginning of your acquaintance,
as she thought the suddenness of your attachment showed it to be a
matter of calculation, and that at that time your manner (particularly
at Church) gave her the idea that you had no respect for religion, and
added with much feeling that if she could think you had a respect
and regard for that most important [page 103] concern, she should
feel as if my happiness were less doubtful. She said that she had not
seen that manner lately. I defended you as I always do, and told her
that intercourse with foreigners had given you a bad habit, not loose
principles. She said she knew nothing in the world against you. I
spoke very freely of my own feelings to you, and she seemed to be
entirely aware of them as was Papa. The very flattering conjecture
that you would not be capable of the same sacrifice for me that I
would make for you and that your affection was not so strong as
mine I mentioned to you this morning, and we parted just as you
said, "You do not think so?" No I do not think so, if I did I would
say but one more word to you, and that should be as summary as
the french Va-t-en [scram!] Your affection has been peculiarly dear
gratifying to me because I have felt from our unhappy circumstances
that I could not appear to you in as amiable a light as I ought when
health and spirits were failing, and besides the difficulties that have
beset us have made it a feeling so entirely entre nous, that it seems to
me ten times more pure generous and sacred than if it were a thing
participated with every body. I have always felt that your continuing
your pursuit was entirely voluntary, [page 104] there is no tie upon
you but that of feeling and none of the claim which the world has
upon people in ordinary circumstances

When my Father expressed his disapprobation, if any motive less
strong than love had influenced you, you could have then desisted
with honour, and at any subsequent period you could retire from the
pursuit and the world that impertinent neighbour could not hold you
responsible. All any body could say would be to assign my Father's
refusal for a reason and no one could (or should, if it depended on
me) blame you. I have not coldly reasoned thus on your affection my
dear Carrington, but have believed fearlessly and confidently that I

have yielded my heart to one on whose warm and disinterested love
I could rely. Mama told me she had always mentioned your visits
to Papa. I told her of course I wished her so to do, that we never
met except accidentally, unless it might be when you had in a few
instances joined me in the street, and which I had requested you
not to do except when I had some companion. She begged me to
think that the idea of watching me never entered her mind. I have
written all this and I do not know what you will think of it; you must
excuse my mentioning every thing so plainly, in a word with the
entire [page 105] frankness which we always use to each other. At
least what I have told you will convince you that I have been explicit
in my declarations concerning you. And now good night. I am weak
and very easily fatigued, but hope soon to be better.

May the time come when our mutual care for each other's
happiness shall be a rich reward for all past uneasiness.

<u>Yours</u>
S.

In the letter that follows, the reference to a big sale coming up is a
reminder of the fact that Carrington in his firm of *Woolsey Ward & Beach*
was in the auctioneering business (above, chap. 1 at n. 2).

Sarah

35   Monday 8. o'clk a. m. March 22. 1830

Mrs Richards has begged me to take tea with her this evening,
that she may have a visit from me before her departure. I am inclined
to anticipate our engagement for to-morrow and beg you to be my
companion in an otherwise solitary walk, that is dear C, if omnipotent
business does not interfere, the only rival I have. I am going about
half past 5, and you will join me "al bivio" [at the crossing]. The book
I enclose merely as a frank to my note, which you will destroy if you
please, for it is a monument of inconsistency, and as such should
perish. I hope your symptoms of scarlet fever have disappeared, and
that your sale today may be a marvellously good one

Yours truly   S.

Sarah

36 [page 106]   June 17. 1830

> I've manufactured for your use,
> A Thread-case, which you can't refuse.
> Well stored with thread and silken skein
> And needles which no rust may stain,
> And "patent pins" its cushion grace
> To make the neck cloth keep its place,
> Tape to renew a failing tie,
> And buttons which may chance supply
> Altho' the things unknown in rhymes
> A treacherous wristband's loss sometimes.
>
> Since in this world all things decay,
> Perhaps upon some future day,
> You'll find that not one thread remains
> Of those which once were ample skeins,
> Perhaps the cushion's sides within
> There may not be one little pin,
> The needle book may be bereft,
> And not a single button left,
> And must the mournful truth be told?
> The thread-case may itself grow old.
> Then think of her who fain would do
> All that affection can for you,
> And let her ready hand fulfil
> The dearest task which claims its skill

The preceding, with its charm of neat verse accompanying a neat little present, is followed after a very long interval by a brief note which certainly has something to do with prying eyes; but I find it as mystifying as Sarah evidently thought it would be to Carrington. Did she wish to prepare a story that he was spending the day in his sick-bed? Or had it anything to do with the fact that his lodging was visible from her house? In any case, there can have been no question of a secret tryst.

Sarah

37 [page 107]   Monday morning November 23. 1830

Will you do me the favour to order the green blinds of your
window to be shut all the day time? I am sorry to make a request
that may give you trouble, but feel obliged to do so, and trust to your
confidence in me to believe I have a good reason as grammarians say
"expressed or understood". Are you well this rainy day? and happy?
"Cose spera

la tua [which is the hope of yours—]
S.

Sarah

38   Monday evening November 29. 1830

I meant to say a few words to you my dear Carrington, which
our last agitated interview left unsaid before your note arrived, so I
will devote a portion of the time allotted to you, in answering your
request. I do not quite understand it however, nor your motive for
making it. The "charges" against you were certainly not facts to be
refuted, but opinions entertained unjustly, but which no declarations
of yours can overthrow, nor would it be anything but unfortunate to
attempt a vindication of yourself to my Father. What he said for the
most part [page 108] you are aware was connected with me as, "your
object in the pursuit being a mercenary one, your want of spirit
in following it against his wishes, his not wishing to contribute to
your support, his personal dislike, expressed in very harsh terms, his
low opinion of you as an individual, the differences between us &c
&c; then [you] were trifling, light, just the person who never would
succeed in life" &c, and forgive me for touching on still another
odious subject, he has seemed to think (an opinion current with
old people respecting young men) that expensive habits were one

bar to your success. This he did not <u>say</u>, and repeated, "he knew nothing against you". Why did you make me write all this hateful detail dearest C.? I have never since that conversation been able to banish it one moment from my memory, it seems to wither me when I think of it. I repeat it, that it is more than useless to say anything in refutation to my Father, it would be departing from your proper position, from what you owe yourself. The only argument which will have weight is <u>success</u>. That is the reward of the most active and indefatigable, and may he who is the help of the fatherless that trust in him, bless your endeavour.

Now let me tell you what has taken place since our interview on the 25th. Mama [page 109] told me that she had promised Papa she would go down stairs during your stay. My Father seemed extremely displeased with me after your visit, much more than before, and scarcely spoke to me for a day or two. I dined that day with Catherine, and gave her the outline of the story in the afternoon. She seemed surprised and sad. I was glad we met at Mrs Johnson's, I had only seen her before a third person. After you went away I told her all. She said "that all that about fortune &c was absurd preposterous". I told her I begged her to invite you when your absence would be noticed. She said, "most certainly, that she had no personal feeling but friendship". I hope you will be on easy terms again but do not forget your resolution to be "guarded", for you are too little so with people in general, nor that she has said, "you are welcome when Sarah is not here"

I hope my dearest friend has not forgotten and will not forget my request to say nothing on this subject. Put it in no one's power to repeat your words or misrepresent them. I shall tell Miss A[spinwall] Mrs Rogers and Mrs Meert[42] part of Papa's opinion. I hope you will remember Miss A's kindness in the beginning of our troubles, tho' with her your resolution [page 110] should also be <u>to be guarded</u>. I told Catherine and Laura that my feelings could not change, for I saw nothing in you to change them, but I could not speak to them, nor any one, of our destiny ultimately being connected with an event we can only allude to. How can I? Nor can I give the world reason to suppose that we are binding each other for an unknown period with the faintest prospect of union. They would say it is most ungenerous in each, and that I ought to leave you unfettered.

But I _have_ dear C, the moment it appears to you no longer best to continue your pursuit, if your feelings or judgment say so, that moment you are free, and no one shall blame you. Do not think hardly that I say this. I wish to be just to you, and to take no advantage of your strong affection. I feel in my own heart an unshaken confidence in its strength and duration. As Byron says, "yet oh more than all _untired by time_". The reposing consoling influence of this I cannot describe, yet I must not hide from myself that were I an indifferent person, and knew the _probable_ trials of hope deferred, intercourse restricted &c &c, I should say "it is impossible, he must be wearied in time".

[page 111] So dear C, do not blame me for alluding to this, but rather think it a proof that my affection does sometimes rise audessus de moi-même [even above myself]. When we shall meet except by accident or in public I know not, but my thoughts are yours.

I would not have you go to Mrs Cadle's[43] for any thing, and am very glad that it is not desirable in any point of view. _I can guess the pleasure_ at this moment particularly. Hier au soir je desirais beaucoup vous dire bon soir mais je ne voyais pas votre lumière. Peu après [yesterday evening I wished so to bid you good-night, but didn't see your light on; a little later] I perceived a flash of light suddenly on the wall which waked me. "était vous mon ami qui m'avait eveillé [it was you, my friend, that woke me]."

Mrs W[illia]m Johnson has a party the 8th. If Laura goes I shall probably accompany her. Can you not get an invitation? I will ask Mrs Rogers to take you if she goes, or perhaps you know some married lady who will do it. Good night, I am very cold, which must excuse this villian scrawl. Good night dream that there are faithful hearts still in the world.

Tuesday A. M. I find this morning that I can hardly read what I wrote last night, but you will forgive it. One recollection [page 112] gives me some hope for the future, that is, Papa's insisting that you can never succeed, and speaking of you as a lover of trifling amusement and expense (not directly but impliedly). If you do succeed in your new business and thro' your own efforts, he must change his opinion, and you at least will be justified, if nothing more, and I must hope that when there is nothing to give ground for opposition, it must fall, Adieu my own love, "il faut prendre les souvenirs pour les espérances" [one must take memories for hopes].

It is better not to answer this, unless you think it absolutely necessary. Do you continue your course of reading? I hope so, and that you will never remit what will give materials for reflection & conversation

✤   ✤   ✤

The reader of the correspondence has now reached to about mid-point. The pace has slackened, the year ends with only six letters between the lovers, as compared with thirty-two in 1829. Mr. Woolsey was winning. At the lovers' meeting of November 25th, Carrington, "agitated" as has been seen, had reverted to that forbidden topic, the "charges" against him; and in the long communication below, plainly Sarah is agitated to the same degree, and suffering greatly. Their problems are not new, but more sharply felt.

39   Thursday December 16th, 1830

Thank you dear C, for the matches which I find answer their end perfectly, and I associate your kind thoughtfulness with them as with many other little comforts.

The poetry was very pretty and I thank you for your trouble in copying it for me, and still more for the feeling which made you like it and think of me the while. [page 113] Have you the original spanish? and do you know the author? I should like the original much. They must be very freely translated for the style of spanish pieces is like a ballad, very simple and unaffected. Notwithstanding you say, "you could not have expressed your thoughts so poetically",

I greatly prefer the language of truth and real feeling which I hear from you to all the flatteries of poetry which must be exagerated and are generally unnatural. In the last "North American Review" there is a beautifully written article on the poetry of the Hebrews, very much in the style of Dr Channing tho' written by a very young man, a student at Andover. I forget the title but it is a review of Dr South's hebrew translations. Will you read it? it would just suit your taste which I remember is for critical writing. Mrs Johnson has the "North American".

Friday December 17.

Now dear Carrington I have a request to prefer to you, an appeal to the most generous part of your affection. It is that you will not urge me to meet you or walk with you. It is delightful to me to be with you, as it is to you, and I know how hard it is to be separated as we are, but my dear C, we have chosen to continue our affection [page 114] thro' all adversity and we must bear this with the rest. It is too hard for me to combat my own sorrow and also your wishes, it makes our few moments of meeting very painful. You can never know the deep mortification and self abasement which a woman feels at the thought she is clandestinely meeting or corresponding with one whom she may love ever so tenderly. You can never know what I have suffered, and how exquisitely painful is my regret that I ever consented to see you except at my own house. This is my only regret for all the rest I will cheerfully suffer ten times more wearysome days and sleepless nights for your sake, but do not oh! do not for the sake of your own gratification in my society, urge me to what I think wrong and imprudent, it will only be worse for both by and by and prejudice more and more my friends against you. Accident will do us the favour to let us meet sometimes, and in society sometimes also, and I will always do what I can to further this object with all propriety, but do let me be the judge for I act against my own wishes in denying your request. Do spare me that pain. Yes Dear C, we must exert our self command and bear like men our present trouble, secure in [page 115] each other's truth and hopeful for the future.

I went to Mrs Johnson's last night, no one there but Mrs Kent and her sisters. I was not well and felt very sad, but for worlds I would not have had you compromise your dignity and gone there. It would have been lowering yourself after all that Laura has said. Do not be hurt my own love by what I have written. You know my heart, a single dream for the future connected with you is enough to send a tide of gladness to it.

I am in hopes of hearing from you soon, that you are forming some profitable business plan. I have no anxiety for you, but I am nervously anxious that you should begin to gain that place in the world which will change my Father's opinion of you, and for the sake of its effect on your own character and happiness I would not have you long in suspense or inactivity.[44] Every body would deteriorate in such a state, and I look to your future course dear C, to prove your affection for me, the reality and disinterestedness of which have been cruelly doubted. Oh Carrington, what a sad lot is mine, with no one to unite with me in my opinion of you, no one to say a kind word for you, our affection pure and constant as it is having as yet led only to disappointment. At times it seems [page 116] as if it would break my heart, but I will not yield to such feelings. You will do every thing, will you not love? that you can do, and I will bear any thing that occurs while I have that cheering idea Good bye

Yours ever

S

Friday 11 P. M.

The little ribbon in the spanish language of colours would mean "faith and constancy". I am writing to say bon soir to you after Mrs R[oger]'s party, but it is growing late and I am cold, yet I will stay a little longer

December 19. 1830

Mama has been ill all day sick, and I have been reading to her. I have read two interesting sermons. Dear C, if you could only know all the wishes I have for you—I never offer a prayer that is not fraught with them.

You will not be hurt dear C, at what I have said in my note. You cannot doubt the strength and sincerity of an affection which has rendered the world a solitary place to me while it is forbidden me to indulge it. But I am so desirous that you should do all right, and that you should stand to all my friends [page 117] in an attitude of dignity and self respect which shall command theirs. They all know my feelings and shall know from time to time that there is no change in them. I am aware dear C, that while I cannot satisfy any claim which my having accepted your affection gives you on me, while that is denied me I have no right to dictate any course of conduct to you, but my desire for your honour and rectitude and success in life and love are stronger than any selfish feelings. "I could not love thee dear so much, Lov'd I not honour more"

> Adieu dear C, once more
> Yours

A resort to her faith seems to become more prominent in the correspondence as the distress of the relationship wears Sarah down, and in the final moments of the correspondence it quite takes over. The development was not unnatural, given the surrounding habits of family worship, her beloved brother's particular piety, the society of persons like Dr. Hodge (above, n. 19) and the Schroeders, and the general expectation of personal devotion to be displayed among the commercial elite of the city.

She would not have been able easily to distinguish between her religion and her morals, of course. They joined in her sense of "duty". The word is a heavy one in her vocabulary, as can be sensed in passages already encountered. In turn, duty which required obedience to her parents' wishes required also "honorable" observance of them, without hiding anything contrary to their wishes. Deceit would violate honor and "delicacy" as well, another term which included a woman's repression of sexual attraction (for example, in the thirty-third letter), at least anything expressed; but beyond that, it included selfless respect for others (in the eleventh letter and again in a friend's, the fifty-second, below). It was always to be expected of a "gentleman", such as Sarah hoped and believed her lover to be (as in the sixth letter); and so, too, she described the man she later married, Charles

Johnson, "possessing the feelings of a gentleman in a high degree."[45] She meant to indicate moral qualities as well as those merely of received style; but the word "gentleman", like "lady", more often did indicate a man or woman with the latter style. A simple "man" or "men" occurs very rarely in the family correspondence; non-gentlemen are referred to by name or some designation of their trade or low rank. Similarly, "women" occur rarely. They are distinct from "ladies", in the forty-fourth letter, below. Mrs. Sedgwick when she encountered the distinction made in her European travels exclaimed in disgust: such a sense of class was never to be found in America;[46] but hers was Republican idealism, not reality.

Sarah

40   Wednesday evening Jan[uar]y 19. 1831.

I wished very much to say a few words to you last evening my dearest friend, but I was detained by a long visit from Mr Pfaefer, and so exhausted by my efforts to entertain him and comprehend his bad english that I had no time left for one whom I have never felt the genant [burdensome] necessity of laboring to entertain. This morning at 12 o'clk Laura and Willy were here and I had an occupation as diverse from the one I would have chosen at that hour as [page 118] possible, viz, making a pudding, but to-morrow (thursday) I shall be interrupted by no dutchmen or puddings either, and will see you just before 12 o'clk. I have to go up Greenwich Street some distance and will you join me at Chamber Street? Put me in mind to tell you what Laura and I had heard the other night which put her out of spirits. I received some books which you sent, so I suppose you have finished some of the studies which have engaged you.

I have lately been reading the first volume which is all that is published of Sir James McIntosh' "Cabinet History of England". You know it is on the plan of Scott's "History of Scotland" and Moore's of Ireland. It is short and brief but I think a masterly account of the political early History of England, and very clear in its abstract of the character of the Sovereigns, particularly of Alfred, Richard coeur de

Lion, the Edwards &c. Miss Kent lent it to me. I read french almost
every evening, sometimes a play from a very voluminous collection
Theodore has, sometimes twenty pages of "Bossuet's discours sur
l'Histoire", which I believe has no end. Then I have in perusal
"letters from the Aegean" by Emerson. I have read little as yet but
it promises to be just [page 119] such a book of travels as would
beguile you of a longer time than you intended.

I did not like to ask Mama directly whether you could call or not,
but I told her what you said about coming in with Mrs Schroeder
and she said it would have excited remark if you had not come in
and she was glad you did. If you wish it I will ask her if she thinks it
proper for you to call. I hate to hazard a negative but you know that
there are few things which I will not essay to do, if you my own love
wish it.

I had such a lovely dream the other night dear Carrington,
portraying such a quiet secure domestic scene of happiness. I cannot
venture to tell you what it was. I never think more deeply on the
future than when I have been reading or thinking on religious
subjects, then the happiness we promise ourselves from our earthly
union seems to me so raised above all the untoward chances of life
and so hallowed and fitted for beings that may win an immortality
of mutual happiness hereafter—but I dare not say any more, or you
will think me an enthusiast

Yours

S.

The book I send as an apology for my note

Sarah

41 [page 120]   February 15th 1831

I have felt exceedingly unhappy for a few days dear Carrington,
and as you once so tenderly told me that my troubles were yours, I
must confess them to you, both for my own relief and to hear from
you something which may give a brighter colour to my thoughts. If

I could only see you in circumstances which favored an unreserved conversation, but I cannot, so I must write, altho' perhaps you will laugh at me for being so much disturbed. A gentleman the other evening (I <u>ought</u> not to say who, so I know you will not ask me) spoke incidentally of Mr [Convers][47] and said he was a very mean man, and upon my asking whether he was considered so as a man of business said, "yes, he did mean and dirty things in business" and another person said, "yes I have often heard that". Can it be true dearest C? Do not laugh at me when I tell you that the pain I felt on hearing this, brought on like a blow the suffering in my side I have spoken of before and my only idea was "could I but ask Carrington, he will tell me if it be true". I have always felt that I had been wrong to show you my anxiety that you should establish yourself as I did, it was not from any want of confidence believe me my dearest friend, yet [page 121] I was wrong, and if on my account you have united yourself to one who has not your own high minded noble ideas of what is honorable, how bitterly I should reproach myself.

Tell me dear C, what you think. That I felt or rather showed so much anxiety on your account when your business was changing, and the hasty declaration I made you the evening we came home from Mrs Rogers' about your leaving the country have always been subjects of great regret, but with you I am sure the clouds which surround us have long since been my apology for being unreasonable. If death were to deprive me of you, I suppose when it should be too late to receive pardon I should recall a thousand instances where I had pained your feelings, but if I err towards you, it is not from the heart. Could you know the constant unceasing concern I have for your happiness—it is the last petition of my prayer at night and the first in the morning, nor do I believe it is ever absent from my mind during the day. But why do I tell you this, when I hope circumstances will one day enable me to prove it more eloquently than by words. I say it to relieve the sadness of my own feelings at the moment, and to plead [page 122] my excuse if I seem officious in my enquiries.

Last evening my Mother asked me what I had in my hand and I told her it was a translation of yours which you had given me. She asked if I had read it, and as I thought she wished to hear it I offered to read it to her. She seemed pleased with it but only said, "he is an excellent french scholar, is he not?" It is the first time you have been mentioned between us for a long period, but I am determined to keep up the recollection that you are dear to me in her mind.

Let me hear from you soon dear C and give me the assurance that if you are allied with any one less noble than yourself, it is not in such a way as to endanger the fair reputation which is dearer to me than life

> Your affectionate
> S.

Sarah

42   Thursday Evening March 10. 1831

You told me dear Carrington that you wished I would send you all my library in the same way with Father Clement, so my book needs no apology as I was disappointed in seeing you this afternoon [page 123] and telling you of our change of plan. We shall not go to-morrow, not till Saturday and I am doubtful whether I go at all. Miss Dwight[48] is staying here, so my time is not quite my own. She enquired with interest for your nouvelles, said it was very long since she had seen you, and hoped you would come to Brooklyn.

I like George's wife, she seems to possess sense and spirit, qualities I have learned to prize during the past year particularly.

Before you came in this morning Laura spoke quite affection-ately of you, and of not seeing you for a long time. I am sure she regrets deeply having ever hurt your feelings, and probably did it in a moment of hasty excitement. Mrs Berger also this afternoon, asked me if you were at Mrs Sheldon's and spoke with regret of having seen you but once since New year, but supposed you had been very busy. I said both busy and indisposed. You surely have no cause dearest Carrington for the low spirits you seemed to feel at Mrs Sheldon's. You do not respect yourself enough. I know no one who is on equally familiar terms with such a number of persons whose friendship is worth having, and [page 124] that too without any thing to assist you except your own character. Such women as Mrs Sedgwick and Mrs Rogers do not like every body, and your standing and estimation are as much beyond the triflers whose existence is in fashionable circles, as you are superior to them. I will not rank the heart that is yours, among your sources of self gratulation, for its talents are for the world to estimate, you alone know its affection and tenderness, but alas! they are of little use to you. I pray you my own love to like yourself only as well as others like you, and you will not be in low spirits again.

My friend G. Pumpelly has just left here, he arrived to day. Mr. H[enry] Dwight thinks of delivering his course of lectures in New york.

Among other people who have been here to pass evenings is the Doct[o]r Eights. He gave me some novel accounts of whaling sealing &c, but I could not like him, because you do not. I am much amused with the "life and times of George 4th". There is much amusing anecdote in it and some eloquent writing. I am also vastly entertained with Madden's letters from Turkey and it is so popular I cannot get the second volume yet. He goes to see Lady Hester [page 125] Stanhope and meets with all sorts of droll adventures.

I must say good night for I am quite ill this evening. If they always oppose the wishes of my heart I fear it will kill me, but no more of that, it shall not, I will hoard a fund of happiness for the future.

Apropos to what you were saying this morning, I saw several ladies who said they were going to the Ball in common ball dress. Mrs Sheldon, her sister and party, Miss Bullus[49] &c, Mrs E. Jones said there would be such a crowd that she would not permit her daughters to go in costume. Mrs Clinton Tallmadge[50] said she should not, and about half were to be in simple dresses, so happily for those whose character is of some importance it is not necessary to "play the fool" as you say. Good night and if I go on Saturday you must receive my affectionate farewell

Yours ever
Sarah

Sarah

43   Albany Tuesday evening May 24. 1831

What would I have given this morning dear Carrington for a
longer adieu, indeed I could almost have chided you for leaving
[page 126] me so soon. It rained all day and I had leisure for so many
recollections. And as this moment I have your pen in my hand, votre
portrait sur moi, et votre image dans le coeur, do you think I could
forget your injunction to write with all these promptings? It is a very
great pleasure to me that I know at this moment where you are,
your very attitude is before me "in my mind's eye", as if I saw you in
reality.

I did not thank you for your attention so kindly bestowed on
my little nieces and Sister [Laura]. Believe my dearest C, that such
a kindness is more deeply felt by me than the greatest possible
obligation from an indifferent person. We understand each other
too well to need professions, but judge by your own affectionate
heart how much any such delicate mark of your affection touches
mine.

Miss Sedgwick came to the Fort from West Point with a Miss
Molinard daughter of the french professor. She was just from Paris,
spoke no english and listened with complacency to even my bad
french, which unless fate smiles on us I shall lose entirely. How
much depends on those same smiles! I am sure if that tide of
happiness could once flow through my [page 127] heart, it would
restore "health to my cheek" more than the skill of a College of
Physicians, but this is a dangerous subject, good night my dearest
friend, may we remember each other in our prayers at the same
throne of Grace, and hold the love of the same God and Saviour in
our hearts as our guiding light

Monday 29th May   Geneva

We reached Attica merely in time to call on Miss Kip and dine
before leaving for Trenton and on our return spent as short an
interval there. I looked with interest at the spot for you had lived

there and regretted not seeing those who knew and loved you. Miss Kip told me that Mr Kirkland told her, that his wife could not live a month with the cough she had. How could he let her go without him. W[illia]m Kirkland told me that he considered her in a rapid consumption. I am afraid you will have the pain of her death my dearest C. but I rejoice that tho' you will feel it deeply, it will not be so severe as it once would have been. May we be spared to each other.

The state of the roads obliged us to come from Schenectady to Geneva by [page 128] canal. We had to Montezuma where the Sineca canal begins, the company of two very intelligent foreigners, men of society who know how to treat a lady. They took a carriage with us to Trenton, and having many mutual acquaintances in this country we soon found them out: Mr Hambro a Dane and Mr Mansell an Englishman of french extraction, whose family live in the Island of Gurnsey. I liked them both, it was refreshing to meet well bred people in a Canal Boat, or Canaille [riff-raff] Boat as one may truly say, but Mr Mansell had a peculiar claim on me for without an actual resemblance, he constantly reminded me of the dearest person in the world, the same height, and in a frock coat the same figure as yours my love. Good night my dear, dear Carrington, pensez à moi, and believe me still the same affectionate

S–

Sarah

44   Cleaveland Ohio June 15. 1831

I wrote you from Geneva my dear Carrington and am in hopes that you have [page 129] also heard of me thro' my sister to whom I have written since my arrival here. She mentioned you in the only letter I have received from New york since my departure.

To say that I have thought of you constantly would be superfluous, you have no fear of being forgotten, it were almost wronging you to suspect you of doubting it, nor have there been wanting some remembrances of you, even in this remote region. I have seen a lady

formerly from Attica who knew you in "days of long syne", and the
only, or rather one of the few men here who use the razor constantly
and preserve a genteel appearance Mrs Hoadly pointed out to me
as resembling you. He happened to be a <u>Hatter</u> but does not have
the insignia of his craft in his air or tournure [appearance], and in
Ohio that is quite an aristocratic business. There is little distinction in rank here although a far better society than I had imagined:
a number of pleasant young married women but no young ladies
scarcely, and what there are, and indeed the married ladies also,
have little leisure and less taste for intellectual improvement. The
gentlemen are rather better, indeed I have seen several intelligent
lawyers [page 130] and one very agreeable German gentleman from
Euclid who promised me a spanish book.

Mrs A[rchibald] Gracie[51] past a day here. I was very glad to see
her. She asked for "our mutual friend Mr Beach" in a way that made
me <u>her</u> friend forever. Only think of the literary Mr [Jared] Sparks
and the illiterate Miss Prime.

I enjoyed my short visit at Geneva exceedingly. We left there
Monday Mor[nin]g and went to Rochester that evening. The day
was distressingly warm, the road bad, and I was much annoyed by
some vulgar foreigners who were our companions. I was quite ill
when we alighted but rest soon restored me. In the morning of
Tuesday I walked before the hour of parting to see the Falls which
interested me much.

Mr Hambro and Mr Mansell joined us again at Rochester in
place of the persons who had made the day before disagreeable, the
road was quite good and I reached Lockport not feeling fatigued
at all. The next morning we went to Lewiston to breakfast, then to
Niagara where at Forsyth's our two companions and ourselves were
the only guests except transient people. It is useless [page 131] to
say what I thought and felt at Niagara. If you had only been with me
it would have been the pleasantest day of my life, the day I spent on
Goat Island. But my companions however agreeable were nothing
to the one I would have chosen, and my pleasure in the enjoyment of
nature nothing to what it would have been if you had shared it. My

dearest C, I must send you this with all its imperfections on its head and try my pillow as the only relief to a most agonizing tooth ache. I am pretty well generally, but either from fatigue of the journey, or debility, I have been hardly awake since I came here. Good bye my own love, yours truly

S.

10. o'clk. P. M. I wrote this last page in an agony of pain which made me unable to close and direct it. It will therefore reach you one day later, but being now relieved from suffering I can bid you more deliberately farewell. You do not forget my request to you at this hour? I am sure you do not. Good night my dearest C. Would that I could say with a word all that I wish for you at this moment.

Sarah

45 [page 132]   Detroit Michigan June 25. 1831

You will see by my date my dear Carrington that I am a hundred miles or so farther from you than before. I came yesterday to this place from mere curiosity and pour passer le temps. Mr and Mrs Allen of Cleveland were coming to pass a Sunday here and return in the same Boat which stops a day and a half. They were urgent with me to join them and I came. The sail is quite pretty, that is the latter part of the way, through the Islands and the scene of Perry's Victory and afterwards through Detroit river. The evening sky was beautiful, the moon rising directly out of the water, and the fine setting sun, and all the peaceful thoughts of such a scene, where should they lead me my dearest C, but to that friend in whose heart I know that distance and absence never effaces my image.

The length of time which elapsed between writing and sending my last was unavoidable, and I am making you my best apology by employing the freedom of my present situation in reiterating every affectionate assurance and kind wish to you. It will not be [page 133] long before I am on return home, tho' our journey for my health's sake will be rather an indirect one. Theodore will return from Cincinati this week, and next my steps will bend to the spot to which all my thoughts and wishes turn. Oh my dearest C, if we could but meet as I could wish, if our reunion were such as we both hope! But I cannot indulge such thoughts. When I dwell for a moment on our situation I am entirely overcome and can scarcely rally a hope for better days.

Laura mentioned in her last that you had dined there with Mrs H[armon] Pompelly[52] and afterwards walked on the Battery the same or some other evening. How eagerly I looked over her letter for some trace of you, and how pleased I was to find your name, of course you were well or you could not have dined out, and in so far I am happy.

I am writing on the floor with my Port-folio for a desk. You will excuse the scrawl which is <u>incident</u> to the accommodations of a Country Tavern, but you told me that these lines would be valuable and tho' I am so soon to return to Cleveland I would write now for fear of an interruption there. Do you know [page 134] two or three times when I have been thinking of you for a moment I have been persuaded that I have seen you, and on a second look have discovered that the person whom I had for an instant mistaken was as unlike you as possible.

I must say good bye to my own love, with every thing that can convey the kindest sentiments of my heart. Au revoir mon ami,

Toujours à toi
S.

Sarah

46   Cleaveland (Ohio) July 11. 1831

When I wrote to you a fortnight since from Michigan I little thought that so long time would elapse before my departure for the home which has all my thoughts and affections. Yet my dearest friend here I am still, at the expiration of the six weeks which I had mamed [=named] as the limit of my journey. Theodore wrote me from Cincinnati that he would be here on the 7th and hoped I would be ready to leave Ohio in a few days, but he has not made his appearance, and I cannot divest myself of anxiety on his account. [page 135] William arrived yesterday and brought me a shower of letters. Laura wrote John that you had accompanied Harman and his lovely wife to Oswego for a few days' visit. I am rejoiced that you allowed yourself that relaxation from the fatigues of business and the heat of the City. And I rejoice that you have added (as I am sure you have) such worthy people as the Pompelly family to your circle of friends. I admired Mrs Bacon's[53] appearance much and her Sister's (Susan's) conversation struck me as being far superior to what one usually meets with, particularly in a village. If I go to Ithaca & Oswego on my way home, I shall hear of you at the latter place, and I know they will speak of you just as I could wish.

I learn some sad things from my letters. What a sad death of Mrs Hoffman's[54] and my friend Mrs Cadwalader[55] is thought to be in a consumption. How mysterious it seems to us that one so useful in every relation of life, so important to her parents, Husband and Child should have her days numbered so early, and Mrs Kerkland[56] too, I have thought of you when her illness has been mentioned, if she had been your wife I think she [page 136] would have been more tenderly watched over. It is wrong to judge without grounding our opinion upon <u>every</u> circumstance, but it seems as if his present illness was a sort of punishment for his coldness to her. Mais trève à ces trifles sujets.

Our return from Detroit was delightful. Our party the only occupant of a fine Cabin and the Lake as smooth as possible. The Captain stopt at Malden on the Canada shore of Detroit River, where we saw Indians from the western shores of Michigan and Superior who had come down for their presents from the British Government. They were more free and wild than any I had ever seen, indeed they had many of them never seen white men before leaving their homes and were undebased with the vices of civilization which is all that Indians seem to learn from us. Their dress was very picturesque, that is, the Sacs and Foxes, who are large athletic men and very gay in their tastes. If you remember to ask me I will describe their head-dress to you when I see you.

Since my return, I have been to dine at Mr West's an Irish Gentleman living near here, whose Wife knows Miss Edgeworth [page 137] and told me many things respecting her. In the afternoon I took a ride with him in his farm wagon, which is merely a box on wheels, no springs at all; there were seven of us in this "wheel machine" as the Wests called it, and we were accommodated with wooden chairs for Seats, having previously rode seven miles and walked two, to reach his House. I was somewhat fatigued, but the motion of the self same wheel machine driven up and down at the rate of eight miles an hour put every thought of former fatigue to flight; I verily thought all my members would be dissevered; a walk thro' woods and brambles of half a mile brought me to the spot we were in quest of, then the rattling Wagon retraced its steps, and after tea we returned home, nine miles or more, of which I had walked two in going out, but was well satisfied to ride on the return. So you see on this day at least I obeyed your injunctions which Miss Silliman delivered to me, "to take a great deal of exercise and grow fat". The latter I must leave to my return, for really I have no time here.

"It never rains but it pours" with frightful [page 138] vehemence to me, I really have been alarmed with the fury of the showers. There are very frequent thunder storms, but I am told in the latter part of July and August, the ground is parched and the streams dried up. From the absence of shade and the nature of the soil in this part of the country, the sun and the reflection thereof are very powerful and painful to me, and the nights are very cool with heavier dews than I ever saw any where else; there is danger from being exposed to them. As to riding one of John's horses is at Twinsb[er]g and the other at Euclid. I have taken some <u>drives</u> with pleasure, but there are not many covered vehicles and the Sun is tremendous. I will not fatigue you with an account of some of the various tea-drinkings which I have accepted among these hospitable people, but pray put me in mind to tell you of the Ball on the 4th of July.

What a long letter! I will write once more on the road somewhere, and not but once if I stay a year.

Believe me more than ever you
affectionate
S.

Sarah

47 [page 139]   August 1831

My dear C,

The Philadelphia Mail this morning brought us the sad news that the hopes of a whole family are crushed in the untimely death of our dear cousin Charles. To my Mother this blow is as if she had lost a son, and my whole care to-day has hardly kept her from sinking under it. The funeral is to-morrow just after the arrival of the Boat, that she might arrive in time, but she felt that she had better not breach them at that moment so Mr Johnson kindly acceded to my proposal to go with her to-morrow morning. Theodore has gone to the funeral. I have been very busy in packing Mama's trunk and getting her mourning ready as far as possible and making arrangements for William and Catherine who are to arrive to-night. Mama is in such a state I am fearful that the noise and bustle will make her ill, but I have given them the upper rooms, to keep the children from her. Mr Johnson has left Laura in my care so that my sleeping apartment will be in Pine Street till his return. Was not he [page 140] very good to go? I write this to you because I have had to make such an effort all day—I want to unburthen my heart to some one I love. One of my Cleaveland friends Mr McCurdy of "McCurdy & Dorrs" is here. He was very kind to me on our Detroit journey, he was of our party and is tho' fat and not very elegant, one of the best hearts in the world, besides being a very <u>good</u> customer. Will you be attentive to him if you see him for my sake

Yours as ever
S.

Sarah

48   September 16. 1831

The agitation into which the subject we spoke of the other day
threw me, was so great that I have not yet recovered my spirits or
composure. I am afraid I cannot explain myself upon it fully by word
of mouth, so you will please read this my dearest C.

I feel now how great was my error in allowing you to continue
to love me, when any opposition existed on the part of a person so
determined as my Father. I never dreamed of so strong a dislike—
you intreated, I was ready to be persuaded, and our hopes cheated
[page 141] us both. All regret is unavailing now, and you know my
dearest C, that my only regret is on your account—for myself I
would willingly suffer all I have for the happiness I have received
from your affection which forms all I can ever know of happiness in
this life.

I promised never to desert you, and never to speak to you of
breaking our engagement. I placed it in your hands to do as you
should at all times wish or think best. Altho' the idea that your
judgment should think it necessary for us to part, and that possibly
indifference on your side might in time follow is more painful than
I dare to think of, yet were you to deem it necessary to resign me,
I should know that therein you thought yourself acting for my good
as well as your own. I should pity you but never accuse you, no
never for any thing, but you understand me. You once told me you
would never ask me to marry without my Father's consent, and I
only promised to be your wife with that, or if I should be my own
Mistress. I am aware how much is due to your untired love and also
of the claims I have given you. I am very desirous that at a proper
time you should apply to my Father in the manner [page 142] we
spoke of. You owe it to yourself so to do, now that circumstances
permit, and to state the reason why you have not done so before,
and I would wish you to repeat the sentiment that you have held to
me, that as long as he thought so unworthily of you, he was right
to object, it was your place to convince him of his mistake by your

conduct. And now my dearest friend you will ask me what I will do in case you fail with him. I will in the first place use every argument to soften him and convince him of my tenacity, circumstances may arise that would justify me in declaring that at some fixed time I will take my own way, but I cannot promise what you think I ought, that I will at all events make this declaration. My Father is now an old man of sixty-five and his state of health has made us fear his sudden death. He has treated me of late far more tenderly than formerly, and I do feel most reluctant to act in direct opposition to him fearing the consequences to my own happiness and of course yours; besides in the opinion of the few who know, you would be justified, but with most people the blame would fall on you as a young [page 143] man opposed to one much older and generally known. I am perfectly aware that I have no right to expect you to wait longer, I know that patience hath had its perfect work, and that if Papa denies you, and if I cannot feel justified in breaking all ties with him, I know that I must bear what to me is the greatest trial excepting to lose you by death, but of that I cannot speak, you must consult your own happiness

You think if I were to marry against his consent it would soon be over, I mean his feelings, but you do not know him, it would never be over. He would give me my inheritance but not back his affection

I do not know what hopes there may be that he will consent. He knows my unhappiness and sometimes I think he must. I have always thought the only chance for us arose from your own success and the estimation in which your own success and the estimation in which you are held by men of business. How far this may have influenced him I do not know, but fear not much as his habits are retired.

Oh Carrington my love if our union could take place with God's blessing and that of my Father!—that it may be so, that that blessing at least may rest on you spiritually and temporally is a prayer I never sleep without repeating.

Carrington took up the invitation that he make his case with Woolsey. He did so by letter. Woolsey withheld his reply from Saturday through the following Monday and for some period beyond. When it was delivered, it was still an unmoved and hostile one, offered to his daughter. He never deigned to answer Carrington directly.

Sarah

49 [page 144]   Sunday evening September. 1831.

Dearest C, I have been most painfully ill ever since Wednesday with severe nervous pain in my head. Until yesterday I scarcely left my bed. I gave your letter to my Father yesterday. He has said not one word to me respecting it or his intentions since, and I presume he has not given you any answer or you would have let me know.

I will see you the moment I have any thing decisive to tell you, at home if possible, and if you have any communication from him you will tell me soon I hope

If you wish me to walk with you, let it be up Greenwich Street. I have much to say to you but would prefer not seeing you while this suspense lasts. That and my illness are more than I can well bear, but I try to support myself. I shall if I am able, ride out to-morrow, for I feel worn out with sleeplessness and pain, but believe me in joy and sorrow

ever yours

S.

Miss Wallace sends me the worst news of Mrs Cadwallader. She was much better for three days after the birth of her child [page 145] which is now ten days old, but an alarming change has taken place and they have no hope.

Monday Evening

You will be happy to learn that a visit to a Dentist this morning in some degree removed my pain, and I hope by rest to-night to feel somewhat recruited to-morrow. I have not had one word from my Father, have you? If you have anything to tell me to lessen this suspense will you write, and request Mary Dwight to retain your note for me. I rode this evening to the eastern part of the City to see our poor old domestic Hagar who is dying of consumption. She was very glad to see me tho' very near death and in great suffering and shows herself so humble a christian that I rejoiced that she was going to a world where there is neither distinction of color or station and where pain and sorrow are no more

yours truly
S.

Sarah

50   Monday Evening 20th May 1832

I have been hoping ever since Thursday to catch your eye that I might [page 146] say good bye to you dearest C, but have been disappointed. I was too ill to go out last week until that day.

At 12 o'clk to-day Mrs Hoadly my brother and myself go to New Haven. I shall return on Wednesday evening, and for a few days shall be entirely alone. I hope to see you then and tell you all I have to tell, and what is more, hear all I want to hear. It seems a very long age since we met my own love, but you must not forget that whether absent or present I am as always yours

(in haste)
S.

While everything seems much as usual between Sarah and Carrington at the time of the preceding letter, as indeed for a long time, with casual items sprinkled into the correspondence—social visits, gossip, shared pleasures of reading—the pain of their impossible situation has evidently continued to chew at them, or at least, at Sarah; for, without one particular reason but rather an accumulation of many, now, a month and a half later, she writes to give him his dismissal.

Sarah

51   July 8. 1832

It is with a head aching almost to distraction and a sad heart that I sit down to perform a painful duty to you my friend. Ever since the bad result of the application to Papa, there have been times when

I thought it needful to request you to relinquish our unfortunate engagement. I then found that my hopes that he would consent if you were in prosperous circumstances were fallacious. Still I hoped sometimes [page 147] and at others you were so unhappy that with culpable cowardice I did not do it.

We have seen little of each other of late and once I was on the point of saying all I felt necessary but could not, nor I fear could I ever were it a personal communication. But now dear C, I must do it. In going on so—for perhaps years longer—I am losing health strength and every thing else. I cannot live in this struggle of feeling. I have been in such an atmosphere of death and sorrow that I have been led to seek direction from God in prayer. The result of my prayers and reflections has been a conviction that I have only one right course to pursue.

My Father has great troubles now in the sad affairs of W[illia]m's firm. He has his family to support which makes it more hopeless that he should incline to me. I have been wrong, very wrong, to let this go on for I was determined never to marry without his consent and might have seen that our case was hopeless, but I did not view my duty as strongly as I do now.

Add to this I have been most cruelly wounded and mortified by what has been said of me and our affairs, I cannot bear [page 148] it. I cannot tell you the anguish with which I relinquish this cherished attachment. You can realize it but in addition to what you feel, I feel my wrong conduct in not at the first breaking off this, and lessening your suffering when your love for me was not so strong. I have wept till I can weep no longer. Dear C, will you pity and forgive me?

We part with the kindest of feelings toward each other. Mine to you I cannot express, thro' the remainder of my life my friendship for you will be one of the strongest feelings of my nature, and it would kill me to fear or know that you had done any thing unworthy of a man or a christian. You cannot think harshly of one, who, tho' her affection has been a curse to you, has loved you as long and faithfully as I have. You are too generous to blame me because my devotion to you has been in vain. Much more would I do had I any hope, and did I not think it wrong. Your letters to me I destroy, dear

C, for in this time of pestilence life is too uncertain to hazard their falling into other hands. I make it one of my last requests to you that you will not fail to do the same [page 149] with mine, but any other memorial you may have from me, I beg you to retain as a token of an interest and friendship which will survive this life. I would also beg you my friend to keep up your interests in such of my friends as you are attached to. The life of seclusion which my feelings will dispose me to lead will prevent our meeting while it is so painful. I know not when I can sustain an interview with one to whom I have been so closely bound, but if you can with truth convey to me thro' my sister or any other friend one word of message saying that you acquiesce in my determination it will be very consoling in my miserable moments. One more request my friend and I have done. The world has been busy in a most ill-natured way with me and my affairs. I need not ask of your generosity to speak of me with respect. You could do no otherwise, but will you have the kindness to say as little as possible on the subject of our engagement or its rupture. It is sufficient for any one to know that we found my Father's objections could never be overcome, and that we part with a high opinion of [page 150] each other. If I have fulfilled my painful task with more harshness than I might, forgive me my best friend. I am ill and worn out with sorrow. I scarcely know what I do write. That we both may have the peace of God is my ardent and constant prayer for you and myself. There is a world of rest, and a tribunal where we shall be judged not by our actions but by our motives. Dear C, farewell—pity and forgive me.

Do not answer this. I cannot bear it now, but think as kindly of me as you can

On the day on which the preceding was mailed, Sarah sent off another letter, this one to Theodore,[57] telling him how "this Spring I have felt so perfectly quiet & tranquil about everything especially as to what may happen in the future that at times I have believed that I have attained to a submission to the will of God & the peace that follows from it." The "future" plainly indicated the outcome or ending of her engagement. In thinking of it she had been able take the high ground, very successfully.

Receiving the letter to end the engagement, Carrington promptly sought the intervention of Elizabeth Devereux. She and her husband George were friends and sometimes house-guests of Laura and William Johnson at the old Johnson place in Connecticut.[58] She could be a good go-between. He made his visit to her and put the case. She shared with him the letter in which she urged it upon Sarah.

Near the end of her letter she mentions Carrington's possible "exile," meaning some overseas job offer he was considering (and see also the fifty-third letter).

52   Copy of a letter from Mrs Devereux to Sarah Dwight Woolsey
                Stratford July 15th 1832

My dear Sarah

I have been wishing to write you for some days past, but a feeble body and a heavy heart have prevented.

I wished to urge you to come immediately here to recruit and cheer me by your dear society, avoiding New Haven as in the present state of your friends there [in the wake of William's failure], you would be exposed to distressing scenes [page 151] without doing good, and you are too feeble to be in the way of your duty there. I say <u>wished</u> because I now see there are some feelings to be consulted, that until last evening I was ignorant of. You will I trust deem it no breach of confidence that Mr B[each] has made me acquainted with the state of affairs between you. I also hope you will attribute my doing or saying anything on the subject to its right cause, a true and deep interest in you both—for you I have felt an affection for years almost maternal and a closer acquaintance with him only confirms my first impressions, and convinces me that he is a man of great worth and most deeply attached to you.

I have seen the pain, I may say agony, which your letter has given him, and you would be shocked to see what these few days of suffering have effected in his appearance. His being without family ties has induced him to centre his all in you, and most distressing is the effort to resign it. In compliance with your wishes he does not write to you, but requests me to say the following (I would premise that knowing Laura's [page 152] feelings towards him, he has been deeply pained by her being made the medium of communicating with him)

"Will Mrs D. say to Sarah that altho' I cannot acknowledge the correctness of her reasoning in regard to our engagement yet having promised to be guided by her wishes, I am prepared to acquiesce. The letters are in N. Y. and I cannot therefore fulfil the request for their destruction. The 'memorials' given me will always remain my most cherished objects, and I entreat that those given by me may be retained. I could not bear to receive them back. Every thing I wished to live for was centered in an affection and constancy I believed enduring as our lives, and I cannot help feeling that utter desolateness which can know no remedy but the grave".

Now may I ask my dear Sarah, have you well considered the step you have taken. I should I am sure do you less than justice did I believe you could ever cast off an affection and engagement of four years' standing and I must think it is done in compliance with a sense of filial duty. Far be it from me to lessen the claim of a child's duty, but I also think something is due to one you have allowed [page 153] for so long to consider himself to have an interest in your affections, and thereby become attached to you, with a feeling which is far different from the evanescent love of a boy. By casting him off you have closed his present and his future, and I must say it is no light matter.

Your Father's wishes should certainly be regarded, but why not let things be as they have been hoping for brighter days. Excuse me my dear I use the plainness of a tried [= a person whose patience is tried], something is due to yourself. The circumstances of your engagement having been so long persevered in against your father's known wishes has given it a publicity and a character it would not otherwise have had, and breaking off will expose you to remarks which your delicacy will and ought to shrink from. Now the worst that is said, is, that you are attached and engaged without your Father's approbation. When it is known to be broken off, you will be exposed to the accusation of fickleness and indelicacy I much fear.

May the Hearer of Prayer guide you in what is best, and he will if you seek his aid. If your attachment is gone, certainly give it up, and tell Mr B. that it is so. It will be best for him, as [page 154] pride will do as much to support him under it. If not, consider well ere you take a step so important to you both, which may condemn you to a single life, and him to one of exile.

I would add what perhaps I ought not, that there are those near you who have other views for you. And now, my dear, I have done. Excuse my plainness, it is because I love you, and my hand writing, for I write in bed. (Don't feel as if you must reply to this, and unless you wish otherwise I will never allude to the subject again.)

It will give me more pleasure than I can tell to see you here as you feel able to come, but if you do not, I will make some reasonable excuse for your not coming. I am only confined for a few days I trust. The family are well, and my news from the South of its usual chequered tenor. Mr D. is better and worse by turns, but he who doeth all things well, will take care of us both, and my prayer is that he may guide and guard you and all who are dear to you

Truly your friend

Elizabeth Devereux in fact wrote twice to Sarah, first in a note to explain her indisposition, also to invite Sarah up to Connecticut, and with an indication that a longer letter would be on the way, regarding Sarah's engagement and Carrington's career plans. The long letter, above, was somehow delayed. Sarah at first responded only to the short one.

Sarah

53 [page 155]   Copy of a letter from Sarah Dwight Woolsey
                                                      to Mrs Devereux
                                        New Haven July 20th 1832

My dear Betsey

I received your short letter this morning (of Wednesday) but have not received any other. I am very sorry that you are in bed still, and deeply sensible of your kindness in writing under such circumstances.

I agree that I am ignorant of the contents of your letter to which you allude and cannot reply. If convenient to you all I shall go to Stratford sometime towards the last or middle of next month when I planned to go, as Bess [sister Elizabeth Woolsey Winthrop] would feel hurt if I left her now. I have only been here five days before in two years.

My ill health is mere debility owing to weakening complaints, brought on, or increased, by long walks when Mrs Rogers was sick. I am getting better and as I mean to take my own way about visiting, hope to escape the fatigue incident to New Haven way of living.

My dear Betsey, I trust Mr B. will take no step, nor accept any offer under his present feelings which his judgement w[oul]d not approve under others. When the business season begins he can form what [page 156] plans the state of things renders most expedient better than now. I am no judge of the advantages of his offer, of course, but should think he might be more comfortable if going to France or England. I thank him for his concern for my health, but rejoice that he is where he can find such congenial society as at Stratford. The tie between us which always depended on my Father's consent I should have dissolved long ago were it not for his wishes, as my fears for the result were much stronger than my hopes ever were except when raised by the sanguineness of his disposition. I am at last convinced that I have been fixed in my choice in vain. My Parents depend on me for comfort almost entirely. My only regret is that the surrender involves the happiness of another

I view life as I never did before, and my only wish is to submit cheerfully if possible to what God in his goodness gives or withholds from me, and if I could see him feel so, and hope that he was seeking peace of mind at the foot of the cross, I should be indeed comforted.

If I am wrong in my resolution I am not wilfully so, for I have certainly acted [page 157] as nothing but a sense of duty could have induced me to, in this dissolving with him, and I have humbly sought direction as to what is my duty. The consideration of his feelings after having so long encouraged them, has, you may well believe not been forgotten, but to persevere in our fruitless, hopeless attachment I am persuaded is not the best for him. My dear Cousin if he has your friendship as I think he has, do you counsel him in the best way for him. Do point out the <u>first</u> great consolation [prayer] and lead him to the second causes which are in every one's power, self control, rational employment and society. If he values my happiness he will try to be happy. I thank him again for his concern for my health, but would by no means wish him to leave Stratford, if he is well there. It is like him to propose it. Do not let him dwell upon this subject in conversation with you, it is the worst way to make any thing wear more deeply and do you advise him not to form plans for the future under the influence of a feeling of recklessness. That would exceedingly pain me.

I presume tho' I have no knowledge [page 158] of the contents of your letter this will be an answer to them. I can never thank you enough for your friendship and sympathy but I love you most dearly

Yours

Sarah

54   From the same to the same
New Haven Tuesday m[ornin]g July 24.1834[!]

My dear Betsey

I have only today received your first letter and though thankful for the freedom and kindness which I have always wished you to express your opinion to me, I was deeply pained and surprised by its contents. Is it possible you can think I have acted capriciously or thoughtlessly in an affair which takes from me the charm of life, that is humanly speaking. Could you know how I have suffered, how long each motive for doing differently which you bring up has dwelt upon me, and with what agony I made up my mind after seeking in my prayers the only guidance under which I wish to walk, you would perhaps feel as if I had done right. The strongest thing was, the unhappiness which I knew Carrington would feel. I care little [page 159] for my own, for even after an act which deprives me of the prospect of ever entering into those ties which constitute a woman's happiness in life, blessed be God there are duties I can perform and beings to whom I am important, so that I am not left to the desolation which I fear is his portion.

My dear Cousin, my only consolation as it regards him has been th[at] he could not misunderstand me, but that, your letter has destroyed. If <u>you</u> think it necessary to urge upon me the considerations you have, I fear he too thinks that I have lightly thrown him away, and forgot at once all that has passed between us, but that is impossible. During the period, nearly four years which our attachment has subsisted, I am sure he cannot forget all I have done to ensure its happy termination, nor that I have never given him a moment's uneasiness. I did not think it necessary to express all I felt for him, but I now say that aside from the approbation of my conscience there is only one pleasureable feeling I can carry on in life with me, and that is, that we have parted with an unchanged opinion of each other.

You tell me my love that I shall be charged [page 160] with fickleness and indelicacy. I hope the quiet of my life will ensure me against the first—you know I am now at an age when a lady no longer receives attention unless she throws herself in society, which I shall shun.

The engagement between Carrington and myself always depended on Papa's consent, that is he always knew my decided intention not to marry without it. Until last fall he never was, since our connection, in a situation which made it prudent to marry. Then he applied fruitlessly to my Father. During the winter I thought it best to break off our engagement, but with a culpable weakness I did not. He thought of going to India, and if he had then left his country, it would have been my wish that he might feel assured of my resolution to persevere. I now think <u>that</u> would have been very unfortunate for him, as I am convinced it would only have been protracting feelings which under the circumstances are utterly fruitless.

It would not certainly have been <u>best</u> to say nothing of <u>right</u>, to have gone on so for years and years longer. Such cruel things were said by the world, which you cannot judge of, that I must [page 161] have denied myself the pleasure of his society—and can you think it would have been best to continue a secret tie, while I could never hope to see him more than any casual acquaintance. With every advantage to make him sought for as a companion if he mixed in society, do you not see that this would in time be only a tie of honour? Without intercourse to keep up his interest in one who would be losing constantly in many attractions, do you not soberly think such a state of things would be very unfortunate for him? As to the question of right, I may be deceived, but I certainly have sought and I hope humbly, direction of my heavenly Father, and the result has been a conviction that I must submit. My Father's claims on me, broken as he is of late in health and spirits appear to me stronger than they have done ever before, perhaps because my feelings of duty are more clear.

If we can be sure of duty by the pain we have in giving up inclination, I may be easy as to mine, for dear Cousin, I cannot and need not tell you what I have suffered. I wish I could hear you say, that upon my statement of the subject you thought I had done best. You say "if your affection is gone, say [page 162] so at once", as if it were possible in the course of a few weeks, with every recollection to increase it.

My dear Betsey if I seem insensible to your kindness, forgive me, it is not so. If I have used less kindness to my dear Carrington than I might, pray him to forgive me. My task was so painful that I could not pause to think of the manner of performing it. Do you use your influence over him to lead him to the Throne of Grace, and do you advise him (from yourself) to use his judgement in forming any plan for life—not act hastily or as he may repent of.

As to the "views for me" which any one may have, I can hardly think any one would so err in friendship for another as to associate them in any plan for so wilful and intractable a subject as myself. Dear Betsey I am sensible, deeply sensible for your friendship, and trust if we do not agree in opinion it is with the best belief in each other's motives.

Affectionately and ever yours

How she adjusted to the decision she had now imposed on the situation is reflected in what she wrote to Theodore, ever her confidant, in October:

news of social doings, visits, her return to her sketching, chapters in the
memoirs of a French noblewoman, and "I am reading something I like
much better—Jeremy Taylor's Holy Living. If I could so live I could possess
myself amid the occupations & cares of the world so as to live above them in
my heart. While my duty was performed, then I should be happy. I mean to
try a strict arrangement of time, so that each avocation shall have its place,
hoping [in this w]ay that I shall escape that confusion of thoughts which
is a moth upon time, as fulness and improvement in every way. . . . I have
just sealed a long letter to Martha [Salisbury, his fiancée], and tomorrow
or perhaps tonight I mean to to Mary Shoemaker—and get that awful
thing off my mind." And here she ends. The "awful thing" can only be the
termination of her engagement, and the need of a strict regimen in her
life is just what afflicts one's thoughts toward the turn of the New Year.[59]

Three months and more passed since the last letter, and Carrington then writes directly to Sarah, passing the letter through Nathaniel
Chauncey (as I suppose: "Mr C."). She replies:

Sarah

55   Saturday Evening Nov[embe]r 3. 1832

I have this afternoon received your letter and cannot rest without
[page 163] answering it. Painful, deeply painful as were its contents
and the spirit in w[hic]h it was written, I have still the consolation
of knowing that had yours not reached me, before I had sent one
intended for you, you would have done me the justice I think I should
do you, if circumstances should arise which made your conduct
appear inconsistent with what I should expect from you.

Mr C. gave me the message you sent me. It was the first time
I had heard your name mentioned saving by Mrs Devereux in any
other than a common way and it overcame me entirely. I could not
answer him, but in a note charged him with a message to you, the
purport of which [was] a request that you would send me by letter
the explanation you wished to give, for I saw not how I could receive
it in any other way, and felt as if I could not summon spirits for an
interview under such different circumstances from what we had met

under before. My health had depended on my composure, I must strive to retain that or be a wretched useless being, unfit from my selfish sorrow to fulfil any of the purposes for which I am placed in the world. Mr C. declined [page 164] this message, or rather he said something to that effect. I have entirely forgotten what, for I was much agitated when he spoke of my note to him, and said what I know meant that he w[oul]d rather not do it. I did mean to acquire that self command which w[oul]d have allowed me to meet you as I wished, as a kind valued friend; but when I turned round on Mr D's steps and saw how near you were to me (I did not know you were behind me before) I could not speak and turned away. I knew and regretted that you would think me cold, but I believed a second thought would be "poor girl, she feels too much to meet me composedly".

The invitation to Mrs Staples'[60] I received in such a way as led me to think she did not expect any company, or I should not have gone. I have been out twice since I came home deceived in the same way, but in both instances have felt that to dance would have been more than I could have borne. I could not be a good enough actress to meet you as I would any other person, to hide the pain which remembrance of the bitter past gave me. I was cold, perhaps. [page 165] I lament it, and if your letter had not anticipated my explanation I should have said so. I trust I may in future be more collected, but I closed the conversation w[hic]h you allude to, so abruptly, because I felt too much to govern, it was no place to look composed, and I preferred showing you how incapable I was of appearing the easy unembarrassed friend, than showing to the world that I was much agitated, which I should have done in a moment more.

How could you judge me so unkindly after all I have felt done and suffered for you, and will you never think that my notions have been (if in your opinion mistaken) yet deserving respect, as they are those which are the fruit of a sincere view of my duty, and indeed all that I could do, taking everything under consideration? But when you read this you will understand me; and I ask it as the only thing you can do to remove the load memory must always lay upon my heart, to form your opinion of my actions from your previous knowledge of my character. That is what I always shall do towards you, and indeed have had an occasion in which to put this in practise lately, when the connections [page 166] of Miss D. insisted so much on your having formed an attachment to her

As to my letters, do what you wish. I care very little about them, excepting that I feared they might make you unhappy. But our feelings were so well known to the public, that excepting that I should feel naturally unwelcome feelings meant for you sh[oul]d meet the eye of another, I should care little, for they are constantly just what I might be expected to say in the painful circumstances under which they were written. I never dreamed of your "making an ill use of them". I judge you by myself—do you follow the same rule, and remember that you have not been the only or the greatest sufferer in the unhappiness which has been thro' my means brought upon you.

God preserve your life, health and give you success in your present purpose. I feel as if my future lot was to take care of my parents thro' their declining age and look forward to nothing but the hope of making myself useful and acceptable in the sight of my Master.

When we next meet I trust it may be "with the smile of [page 167] welcome". It will be, if I can command smiles, at any rate, tho' my cup must be poisoned by the feeling that my injudicious encouragement of feelings, which had so little hope to guide them, has been such a thorn in your path. Yet the idea of your friendship wherever you may be will be an indescribable pleasure to me. I am sure you understand my feelings now, and that you will view me with indulgence.

I am very careful not to mention the subject to any one voluntarily and if I am ever obliged to speak of it shall do justice to your treatment of me at any and all times, as well as to your character in general.

And now farewell my friend with the reiterated assurance of as warm a friendship and interest in your welfare as I am capable of feeling, and of your good wishes, too deep for words. I am yours sincerely

S.

Sunday Nov 4th 1832

I enclose my letter to add a few lines to what I wrote in haste last night.

I know you will feel troubled that you wrote what you did, and at the pain it [page 168] gave me. But do not feel so. If absence or the death of either should forbid a continuance of friendly expression in our accidental meetings, I shall rejoice to hold this assurance of your friendship for me particularly as in a moment when I thought my life was drawing to its close, I destroyed <u>most</u> of your letters, <u>all</u> that my prejudiced eye might misinterpret and enclosed <u>one</u> souvenir of you with directions to be sent you unopened in case of my death.

You too will be glad to think that if I ever did utter "an unkind word" it was from any thing but an unkind cause. Perhaps it would have been more consistant with the line of conduct I think honorable on my part not to have expressed what must distress you, namely in how slight a degree I have recovered my composure but I repelled with indignation the idea that you had already forgotten the events of years as unworthy of you and inconsistant with my knowledge of your heart and character.

From you I ask your friendship and <u>justice</u>. The world was loud in its censures of my conduct during our engagement, and now blames [page 169] me for ending it. I sought not its approbation in either, and I must add its censure to all I have to bear, but <u>yours</u>, after all that has passed may be natural on your part but I cannot bear it. When weighed down to the extreme of ill health and spirit, worn out with the contention I had kept up for years with my nearest relatives, seeing no hope for the future, but a continuance of the same difficulties and embarrassments, I sought to perform what I honestly thought, and still think both the course of duty and what was best for both. I knew I was resigning all individual hopes and prospects, that a solitude of soul must succeed, and a state of mere tranquility was all I could hope to attain to. At least it has been as severe as I expected. To add to my suffering the idea that you feel as bitterly as one sentence of your letter would convey would be cruel and unworthy of you.

But those feelings arose from my unfortunate error w[hic]h I lamented at the time, that is, that I could not meet you with the free disengaged air of a mere friend, and sheltered myself in reserve. After [page 170] what I have said I know they will pass away, and in our widely separate paths, wherever yours may lead, you will carry with you, and I shall keep by me, the assurance of a friendship as sincere as our attachment was unfortunate.

I trust your expedition does not involve danger [from yellow fever]. I know not the state of New Orleans at this season, but the same Providence will attend you, and to him I trust you will commend yourself. It is a great comfort to me to remember my friends in my prayers, and before that Searcher of Hearts whom I dare to appeal to for the purity of the motives of my conduct towards you, I can safely dwell upon your welfare here and hereafter.

farewell kind friend

Sarah

56   Sunday December 2. 1832

I have a few words to say in my own justification, that before we part perhaps forever, a kinder judgment of me may be formed in your mind. I wished to <u>say</u> them should accident give me the opportunity of speaking without a witness, [page 171] yet when we met to-day your manner took from me the inclination and power to say any thing. This should teach us both, as I am sure we desire each other's friendship, to bear in mind that we ought not to think of <u>manner</u>. You were hurt with me once, and I know your consideration that I had no reason to be hurt with you. Those who have been in the habits of intimacy which we were, must feel unequal to assuming the easy manner of mere friends unless when assisted by the presence of indifferent persons.

I did hope that you would have done me justice and have acknowledged that sad as is our lot, I could do no otherwise, but I suppose it is expecting too much, at least until time should soften the blow and reason view the subject in a truer light. Yet much as I have suffered, more since the excitement of feeling is over, which always attends a great effort than ever before, I must still think I had no choice in what I did. I never said or thought I could marry against my Father's consent, and when I became convinced that <u>nothing</u> would alter his determination what could I do? I certainly thought as any one would [page 172] that his opposition would be given up, and wonder at the strength of the sentiment on his part which withstood my perseverance and pleadings. Could I have foreseen all in the beginning certainly I would not have given you all the mortification that has followed, but after all I went through (buoyed up by some hope, and then found all fruitless, and my health in such a state as to excite alarm in indifferent persons even), to be obliged to relinquish all, and be blamed by you—Oh it is too hard. You can never know what I suffered during those four years. The irritation in which my Father was constantly kept by his knowledge of my attachment, of course produced a feeling towards me, and influenced his manner to me to a degree which made my life wretched.

It is no use to tell you now what were my trials then. Had I the feelings of submission at all times which I feel at some more tranquil moments, I should be more comfortable, but alas, I can only pray for them for us both. Our unhappiness admits of no remedy, save in the spirit which God gives us to bear with it. May you claim the promise made to such as [page 173] trust him.

The considerations I have alluded to, will I trust in time make you judge of me with indulgence. I have poisoned your cup, let it plead my forgiveness that my own has been sufficiently imbued with bitterness. You cannot blame my motives, you may think me mistaken weak or over persuaded, but you cannot accuse me of instability of feeling or worldliness, unless you think my character at once transformed from what you have always known it; and for my apology for what I have done, let my wasted youth, blighted hopes and sorrowing heart speak.

Mrs Devereux is your sincere friend I am sure, and for Miss D[evereux] I spoke to her of you freely and she expressed herself most warmly. Had not her kind well meaning but giddy and injudicious friend Miss L. so talked and acted as if she thought

Miss D. the object of your pursuit those silly stories would not have been abroad and her friends would not have acted so absurdly about your seeing her.

I have lived in so recluse a way that I know not what the world says of us. My friends respect my feelings too much to allude to the subject. I suppose however the usual uncharitable judgments are [page 174] framed of me, yet as other things are so much nearer my heart, I care little for it. I shall ever maintain silence on the subject unless I should hear you blamed and then I will speak.

I know I have said all and more than I wished, but as these are perhaps the last words my hand may ever pen to you, I may be allowed to say how much I value your friendship. Should time soften what we feel, you must allow me the place of Sister. <u>Now</u> I <u>claim</u> nothing, only <u>ask</u> your kind judgment of me, and if you will give me one small share of the good wishes and prayers I constantly give you, I shall feel consoled.

I shall sacredly retain the papers entrusted to me, which I trust may be returned to you when I am no more.

One word more. I am aware that I am passing that period when with the bloom of youth vanish the attractions that females possess. With your sex, it is otherwise, and "younger and fairer you'll another see". Should this be the case remember that my last farewell contains a prayer for your happiness in <u>all</u> circumstances.

And now may God bless you a thousand and a thousand times, is the wish of your most true and sincere friend

S.

The concern with which Sarah closes the preceding—that she is on the edge of being unmarriageably old—was a natural one, at twenty-eight. Theodore, the most recent in the family to take a wife, had first found the girl in her teens, and in one of her letters, triumphantly young, she speaks of a woman of her own acquaintance recently reduced to a hideous match—"the lady a Miss Gardiner, over thirty years old and I suppose very accomplished and agreeable—she certainly has had <u>time</u> enough to become so."[61] In fact, Theodore's bride was of the most ordinary age when the marriage finally took place, delayed for reasonable reasons of property transfer and the building of a house: she was twenty-one. But her sex anticipated marriage in some realistic way by their mid- to late teens.[62]

Sarah

57 [page 175]   September 3.^d 1833

    I am unwilling to trust to the uncertainties of absence the papers which I believe you meant to be returned when you should arrive from New Orleans. I ought to have returned them, and have been still more faulty in not returning a year ago the gift of affection which I had no longer a right to keep. I was very wrong, but a dread of returning to painful associations must be my apology.

    When I had promised my Father that in no circumstances could we be more than friends, I hoped we might be friends always, but my conduct has been marked with avoidance which you may have been surprised at. I told you a year since that unkind things had been said of us, or rather of me. They have been repeated to me frequently this season with the exaggerations of time and distance to deepen their malignity. I can only be silent, leaving to God our own hearts and each other their refutation and the opinion, dear indeed, of the uprightness of our motives and intentions; but they have obliged me to adopt a formal and constrained avoidance, instead [page 176] of the open friendliness I would wish.

    The time may come when all will be forgotten and I may prove my desire to be your friend. Providence forbade any thing more, and I trust you feel as I now do that however severe, all has been for the best.

    May She who will fill a nearer place, be as worthy as you deserve, and may you be as happy as I hope

Your friend
S. D. W.

(May 1834)

[page 177]

"I never nurs'd a dear Gazelle
To glad me with its bright black eye,
 But when it came to know me well
And love me—it was sure to die"

 Yes thou must die, thy footsteps fail,
 Thine eye is hollow, and thy cheek
 Tho' yet the crimson hues prevail
 'Tis not of health's bright reign they speak,
Ah no! ah no! that hectic spot
Too plainly tells thy coming lot.

 Yes thou must die, and I must stand
 Dearest! beside thy dying bed.
 And press in in[!] mine thy wither'd hand,
 And gently raise thy feeble head
Wet thy parch'd lips, and wipe thy brow
'Tis all thy husband's office now.

 This painful task shall still be mine
 I'll bend to catch thy faintest tone
 And watch thine eye, thy spirit's shrine
 Till from its orb all light has gone
And then—no other hand shall close
Thine eye lids for their long repose.

 And dost thou think that I can bear
 To wander thro' my lonely home
 And meet no cheering welcome there
 No gentle murmur, hast thou come"
[page 178] No lovely smile, no answering voice,
To bid my weary soul rejoice?

 To sit by my deserted hearth
 When care and toil the day have spent,
 And muse upon thy truth, thy worth—
 Our tranquil days of sweet content
And lose myself, and turn to press
Thy downy cheek with fond caress.

It cannot be, no dearest no!
When thou art number'd with the dead,
I feel the stroke which lays thee low
Will fall resistless on my head.
We'll love while life shall grant us breath
And undivided be in death.   1831

"Written" (by Sarah D. Woolsey) "Aug[us]t 3.ᵈ 1826 after visiting
my dear Mother's grave".

1

I stood and wept upon the spot
   Where I have wept for years
When first I learnt my future lot
   Would be traced out in tears.
Here, ere I scarce had known thy power
   Or felt a Mother's claim,
Here, when in early childhood's hour
   A mourner sad I came.

[page 179]

2

And here while youth's warm blood is high
   Alone, unmark'd I stand
And think upon thy hapless eye
   Thy thin and pulseless hand,
Thy heart so noble and so kind,
   Thy spirit free, yet tamed,
Oh why for thine immortal mind
   Was such frail casket framed.

3

Oh can I turn me to the wave
   To pleasure's ceaseless din—
My Mother! from thy holy grave
   Turn to the world and sin
Oh God in mercy let me bear
   Within my soul thy light,

Which blest my heart while weeping there
  Too high for earth to blight

4

And should an earthly idol stray
  Between me and my God,
And he should bear my hope away
  I'll bow me to his rod,
And murmur not, altho' from me
  My heart's best good is riven
'Twill lead my spirit on to thee
  To share thy bliss in Heaven

1834

With these verses, all softer—not to say bleating—sentiments in the record give place to anger, and, under more or less control, it is anger that dominates the conclusion of the story.

Well in the background is the happy discovery by Sarah of Charles Johnson, and of Sarah, by him, which gives a tone of settled intimacy to their correspondence by the summer of 1834.[63]

[signature]

[page 180] Letter from William Samuel Johnson Esq
No. 58   29 Warren Street Jan[uar]y 30. 1835

  H. C. Beach Esq
          My dear sir
      As long ago as the middle of October last, Miss Woolsey requested me to see you, in reference to your continued correspondence with her, and particularly with reference to letters she had then lately received. I promised her that I would do so, and once I called at your office for the purpose but you were out. A very natural reluctance to approach the subject, arising out of my regard to you, the delicacy of the subject and my affection and relationship to Miss W. has prevented me from speaking on the subject at any of the meetings we have had, and indeed I hoped that your own discretion

would induce you to stop your communications to her, and to erase all traces of her from your heart. Your letter to her of the 26th instant, has revived the subject, and shown me that my hopes were vain.

Your letter is before me, and like the other letters to which allusion is above made, has been seen by the immediate family of Miss W. I will answer your Notes, Miss W. will not. You inquired when she was to be married and the "very day". This is a question which I apprehend you have no right to ask, any more than any other man. Your engagements (if any such ever existed) have [page 181] been dissolved, and thus the relationship (if any) terminated. From thenceforth, you became as two indifferent individuals. The right of each party to dissolve any such engagement, when it exists, is absolute, and when dissolved, it ends. Still I answer your question. Miss W. is not to be married immediately, the day of her marriage is not fixed.

In your late Note you express your surprise at receiving a Note of invitation from Mrs. Johnson, and you inquire whether Miss W. "had any agency in sending you the Note". Your surprise has very much surprised Mrs Johnson and myself. We had supposed that our expression of friendship for, and interest in you, as manifested in both conduct and language, had been so uniform and consistent, that it would have been a cause of surprise with you had Mrs J. omitted to invite you to her house, on an occasion when the invitations were far less general than the late one. If our conduct and language have failed to express to you such sentiments, they have done us injustice. We have a strong friendship for you personally, and there is no one who will rejoice more in your welfare and prosperity and happiness, or sympathise more truly in your afflictions, should they overtake you than Mrs J. and myself. Mrs Johnson [page 182] invited you to our house where we are always pleased to see you. Your non-acceptance of the invitation did not surprise us. It was left to your judgment and feelings to come or not, and it would have given us pleasure to have seen you. Miss W. did not know that you were invited here until she received your Note. She had no agency whatever in your being invited here.

Let no false inferences be drawn from the above expressions of interest in you; they have no connection whatsoever with the affairs between you and Miss W. and last of all things are they intended to bear any implication even of censure of Miss W. The subjects are entirely independent of each other.

You must be aware, or if it has not occurred to you, a moment's reflection will make you realize that your attempts at a correspondence or communication with Miss W. now that your former intimacy has terminated are extremely unpleasant to her, and her protectors, indeed that they are improper. I think that your very good sense and gentlemanly feelings will prevent their recurrence. You know my affection for her, and my feelings know scarce a shade of difference in the allegiance I owe to her and to my own Sisters. The expressions of hatred and detestation [page 183]—I do not note them to censure—which you have used in respect to Miss W. evince, that no kind impulse induces you to seek knowledge of her. You should suffer no other impulse to influence your conduct.

Long since Miss Woolsey requested you to destroy her letters. Afterwards in a letter to her, you said that you never would do so. She now requests that you will restore her letters to her. It will give me pleasure to receive the package for her. I know of no good motive that should induce you to decline the request, and can hardly think that you will decline it. I presume you feel like every other man of honor no desire to keep that, which is attended by no pleasant associations, and may by possibility give uneasiness to one whom you have no desire to injure. Your desire must be to get rid of that, the keeping of which can do you no good, and will gratify another to possess. Your expression before cited was made long ago and under feelings which I hope time has obliterated.

During our long acquaintance and frequent intercourse, it is seldom that your affairs with Miss W. have been a matter or remark, and then I believe only when there has been a special cause [page 184] for it. I have avoided them, because no good could arise from the discussion, it might give pain, and I wished to prevent our personal feelings towards each other, and our personal intercourse being affected by them. My desire still remains the same. I know of nothing in this letter which requires an answer, or of anything in the occasion which has given rise to it, that should affect our conduct towards each other.

It will be my study to forget this letter as soon as it is sent to you, to meet you as if it had not been written, and always to manifest to you that I am in truth and sincerity

Your friend & Servant

W[illia]m Sam[ue]l Johnson

H.C. Beach

No. 59   New york February 4. 1835

W[illia]m Sam[ue]l Johnson Esq
No. 29 Warren Street, New york
Dear Sir

I must apologize to you for presuming to reply to your letter of January 30[th] as you evidently did not intend I should do so. There are however some things in it that ought to be explained, and which my sense of propriety would have kept from the knowledge of every person on Earth [page 185] but Miss W. But as she obliges me to make explanations to another, I cannot choose.

When Miss W. admitted what you are pleased to term "your engagement (if any ever existed)", there were certain Rings, containing each a lock of hair, exchanged, and it was agreed with many solemn vows, that should the feelings of either change, the rings should be returned.

In a note to me in January 1829. Miss W. says, "Did you understand what I said to you as we parted? It was that you should give to me the very ditto of the simple Ring, which, if you follow Pelham's rules, is such an one as a gentleman may keep. I have worn it many years, but will wear its substitute with much more pleasure". In another Note soon after, "My Father says if I choose to marry you, it must be without hope of his consent. This I know your feelings would revolt at, as well as mine. Alas for us both. We are doomed to unhappiness, for what I told you the last time we met at my Sister's" (that if she did not marry me, she would never marry) "must ever be true on my part. But for you who have no home, no friends, if you can ever be happy, think not of the heart you have gained, and the hope which is taken from you, if you can be ever happy with another, think not of me, and I will try to be glad [page 186] that you are happy and forget the past. If this does not happen, if you retain unchanged by time the remembrance of my love, recall to mind all I have ever told you, look upon the Ring, and remember that as long as I do not take from you this token of my affection my heart is still yours" (the latter part of the above is written, <u>in the original</u>, in french).

Hearing Miss W. was engaged to Mr Johnson (and indeed if I am not mistaken being told so by yourself) I presumed she would send me her Ring and ask for mine, but in the hurry of a new engagement, I supposed she had forgotten the (to her) trifling circumstance. I intended on the "very day", to have sent her the Ring now in my possession, and that is one reason I wished to know the "very day".

There was another reason which is of no consequence here. Had Miss W. told the simple fact, directly or indirectly, I should have been satisfied, and the false position, the request and the course she has pursued have placed me in, would have been avoided.

As to whether <u>an engagement ever existed</u>, I will give Miss W.'s words from her letter of January 1st 1829. "I am frequently enquired of whether the report of an engagement between us is true. I say not, but that we are the best of friends. Is this wrong? What [page 187] can I say? The tie tho' indirect and unacknowledged is binding on feeling and principle, and I hope makes you easy, may I not say happy?"

In a Note soon after she says, "You seemed hurt that I mentioned that you might be happy with another. I wrote from the impulse of the moment, I hardly know what, and only admitted that sentiment when I contrasted my situation with friends and home with your lonely one, and felt that you were most to be pitied. But cher ami, neither your imagination nor wishes can paint my attachment more fervid than it is. This unhappy circumstance" (alluding to her Father's decision) "removes all disguise & I feel it no departure from feminine delicacy to say so, conscious that my heart is in the safe keeping of an honorable and upright man".

I hope these extracts and they are but from four among more than fifty letters, will settle the question of engagement and it is to be recollected, they were not from a novel-reading Miss of fifteen, but from one of more than ordinary powers of mind, and who had attained an age when women are usually allowed to judge for themselves.

It was I believe more than a year since Mrs Johnson had invited me to a party, and I was therefore surprised at her [page 188] invitation. Miss W. might wish an invitation, to convince me how entirely the past could in her mind be obliterated by the present, and to show with what unconcern she could meet the man who was weak enough to believe in her truth, but I was wrong, I own it, and am sorry I indulged the suspicion.

One word more as to Mrs Johnson and yourself. During the early part of my acquaintance with Miss W. I was told by her that Mrs Johnson was to her the dearest person in the world, and that she hoped I would make her <u>second</u> in my heart. This I found an easy matter, and I used playfully to ask dear little Sue [the Johnsons' daughter], to place me <u>third</u> on her list, as she was <u>third</u> on mine. Sometime I think in 1830, Mrs Johnson endeavoured to persuade me that I ought to relinquish the idea of marrying Miss W. and among other things intimated as I thought that her sister's marrying me, even with her Father's consent, she should consider a stain upon the family. However true this might be it was not agreeable to hear it intimated. This conversation did not however cause me to do the slightest injustice to Mrs Johnson's fine mind and excellent sense, and it was the very circumstance [page 189] of being regarded in this light by one to whom I was really attached that pained me, and since that day I have never been even spoken to by Mrs Johnson without the intrusion of this unwelcome idea.

Her treatment of me as well as your own, has been at all times kind, and even more than kind, and for the trouble I have caused and am causing you, in this dark page of my life, I would it were in my power to show how much I thank you. Perhaps that power may one day be given me. As to Susan, the avowal that my New Year's visit gave her pleasure, was to me, the most agreeable incident of the day.

As to expressions of hatred and detestation, if they are unpardonable from me, are they commendable from Mr Woolsey. Mrs Chancellor Kent once asked me why William Woolsey and myself dissolved partnership. I answered by asking her, if she should wish her son to continue connected with yourself, should she know that Mr Woolsey took frequent occasion to speak disparagingly of him, that he represented him as of a fickle, changing, trifling, disposition, as not a man of business &c. She replied "not an hour". Now this was my situation for nearly three years. There was no intercourse of advice and counsel in our affairs, that would have been [page 190] so useful to us. With me, he never would communicate, and William always trembled in his presence, and to this want of confidential communication our dissolution was mainly to be ascribed, as well as William's late entire loss of property. My partnership afterwards was formed not in accordance with my judgment, but because Miss W. was anxious her Father should not be able to say I was "out of business."

But to return, so far was Mr Woolsey's hatred and detestation of me carried, that he declared "that if his daughter married me, and I remained in New York, <u>he</u> would move out of the city". The common civilities between man and man have not been observed towards me on his part, my letter to him has never been either returned or answered; indeed my standing unsustained by family interest or powerful friends induced Mr Woolsey to suppose that my feelings, or interest or welfare, were not of the slightest account. Situated as you have ever been in the world, surrounded by persons whose duty and business it was to aid you by every means in their power, I say thus situated, you can hardly conceive how discouraging and blighting the influence of a contrary spirit evinced towards you would [page 191] become. At times it preyed upon me to such a degree, that like George, in the Vicar of Wakefield, "I regarded myself as one of those vile things that Nature designed should be thrown by into her lumber-room, there to perish in obscurity".

But I have lived through it all without losing in character or reputation, and not even the frowns and predictions of Mr Woolsey, nor the loss of all I hold most dear, have broken my spirit. And as to having given Miss W. any trouble, except in this request, I have not and I hope you will do me the justice to believe it. I have not for a long time gone to a party where I supposed she could by any possibility be invited. I have left off visiting except at long intervals at houses where I might meet her, your house among the number, and her name seldom passed my lips, for I ask no person's sympathy.

With regard to the letters, I have but one answer to make. I will return or rather restore the Books and other small tokens of affection (given me by Miss W.) of various descriptions, if she wishes them, but the letters I shall retain. They are <u>mine</u>, they were written <u>to me</u>, I have paid dearly for them for they will cost me the happiness and repose of a whole life. The extracts [page 192] given to day would never have seen the light had it not become necessary to defend myself from the charge of seeking a correspondence. Miss W. cannot even now, with all the cause she has given me for breaking faith on my part, put her hand upon her heart and say she has the slightest suspicion that I will make a bad use of them.

The ridicule which the world always casts upon the want of success in affairs of the heart, and the quick march of my successful rival, who, the word said, was engaged even before my miniature was returned, did sting me to the quick, and I have doubtless applied harsh terms to a conduct I could find nothing in Miss W.'s previous life and feelings and a confidential intercourse of four years to warrant.

But I have now done with this subject and as my former notes were "seen by the immediate family of Miss W", I hope this letter also may be shown them.

I am aware that after this making as the Spaniards say "a clean breast of it" you may not be willing to treat me as if <u>I had not answered </u>your letter. If so, it will give me great pain, for my heart tells me, that however [page 193] it has been taught to distrust almost every-thing and every-body, it never distrusted the sincerity with which you have always assured me, you were my friend, as I am, and shall ever be, however you may receive this,

Very truly Yours
H. C. Beach

No. 60   29 Warren Street Feb. 6th 1835

My dear Beach

I acknowledge the receipt of your letter of the 4th inst., and notice some of the contents. To prevent misapprehensions & to assure you that nothing in the correspondence or connected with it, affects in the slightest, the regard I have always had for you, I fear from some slight things in your letter, that I may have given you pain. If such is the case, the pain I have occasioned you will come back in the form of agony to me. I used my utmost caution not to pain you, but the sound and healthy cannot imagine the sensibility of the afflicted. If my caution has failed, I pray you find my excuse in that principle.

You mistook me, "I did not intend" that you should not answer my letter. I intended to render an answer unnecessary [page 194] and thus leave you entirely free, to not answer it or to answer, as your judgment or feelings might dictate. I think you did right, to answer it, as what you have written proves.

The contents of the letter surprize me. The information I <u>did</u> not possess as to particulars, but what I had observed before prepared me for its general character.

I wonder that the rings have not been exchanged, though I have an impression that Miss W. once spoke with me about them. The impression is however so slight that I dare not trust myself as to the purport of the conversation. Your idea of returning the ring on a particular day, may be a natural one, but will it not be better that you abandon it.

You notice that it was more than a year since you have been invited to a party at our house. I notice this to show you that you have not been overlooked. I believe that it is all the time that you mention, since we have had a party that was not so small, as not to bear the name, so small, that it would have been an insult to have invited you if Miss W. was to have been present. Last May, we buried our little boy, of only six weeks of age, and since that [page 195] period and for a long time previous, we saw no company except most familiarly.

Your attachment to our little Suzy, and hers to you, has not failed to touch her parents' hearts, and you must have seen it, in the measures we have from time to time taken to promote your intercourse. Her attachment to you seemed to sooth you and to warm your heart and it pleased us, to see her in the office of administering comfort.

I recollect the interview you had with Mrs Johnson in 1830. It was one of a great deal of feeling, and you mistook her meaning, and ever since that interview I have been under the impression that you did mistake her. The expression from which you took the wrong idea, was a strong one, but was never meant by her as conveying in any respect the idea that your marriage "would be a stain upon the family", or any thing like it. She never possessed the sentiment and never intended to express or imply it.

Since I wrote my letter to you Miss W. has corrected me in one fact. Your letters have not been "seen by the immediate family of Miss W," Mrs Woolsey is the only one of the family, and I [page 196] believe the only person who has seen them. Mr Woolsey knows nothing of them to Miss W's knowledge. The last I had before me when I wrote to you.

I forbear to notice the remaining topics of your letter, not because I do not approve of what you have said or because there is any thing I would disapprove or censure, but simply because a notice on my part can do no good, and because there is no call upon me to notice them further. I have always entered deeply into your feelings and regarded them with acute sensibility, and regarded you with a strong and honest friendship. This correspondence I regard as an episode in our intercourse, totally disconnected with the general plan, a scene in other characters and not affecting, or to affect the unity of character which belongs to us and in which we have heretofore appeared. So viewing it, I shall when we meet, lose sight of this correspondence and take care that it lie by in recollection as forgotten. I remain as heretofore sincerely and truly

Your friend

W[illia]m Sam[ue]l Johnson

[page 197] P. S.

I have not seen Miss W. since the receipt of yours, and yours yet remains with me; it will go to her to-morrow A. M.
Feb. 7

Mrs Johnson asks me in a Note to add to my postscript. I quote her language. "That a connection with him (you) was never otherwise than a respectable one in my (her) view, but a clandestine correspondence and acquaintance was always a stain upon any family in my (her) opinion".

Mrs J. has seen this letter but not read yours to me.

H.C. Beach

No. 61   February 7. 1835

My dear Sir

So much pain has been caused by not being frank and open in the affairs to which your late letters and my letter of the 4th inst. allude that I earnestly request that Mr & Mrs Woolsey and Mrs Johnson will take the trouble to read <u>my letter</u>.

I shall then be sure that I am not misunderstood

Most truly yours

H.C. Beach

To W[illia]m Sam[ue]l Johnson Esq

Wm Samel Johnson

No. 62 [page 198]   New york Feb.y 19th 1835

My dear Sir

I am again in fault and for a reason I know cannot be received as an excuse. Half of what I ought to do, is left undone, and this among other things. Nearly a fortnight since I received the enclosed Ring, with a Note from which I extract the following.

"Miss Woolsey returns the Ring which was retained for fear of awakening painful feelings. She has read with the same pain some portions of Mr B's letter to her brother[-in-law], that she felt when some expressions of his were reported to her, but they will be alike forgotten. She never thought of denying what he seems to wish to prove, she is as incapable of that as of any insolent parade of indifference towards him or any feeling but the most heartfelt wish for his happiness, and respect for his sorrow. She cannot forget the period when her desire for his happiness, with a mistaken belief in the result led her to carry the right of remonstrance far beyond the duty of a child. Regret for [page 199] this, and for the effect she has had on his happiness, must ever be her most bitter recollection. She must still hope to hear that he is prosperous and happy, and the voice which assures her of this in distance and retirement will be most welcome"

To   Your friend & servant
   H. C. Beach Esq   W[illia]m Sam[ue]l Johnson
      No. 7 Broad Street

H.C. Beach

No. 63   New york March 26. 1835

W[illia]m W. Woolsey Esq
    No 59 Greenwich Street
        Sir
    In the month of September 1831 I had the honour of addressing you by letter. As I have never been favoured with a reply, I would respectfully request that my letter, may be returned to me

        With much respect
          Your obed[ien]t Servant
            H. C. Beach

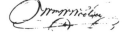

No. 64   Saturday March 28. 1835

Mr Woolsey with his respects informs Mr Beach that he has not
been able to find the letter of September 1831. [page 200] which Mr
B. requests to have returned to him. It has been mislaid, but shall
again be searched for, and if found, it shall be enclosed to Mr Beach

No. 65   Monday April 20. 1835

W[illia]m Sam[ue]l Johnson Esq
        Dear Sir
    I am told that on Tuesday Miss Woolsey will be married.
    I am determined to keep no gifts of hers after to-day, and shall
return them (the gifts) to her Father, with a Note stating my feelings
in regard to his former treatment of me.
    In my Note I may have occasion to make extracts from our late
correspondence, and it is because it may be necessary to do so, that
I take liberty, of informing you of my determination

                     With much respect
                     Very truly Yours
                     H. C. Beach

No. 66   37 Liberty Street Apr. 20. 1835

H. C. Beach Esq
        Dear sir
    Your Note of this [page 201] morning is received. In addition to
the "Gifts" I should advise you to return the <u>letters</u>, and the copies
of them, it is said you have taken. I recollect the determination you

expressed in reference to them, in a Note to me; but still it is not too late to do what is right and honorable.

There is nothing in any of my letters, that I am unwilling Mr Woolsey should see. The time and mode you have selected, of returning the articles must be considered your own. Miss W. has authorized you to return them through me

> Your very ob[edien]t s[ervan]t
> W[illia]m Sam[ue]l Johnson

H.C. Beach

No. 67   New york April 18[th] 1835

W[illia]m W. Woolsey Esq
        No. 59 Greenwich St.
                    Sir

Your Note of March 28[th] is received. You have not seen fit to return me, my letter of September 1831. and as your daughter is to be married on Tuesday next, I have no time to lose in accomplishing what I intended to do before that event should take place [page 202] which is this. I intend to place before you the nature of my engagement with your daughter and my view of your treatment of myself.

On the 30[th] of January last W[illia]m Sam[ue]l Johnson Esq. wrote me a letter from which I make the following extracts. See Page 180. The part of the letter which is written in Black Ink was sent to Mr Woolsey

Mr Johnson received from me the following answer

See Page 184. Letter dated Feb. 4. 1835

W. Johnson answered my letter of the 6[th] of Feb[ruar]y and I make the following extracts from his letter

See Page 193. The part of the letter written in Black Ink

To the above letter I sent the following Note in reply which ended the correspondence

See Page 197. Note dated Feb. 7. 1835

I had forgotten that W. Johnson wrote me on the 19[th] february (See Page 198) enclosing the Ring refered to, and the ring in my possession was immediately returned to him.

I now take the liberty of returning [page 203] all of Miss W's gifts to me, and will add but a few words. Until the engagement was broken off, I took every step in accordance with her wishes, and was repaid with—<u>desertion</u>, and at the moment I most needed kindness. I was always treated with disdain by yourself, and the weight of your opinion has arrayed against me in public, even when connected with your son. I was pronounced <u>fickle</u>, <u>changeable</u>, and not a business man, when you would not deign to inform yourself as to whether or not, the charges were true and I thank heaven that my present situation is a full refutation of the assertions.

There are honorable men of the first standing in this community, who view the matter as known to the world, in the light most gratifying to my feelings, and who are glad to find I did but bend, not break, under an accumulation of evils, that made life for a time a burthen.

One word of real kindness on your part would have effected your object and spared your daughter and myself years of unhappiness. You would not speak it, <u>because I had dared to be independent</u>.

With much respect &c

H. C. Beach

The ringing notes of indignation, amounting to fury, that close the letter-book and the story there written out, make a very proper ending. It was and is right that Carrington should have the last word—right, because he had been wronged. The degree could hardly have been guessed. It finally bursts through mannered restraint and genteel circumlocution, quite unexpectedly, where before, only Sarah's pain had had a voice. A great deal of suffering can be sensed in all three principals of the drama; for we may suppose Woolsey himself to have been hurt even in his tyrannizing.

But his position needs the explanation of another chapter to be more fairly understood.

THE Sarah's Last Choice

A s her letters show, Sarah chose to turn away from Carrington and marry Charles Johnson. She could have defied her father about the first engagement but in the end decided not to. Instead, she gave up Carrington, hoping in time to find (or already certain of) a happy, natural alternative. All, quite straightforward and obvious, so it seems.

Governing the situation, however, from the opening words of the surviving correspondence between herself and her first love, was a choice her father had made. It topped hers. He would have none of Carrington, at least within the family. He defended the older, masculine, American aspect of that polarity which was sketched in the first chapter, where young Carrington and Europe and the Romantic lay at the opposing end. "Mr. Woolsey's choice" might then be another, perhaps a better title for this chapter, since what he judged best was ultimately what Sarah accepted.

127

And what sort of a man was he, to do as he did? The answer lies partly in the past, since his family's was a prominent name in the city and he cannot be imagined careless of the fact. An ancestor had been brother to King Harry's great cardinal, later supplying a nickname to his descendant among the businessmen of New York. The Woolsey line had run down through seventeenth-century settlers to the New World. Some had prospered greatly in the city. Among them were certain Jews and Tories; but these had been converted to better-received communities, had married well, grown rich, and in Woolsey's own day (1766–1839) could be looked on as a source of pride. He could be proud of them just as he could of his first wife's family, the Dwights of New Haven, and of his second, the less eminent but more than respectable Chaunceys (one of them, a judge in due course).[1]

His father had been a prominent merchant and he himself was named after another, William Walton; he had served his apprenticeship from the age of fourteen as a clerk, in the 1790s joining the well-established and more experienced Moses Rogers to make a firm on Pearl Street that sold hardware—nails and saws and all such things—in a town blessed by a more or less perpetual building boom; so there was a lot of money to be made in that line. Rogers married his partner's half-sister, adding an element of kinship to the affair. He later had the idea of refining sugar and Woolsey joined him in that, too, and they dealt very heavily in it.[2]

But I need now to explain one part of my strategy in this chapter before I go further. I aim to show, among other things, just how important one's family was, in the small world here under examination; and if I offer a lot of detail, there is the reason for it: its weight in the making of decisions about one's children.

To continue along this line, then: Woolsey's ties to New Haven dated to the marriage of another half-sister to that Timothy Dwight whose father-in-law was Jonathan Edwards, once president of Princeton, and who was himself to be father of a president of Union College. This Timothy Dwight presided over Yale from 1795 to his death in 1817.[3] The home town of Woolsey's in-laws was a natural place for him to find his first bride, the mother of his children, and a second time, after her death, to find his "Sally". Sally Chauncey, as she had been, proved a loving step-mother to

Sarah, Theodore, the twin boys John and William, Elizabeth, Laura, and Mary Anne.

For a time, Woolsey conducted his business in New Haven. He had sold out the New York end to his nephew Benjamin Rogers, with an agreement to leave that city's hardware markets to young Rogers uncontested for a decade (1805–1815); and during those years Woolsey became deeply involved in all the commercial affairs of his place of exile, call it. A particular focus of his activities was the ill-omened Eagle Bank. In everything, his in-laws proved of great help. When he returned to New York they continued, both Dwights and Chaunceys, to correspond regularly with him, to join in commercial ventures, to invite his help in the managing of their money, and to pay cordial visits to his home.

In New York, Woolsey's brother George (George Muirison Woolsey, 1772–1851) married a certain (Jane) Abby Howland, and their son Edward in turn married Emily Aspinwall. Both Howlands and Aspinwalls were important in the city and in Sarah's life, as her letters have shown. They worked together: John Aspinwall, like George Woolsey, had married a sister of Gardner Howland partner to brother Samuel Shaw Howland, and in time *G. G. & S. Howland* took in their nephew William Aspinwall as a partner. Mr Woolsey must have measured them all in his own way, particularly John Aspinwall, his contemporary and fully his match in wealth and prominence. The Howland brothers' ads for dry goods could be found right in the middle of the pages of the *New-York Daily Advertiser*, just like *Woolsey & Rogers'* for hardware.[4]

With Gilbert Aspinwall, Nehemiah Rogers (brother of Moses Rogers, Woolsey's partner) did business as *Rogers & Aspinwall* till he retired in the 1790s. Moses, too, retired late in the same decade, handing on his position to his son Benjamin Woolsey Rogers. This son married the daughter Susan of William Bayard, another prominent merchant, while Moses' daughter Julia Ann married Francis Bayard Winthrop of *Winthrop, Rogers & Williams*. After her death in 1814, Winthrop was married again, to Woolsey's daughter Elizabeth.[5] The names Bayard and Francis Winthrop have been seen in Sarah's letters and occur very often elsewhere in the Woolsey correspondence.

Just like the business of politics for the Hapsburgs, the business of money-making for the merchant class of New York was inseparable from family. The two were one. That was a given, and well established by the 1790s when Sarah's father came on the scene and learnt the rules.

There remains one other family often mentioned and worth folding in to the texture of Woolsey relationships, mercantile and marital: the Gracies, beginning with old Archibald (d. 1829). He established the line which is today still a great shipowner, and in that connection also he went into marine insurance on a grand scale. In due course he married Esther Rogers, sister of Moses, Nehemiah, and Henry. His son Robert Gracie joined Henry F. Rogers to make a firm *Rogers & Gracie* (Henry F., son of Henry and nephew to Moses and Nehemiah), after young Henry had quit his partnership (1811–21) with Francis Bayard Winthrop. Henry Rogers' brother J. Smyth Rogers married a Winthrop; Robert Gracie's son James formed a partnership with one of the New York Kings, later, in an expansion of the legendary firm *Prime, Ward*.[6] These various ties, particularly to Rufus King and his line, reach beyond commerce very deep into the political history of the period that is Mr. Woolsey's and Sarah's; but none of that need concern me.

Family business extended across the generations and the country, alike, through the use made of sons during their apprenticeships and early careers. As Woolsey while a boy had gone to work in a suitable office, no doubt by his father's arrangements, so had and so would, in the future, other boys eager to get ahead. The city received a steady flow of aspirants from Yankee parts, on which Joseph Scoville comments in his memoirs. They had mastered their letters out of a common reader so very common that its royalties made its author rich, and he gave his name to a part of town (Murray Hill); and their numbers, they learnt out of another equally standard text (Daboll's) which prepared them for accounting—and then, there they were, ready for fortune.[7] Mr. Woolsey received a number of requests to take in boys and train them in his firm;[8] he settled his own eldest son into the law office of an in-law, the latter offering or rather pressing the idea of an apprenticeship as a generous kinsman should; and he found uses for his other sons, the twins John and William, as his trainees and deputies in his own affairs, the one as a lawyer, the other as a young businessman, on missions to Georgia or Ohio territory. He used other young relatives. After all, you can trust your own flesh and blood. That belief has controlled arrangements in every land across all time.[9]

You could trust them, but, as will appear a little later, you could be wrong. One that went wrong involved Woolsey's brother George Muirison (1752–1851). He was for years resident in Liverpool and go-between in cotton trade for the two of them. Before he took up residence in England, they had had no major position in the commodity. It was kinship that was thought to justify and enable the outreach of commerce to Europe or the East. A great many houses sent out their juniors, whether a son or a son-in-law, as supercargo on a commercial voyage, who then stayed on for a time at the other end.[10]

In the 1790s, Woolsey with his brother-in-law Moses Rogers had already turned some of their extra capital into real estate. More purchases followed into the period of interest here.[11] The hardware market had been a good one; cotton proved risky but there were many profitable years; and sugar certainly paid well. With his profits Woolsey bought land in Connecticut, more in the Ohio territory, upper New York State, and of course in the city. He lent money at interest and bought shares in banks, where he sometimes served as director; served as president of an insurance company from 1804 on; invested also in roads and canals, being one of the fifteen men chosen as a committee to celebrate the opening of the great Erie (along with John Pintard, William Bayard, Cadwallader Colden, . . .).[12] He knew all about all sorts of stocks and enterprises, and advised his relatives what to get, being seen by them as wise and successful in the world of commerce. He could take advantage of the dynamic nature of the urban economy and its growth in number of residents: nudging 200,000 in the period of interest for the present study. Its rate of growth had been and would continue to be gigantic, and it served a still more gigantic market.[13]

A document signed by Woolsey and other prominent businessmen sums up their claim upon the world and history:[14]

> This City owes its present magnitude and opulence entirely to it being the great market to which dealers resort from every part of the Union, for their supply of Merchandise. The goods required,

annually, for this purpose, amount to at least one hundred millions
of dollars, and are sold by mechanics, wholesale grocers, and the
houses in Pearl Street and its vicinity.

Accordingly, as it might seem, a good profit, even a fortune, was to
be made in providing anything whatever that filled a real need; so the
purveyor of a specialty like drugs (James Scott Aspinwall son of Gilbert) or
mahogany (Cornelius Cadle) could grow rich; or a purveyor of something
much more regularly in demand like tea (John Jacob Astor) or sugar (Isaac
Roosevelt, rival with Woolsey and Rogers) or sails (George Warren) or
what one wore (dry goods, from the Howlands); or, most common of all
because a requirement of life itself, food. Grocers, wholesale or retail or
mixed, on such good streets as Greenwich, were many indeed: Samuel
Tooker and Tooker's son-in-law, or Luman Reed, patron of painting, or
others from millionaires down to the merely prosperous.[15] The roll-call of
all such names and their stories might make the city sound like the heaven
that capitalists ever dream of.

Replete with litigation, naturally. Every family and firm had to have its
defenders in court, because there was a great deal of bitter fighting over
money. Woolsey's lawyer sons and in-laws were no more than representative. He also numbered many others of the profession among his friends
and acquaintances: George Strong and James Kent, to instance two of the
most distinguished. Lawyers were much on the scene.

For, from the close of the Revolution to well past the period here
under review, the economy was subject to wild swings, some national,
some sharply felt only in one city or another. New York had its full share of
troubles. In the very simplest terms, what could go wrong was the fabric
of indebtedness in which a misadventure, let us say a sudden change in
the price for cotton in England or something still more specific like the
failure of a ship to survive its voyage, bankrupted one man. What he
owed could not be collected by another, whose bills came due, and he
too went down; so the series extended itself, with consequences to be
fought over in the courts. Multiplication of banks, imbalance between
specie and liabilities, and other causes of this economy's fragility, do not
concern me.[16]

As kin turned most naturally to kinsmen in their financial distress, the problem was often a family one. With this, Woolsey was familiar.[17] "Among the many painful situations a man is liable to be placed in, that, which obliges him in defense of the reputation of himself, and the honor of his family, to make disclosures, unfavourable to those with whom he is connected by affinity, is peculiarly distressing . . . some circumstances were connected which for the honor of the family it was essentially necessary to keep from public view"—so runs a public letter drafted by Woolsey's brother to refute the charge of bankrupting an associate by too harshly calling in a loan. The person in distress had been a Howland, the persons accused were several, George Woolsey and John Aspinwall among them.[18]

Or the problem might be more remote. A farmer after a bad year had to borrow from Woolsey on the security of his estate, and still couldn't make his payments, so he must be sold up. He had only a cow, a two-year-old steer, nails, screws, hinges, articles of glass, several small mirrors, and (what might fetch the most at auction) some quantity of ribbon: in total, not $2,000. Woolsey's agents worry the matter in their letters to him: how could the inevitable loss (not to the farmer, needless to say) be minimized?[19]

Or, last, the problem appears on a large scale. "I learn this evening by a source on which I rely that Arthur Tappan has failed," so Theodore informs his father; and continues, "I write now in haste for the purpose of knowing what Mrs. Salisbury [Theodore's mother-in-law] ought to do with regard to his note for $2205."[20]

In fact, fallen though this well known silk-importer was at the time, below his great wealth of only a year prior, he survived. Yet it was all too believable a rumor, of a sort that a writer of the time could comment on and exploit for novelistic purposes. "These fashionable people, who most pride themselves on their prerogative of exclusiveness, feel the extreme precariousness of the tenure by which they hold their privileges. A sudden reverse of fortune, one of the most common accidents of a commercial city, plunges them into irretrievable obscurity." And once again in contemporary fiction, "Of all the various professions, occupations, or employments of life, none perhaps afford greater vicissitudes than that of the merchant. None exhibits greater changes of fortune; none lead through more trials and difficulties; none expose their votaries to severer hazards of shipwreck, both in money and reputation. . . . Of those who engage in mercantile pursuits, it is estimated that not more than three of every one hundred retire with absolute wealth, while nine out of ten become bankrupt."[21] The author of this last describes himself as a merchant, calls his work *Pearl Street*, and writes in the very year of the Tappan rumor. His was a piece of entirely permissible fiction, accepted by all readers because they knew it to be an accurate reflection of real life, or close to it.

Or a third witness, calm wise old John Pintard telling his daughter in a letter of October, 1825, "Commercial men are very gloomy. Every day almost produces failures."[22] He mentions in other letters of other years the destruction of people in his own circle whom anyone would have judged secure from misfortune.

And Joseph Scoville, so often quoted in my pages thus far, and rightly, because of his experience and carefulness in speaking from it—he not only mentions numerous failures spread across the period I focus on, but speaks of their likelihood in just the same terms as the novelists or as Pintard.[23]

My object here is not economic history, certainly, but a look into Woolsey's world and consequently into his mind and its tendencies. Just so, to understand what an advancing infantryman may be thinking, one must know what a minefield is, and, by the man's side, count the stretchers that pass him on their way back from the front. In them might be his friends. Among the failures in New York were, at a certain moment, the De Peysters and the Coits, whom Sarah chats about in her letters. Woolsey knew them well in business connections and at worship. They failed and went under, and many others like them: his principal domestic hardware supplier, or George Warren of the sailmaking firm.[24] In 1834 he wrote, "There are failures here every day. None has occurred which concern me"—as yet.

You could negotiate the hazards of the commercial world with caution, or you could go for broke, or for an intermediate course, depending on the tendencies of your mind. Woolsey chose a middle course. His measure of success, however, required, if not some willingness to gamble, at least full confidence in his own ability to weigh the odds and to act decisively. I have mentioned how he was used to serving as the clan-oracle on what to invest in.[25] Though there is no sign of his taking real risks, he did engage in deals that needed to be concealed.[26] Some may have lain in documents that were at some point evidently culled out of the family papers. Naturally, a businessman was well advised to keep his own council. Anyone who expected to find out very much about merchants "should," as Scoville said, "reflect upon the difficulty of actual knowledge of affairs that most men keep secret. The most secret class in the world, and the most opposed to any sort of publicity about himself, is the great merchant."[27]

One matter kept dark was embezzlement from George Woolsey's firm by his son Charles, resident in New York as the firm's agent, with liabilities which involved the other son and could not be repudiated without destroying their future credit. Need the father's legal connection with the sons' actions be made public?[28] Some years later he is found again in the collection, in another letter, long and agonized, asking Sally, his sister-in-law, to intervene with her husband on his behalf. He confesses himself to be the disgraceful cause of his own and his family's distressed circumstances. He has withdrawn from decent society and is eking out a life in Genoa. Whatever the story behind it all, he will not sign his name to it; nor is there any sign that he got any financial help from his brother.[29]

Woolsey himself had two serious setbacks through a son and a son-in-law. The son William (1796–1840), it may be remembered, had formed a partnership as an auction house, *Woolsey, Ward & Beach*, in October of 1827, which was reported doing well toward the end of the year. The reporter is a cousin of William's and Sarah's, Charles Frederick Johnson. The name will recur.[30] They prospered until Ward quit the firm in 1831 for a place with *Gracie, Prime & Co.*, and *Woolsey, Ward & Beach* closed its doors. William then sought out new partners. His father, to Theodore, still in Europe (July of 1832), explained the upshot, with ruthless clarity:[31]

> You will (ere this) have been apprised through Mr [Francis Bayard] Winthrop that your brother William and his concern have failed; it is needless here to enter into an explanation of the causes which produced it; suffice it to say, the connection was unadvisedly made, the business was carried to an extent beyond the means, they have had a falling market the whole time to contend with, and great failures among the debtors—the other partners when the firm

commenced were bankrupts, a great deal more than the capital they pretended to bring into the house has been applied to their own debts, and one of them Mr C[onvers] has abstracted from the property of the firm considerable sums for improper purposes, these last causes I wish at present not to go beyond you and Mr Winthrop.

In December last they applied to Mr Conver's father-in-law, to me, and to Mr [Benjamin] Poor, a friend (he having recently gone to England) to aid them; their statement would in any case except one relating to a son have induced me to refuse, but I reflected that I was supposed to be a man of some property and it would be deemed unkind if I did not give that aid to so near a connection which might enable him to go on with his business; many circumstances which have since come to my knowledge were then hidden even from William, and Mr Poor's expedition to England had not then resulted in the loss of at least 10,000 doll[ar]s. I agreed to aid them . . .

Notice Woolsey's reasoning: it would damage his reputation if he left his son to suffer. But saving him would cost him no less than $30,000. A year later, in retrospect, he saw in the affair the fault of William, who "plunged into business without consideration and in company with a rascal and a feeble minded man well meaning but capable of being acted on and lead [!] to do very improper things. I see no other fate for William for a good while but to come to rely on others for support of his family."[32]

The son-in-law problem was more serious. Woolsey's second daughter Mary Ann Woolsey Scarborough (1793–1871), after the death of her first husband in 1816, married a lawyer, George Hoadly, whom she met during the family's New Haven years. Woolsey was there president of the Eagle Bank employing as cashiers both Hoadly and Francis Bayard Winthrop, husband to his second daughter, Elizabeth (1794–1863). It was a family concern, of which Hoadley became president when Woolsey moved back to New York in 1815. But Hoadly, like his cousin Charles, could not resist the urge to get rich more quickly than seemed likely to happen in the natural, leisurely, honest course of things; so he took out bank money and speculated with it for his own account, and was caught in 1825.[33] Some of the funds he used had been invested with him by Woolsey on behalf of the American Bible Society, of which Woolsey was the devoted and long-term treasurer; more still, a very great deal more, was Yale money most enthusiastically invested in it by the college's treasurer, James Hillhouse, another Woolsey kinsman.

The newspapers got hold of all this. Woolsey offered an angry defense of his reputation; Benjamin Strong signed a Bible-Society declaration that Woolsey had always acted properly. In New Haven, others absolved Hoadly, who remained in his position until he was sent to be held in jail in the summer of 1828 and by the fall, convicted of fraud. "His conduct has ended in ruin and disgrace," his brother-in-law Winthrop concluded.[34] It was inevitably Woolsey who must step in to make good much of the loss. Before long, Hoadly in Ohio had begun again what was to be a most successful career in law and politics. America! indeed a land of opportunity. Theodore, however, never forgave him.[35]

Such was the family news in the later twenties and early thirties of the century, when Sarah and Carrington were engaged in their correspondence—if they were not engaged, as Woolsey determined, in any other way. He might have supposed that, in commercial affairs, he could trust his own kin; and that was certainly the conventional wisdom. But he had discovered he couldn't trust even those closest to him. Confronting another candidate for admission to the family, he could afford no more mistakes; and perhaps he was all the harder to please, too, in Carrington's case, out of the galling circumstance that Carrington's business reputation had ended up in pretty good repair, after the closing of *Woolsey, Ward & Beach*, while William's was in tatters.

Now Woolsey must set himself to protect and recover the health of *Woolsey & Co.* —for such it was, the larger family, like those other families of the merchant class that he belonged to: each one a business enterprise literally, or almost so, each with a president or joint presidents such as himself on whom the responsibility for everyone must fall.

Ubiquitous and continual as bankruptcies were over the decades here being described, fraud (if I can trust my reading) seems to have been quite rare. The fact may be explained by the weight given in the business community to trust. Whatever would inspire this was essential to a man to get ahead. Risk-taking and eager ambition might be characteristic, noted, and generally admired (with some disgust registered by "old money");[36]

but earning a good name counted for even more. Without it, a man was nothing. Let him be banished to Ohio, to Genoa! or left to lurk at home like William until his faults were more or less forgotten. It was one's name that gave one credit—trust, that brought in business and eased one's payments or rates of interest. To be known as reliable in all things, accurate and exact in one's reckoning, even to a degree predictable in one's behavior, marked out the successful businessman.

In estimating reliability, the community made all the figures readily available, as its periodical literature makes clear; and what could there be of relevance to a business estimate that was not quantifiable? But the question would in those times have been by no means rhetorical: character and reputation were of interest, of the very greatest. They were discussed continually.

For example, John Pintard introduces "an amiable young gentleman Mr. [John M.] Woolsey, son of William W. Woolsey Esq.r & partner, who is going to N[ew] Orleans to look after their concerns. He is . . . very correct and pious. He is" a Presbyterian, "and should be further introduced to the Rev. Mr. Larned to whose denomination he belongs." Or the same Pintard contemplating a purchase that will be noted by others as extravagant sees he must be ready to explain it; otherwise people "would suppose that I had hidden resources which were wrongly got."[37] Experience had taught him that one's spending habits were routinely noted and discussed.

A novelist imagines a firm to write about: "The house of Thomas Steady & Sons was famed for its accuracy in the transaction of business, as well as for its promptness in the discharge of its pecuniary engagements."[38] The description was meant to be exemplary, as the name chosen for the firm. It is confirmed by that compiler of people's worth, Moses Beach, noting someone most beautifully rich, to the amount of $400,000, though he had started from nothing: "In his business [of sail-manufacture] he was industrious, scrupulously exact, and rigid in justice. By his reputation for integrity, he procured large accessions to his business."[39] Readers would want this latter information as much as the total of the man's dollar worth. Regarding a younger member of the business world, a second novelist imagines a seasoned person offering "my secret opinion of this young man. He can never himself make a good lawyer or a good man. He is too light and fickle"—exactly what Woolsey thought, or feared would be thought by others, of Carrington Beach.[40]

Regarding still others, Hoadly writes to William, Woolsey writes to Theodore, sketching character. Reputations were quoted like prices on the Exchange.[41]

And a word more on that Moses Yale Beach, the compiler, who published an alphabetized booklet instantly in great demand and updated every few years. It covered more than a hundred of the commercial class elite, giving to some a biographical sketch of a few or many lines, to all of them a figure of total wealth so far as Beach could learn it. He seems never to have been at a loss. Considering how close-mouthed the merchant class had to be, it was a wonder he could be so successful; but, quite aside from any informants among clerks and the like, in fact a very great deal of up-to-date information was available in print. Some provided a rough ranking in the form of subscriptions to good causes, where, however, notorious names of great wealth might never appear.[42] Skinflints.

The various reporters most often used in my account drop dollar figures into their biographical mentions quite easily, suggesting they had in their heads a good idea how much most businessmen, including lawyers, were worth. In particular, Joseph Scoville describes the bankruptcy and recovery of a certain Arthur Tappan, silk jobber, in the 1830s. He has appeared in these pages already. He could widen his market where he could trust it; but where was that? To whom among his customers could he extend credit for a time, being confident of repayment? "He would inquire about all such individuals. . . . No detail would be forgotten by the inquisitive merchant. This information Arthur would store away in a very retentive memory;" and when his silk ran out and he had to find something else to sell, it was just this information through which he recovered his place in the city. He set up as a firm consisting of himself and his brother Lewis, and then with Benjamin Douglas, and eventually as *Dun, Boyd & Co.*, and now *Dun & Bradstreet*. They could sell you information about a man's worth, marital status and derelictions, drinking habits, politics, and record of church attendance.[43] Demand was instant and Tappan was back in the action.

I should interrupt at this point to make clear a second part of the strategy of this chapter: as I meant to draw out the importance of family in Woolsey's decisions, so I would like to emphasize the importance of public opinion in his decisions. The public he thought of, the audience before which he acted out his life (as we all have such an audience, big or small), can be identified both through the family papers and other sources around them.

There were the city's churches, first: indeed important, important as an element in the fabric of trust that I have been describing. Over the period of Sarah's youth and engagement, as it was later recalled, "most of our merchants and prominent business men were men of piety, and were religiously useful. They were attached to some church—and were usually engaged in the process of Sunday school teaching" (though not Woolsey himself).[44] There are all sorts of demonstrations of the fact: among them, Lewis Tappan, editor of the *Commercial Advertiser* from 1828 on, whose private journals then and for many years prior he filled with records of the sermons he had heard; or the business-oriented *Daily Advertiser* of July 16, 1825, printing generous extracts from a review of the Rev. Timothy Dwight's *System of Theology* —that same reverend voice at Yale that had so wonderfully chastened the student body and won them over to the New Divinity.[45] It was this doctrine in which Theodore Woolsey and his seminary friends were so immersed.

Its arminian or semi-arminian teachings were entirely compatible with the choice of life and values that best suited the merchant class, assuring them of their state of grace so long as they were reasonably honest, observant of worship—and prosperous.[46] Men who worked with their hands, lowly scrabblers, the Rev. Dwight viewed as "shiftless, diseased, or vicious," in exactly the way Woolsey regarded his fellows who succumbed to yellow fever: "Papa says that every case as yet can be traced to intemperate habits, bad dirty living or imprudence of some sort." So Sarah in a letter to Theodore.[47]

As a moral corrective, nothing counted for so much as religion. Its propagation Woolsey faithfully supported through the American Bible Society, as was mentioned. There he would find on the Board Rev. Timothy Dwight, Rev. James Milnor, big merchants like Arthur and Lewis Tappan, Isaac Carow, John Adams who took over from Woolsey as treasurer, and others of the set, served by their immemorial humble secretary, John

Pintard.[48] All were Woolsey's friends and acquaintances. Theodore was a member of the Society and its supporter, too.

Theodore's work in theology during his seminary years involved him fully, witness his letters to his family and especially to his friends at their studies elsewhere. People of his intellectual bent such as Tappan savored sermons as food for thought, and, of a Sunday, ranged about among churches in search of the reward of an outstanding preacher.[49] Woolsey, too, had a mind for the matter, and offered views characteristically firm and peremptory, not to say dismissive (". . . if it is not a dispute about words," he says in comment on something Theodore had ventured, "it is a question of a nature too metaphysical for discussion. The topic of the imputation of Adam's sin is of the same nature; about either, people may talk for months without gaining a valuable idea . . .").[50]

Besides its value in moral instruction, however, religion for most of the Woolsey set served in at least as important a way to knit that set or society together. Ministers might be born into it, as Theodore could have claimed had he continued in his seminarian ambitions, or like his sister Laura's father-in-law, the Rev. Samuel William Johnson; ministers might marry into it, as the Rev. James M. Mathews did, indeed into John Hone's family (Sarah disapproved—Mathews was too old); they might live next door to their parishioners; they might be received as guests (a damper on the dancing); and among their neighbors, their daughters (long on respectability if short on dowry) might find husbands. A symbiosis: serving others' faith, ministers themselves can "never get on and become very great, very good, or very popular, until they can spot in their congregations and audiences fifty or a hundred extensive merchants."[51]

And for their part the extensive merchants came forward as vestrymen or elders, in an endless list. To instance only those persons whose names show up in documented relations with the Woolseys, there is John Adams in the Presbyterian church on Cedar Street, elder for forty years; Pintard, for decades a vestryman in the Church of the St. Esprit (and kin to several ministers), while, at Trinity Church, though there are no full records, among the wardens or vestrymen were George Warren, Gardner G. Howland, Richard Cadle, William Bayard, Nehemiah Rogers, William Johnson, Philip Hone, Jacob Le Roy, Isaac Carow, and Moses Rogers, all of whom figure as kin, friends, or acquaintances in the Woolsey letters and have appeared in other contexts, too, above.[52] In Trinity, their friend Rev. Schroeder became assistant rector in 1827.

Among some fifty city churches of the time, ground plans of the principal ones allow us to visualize the experience of belonging and being present in them, so as to bow and smile to others in the congregation, perhaps invite someone not of the family into one's pew, and at the doorway on leaving discuss Sunday hats, children, proposed outings, cost of oats for the carriage, and accumulating infirmities. In this way, Pintard met young John Woolsey for a chat. It was not uncommon to spend a Sunday morning at some other place of worship than one's own, as the Pintards' house guests did on another day in the company of Sarah Woolsey to the Dutch Reformed Garden Street church of Rev. Mathews; but the elite among the commercial classes favored the Episcopalian. There were a dozen such, including Grace Church on Broadway and especially Trinity Church with its three broken-off chapels, bearing saints' names: St. Paul's between Fulton and Vesey Street (no. 14 on the adjoining map), St. John's on Varick from 1807, and St. George's on Beekman Street from 1815 where Rev. James Milnor held forth.[53] He has appeared as Foreign Secretary of the American Bible Society, working closely with Woolsey.

Pintard in 1825, when St. Thomas in its refurbished form emerged on Houston Street ten blocks uptown from Laight Street (no. 1 on my map), bought a pew there. It cost him $400, but uptown meant down, in social terms; so he had no trouble selling his old family one at Grace Church for that sum. At Grace he confessed to having felt "overshadowed by wealth and arrogance" and all too conscious of his "insignificance, I mean in the bank-book way." The price he paid even at St. Thomas, however, needs to be measured against what a man could scrape by on in New York, per annum, around $250.[54]

Among Presbyterian churches, that on Cedar Street (on Duane, after 1835) was by far the "best". Its pew-holders numbered, among others, the families of Elisha, Benjamin, and Levi Coit, including J. Howland Coit and Miss Coit, friend of Sarah's; John Aspinwall behind Levi; George Woolsey across the aisle; Mrs. Staples, also in Sarah's letters, her intimate and hostess; Gerald Lathrop; Mrs. Whittelsey; Ralph, then James

Olmstead; Mr. and Mrs. Roderick Sedgwick; Mrs. Gardiner Howland; Tappans; various Ludlows, mentioned there, too; Sarah's sister Laura and her husband William S. Johnson; Miss Le Roy among the family or kin of Jacob, and Sophia Wyckoff, Benjamin Strong, and Archibald Gracie.[55] All these whom I select were not only in the Woolsey circle and so of interest, here, but many of them very grand presences in the city, and so of interest to everybody.

"Locality has much to do with marriages," observed old Scoville as he reflected on New York; "young clerks at boarding houses went to Sunday school as teachers, and became members of the Presbyterian church that had the richest members and prettiest daughters. Their piety game was the card that won in every instance."[56]

There were equally good pickings among Episcopalians. At St. Paul's, family pews were owned by Nehemiah Rogers, William Verplanck, and Ralph Hodge—the last, like other members of the congregation, holding two pews.[57] Again, I cite only names of known friends and acquaintances of Sarah's family, without explaining also what great business interests they represented.

In Trinity church itself, far larger and grander, possessed of ample grounds, and staring, nose in air, down the length of Wall street, there were pews bought by many Woolsey friends: no less than six by Ludlows, two for Frederick DePeyster, a pew each for Benjamin, William, and Nehemiah Rogers in addition to the latter's at St. Paul's; Philip Hone mentioned above as a vestryman; Jacob and Herman Le Roy together and John Aspinwall; William and Susan Wallace; William Walton after whom Mr. Woolsey was named, but holding a pew surrendered before Sarah comes into the picture; and other Woolsey kinsmen, William Bayard and Francis Winthrop, the latter a trustee along with the Le Roys.[58]

"How many youths attended devoutly every Sunday at Trinity to see the Miss Carmers?" exclaims Scoville. He is recalling the lovely daughters of a vestryman, someone successful in the hardware business like Woolsey, but on a smaller scale, on Pearl Street.[59] At the not-so-grand Grace church, when Henry Laverty bought a pew, and was asked "why he chose that church in prefference to any other, he replied, Why Madam, there is more carriages attends that church than any other in the city, and I wish

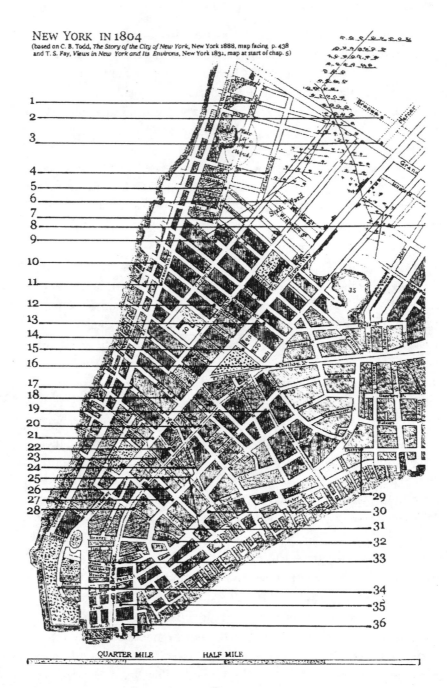

NEW YORK IN 1804
(based on C. B. Todd, *The Story of the City of New York*, New York 1888, map facing p. 438
and T. S. Fay, *Views in New York and Its Environs*, New York 1831, map at start of chap. 5)

QUARTER MILE   HALF MILE

Fig. 4a

Mr. Woolsey's and Sarah's 'village'
Their known friends, acquaintances, and associates

CHAMBERS STREET
Backus (Mary Ann widow of Thos.) 1833-34
Haggerty (John) 1827-34
Ludlow (Francis) 1826-27
Richards (Nathaniel) 1826-35
Wyckoff (Henry) 1828-34

WARREN STREET
Lathrop (Frances widow of Chas.) 1827
Lathrop (Gerard) 1833-34
Schroeder (Rev.John F.) 1826-27
Sedgwick (Henry D.atty.) 1826-27
Sedgwick (Robert atty.) 1826-35

MURRAY STREET
Berger (Dr. Francis) 1826-35

VESEY STREET
Curtis (Edward & George) 1832-35
Tallmadge (Frederick A. atty.) 1826-30

GEORGE STREET
Curtis (Edward & George) 1830-35
Tallmadge (Frederick atty.) 1826-30
Tallmadge (James atty.) 1833-35

CHATHAM STREET
Charles (Robert) 1820

WILLIAM STREET
Cadwallader (Dr. P.) 1826-30
Leroy (R. E.) 1829-30

MAIDEN LANE
Schenck (Peter H.) 1827-32

DEY STREET
Coit (Elisha) 1827-32
Olmstead (Ralph) 1827-28
Woolsey (Charles C.) 1830-31
Wyckoff (F. S.) 1827-29

NASSAU STREET
Verplanck (Samuel atty.) 1828-34

CHERRY STREET
Silliman (William atty.) 1827-35
Olmstead (Ralph) 1829-32

LIBERTY STREET
Coit (Elisha) 1833-35
Johnson (William S. atty.) 1826-35
Kent (James atty.) 1826032
Kent (William atty.) 1826-32
Olmstead (Ralph) 1829-32

MERCHANTS' EXCHANGE
Carow (Isaac) 1827-30
Dwight (Theodore) 1827-35
Olmstead (Francis) 1831-35
Richards (C. H.) 1827-33

TONTINE COFFEE HOUSE
Dwight (Theodore) 1826-27

GREENWICH STREET
Bailey (H. C.) 1832-37
Coit (Elisha) 1826-27
Curtis (William B.) 1826-28
Donaldson (James) 1826-28
Hone (Isaac) 1827-34
Howland (Gardiner G.) 1826-30
Howland (Samuel) 1826-35
Leroy (Daniel) 1826-27
MacMullen (John) 1826-35
Olmstead (Francis) 1827-28
Rogers (Nehemiah) 1827-34
Verplanck (Gulian C.) 1826-34
Whittelsey (Jared) 1827-29
Woolsey (Charles C.) 1827-28
Woolsey (William C.) 1827-33
Woolsey (William W.) 1826-37

PEARL STREET
Bailey (Nathan) 1826-35
Bayard (Mrs. Eliz. widow) 1827-
Beach (H. Carrington) 1828-31
Carow (John) 1827-34
Curtis (George, atty.) 1829-30
Haggerty (John) 1827-34
Laverty (Henry) 1827-34
Meert (Joseph M.) 1827-32
Olmstead (Francis & Ralph) 1826-27
Phillips (William) 1826-35
Richards (Nathaniel) 1826-35
Rogers (Benjamin W.) 1827-32
Rogers (Nehemiah) 1827-34
Sheldon (Frederick & Henry) 1826-28
Stone (Joel) 1827-29
Verplanck (Samuel atty.) 1828-34
Woolsey (John M.) 1826-30
Woolsey (William C.) 1826-30

PINE STREET
Johnson (William S.atty.) 1826-35
Kent (James atty.) 1826-32
Kent (William atty.) 1826-32
Schenck (Peter H.) 1833-35
Sedgwick (Henry D.atty.) 1826-27
Sedgwick (Robert atty.) 1826-27
Silliman (William atty.) 1826-27
Staples (Seth P.atty.) 1826-27
Stone (Joel) 1830-34
Van Ness (Edward atty.) 1827-28
Wallace (James D.) 1826-28

BROADWAY
Beach (H. Carrington) 1831-33
Bullus (Mrs. John) 1828-33
Bullus (Dr. Robert) 1831-35
Donaldson (James) 1834-35
Haggerty (John) 1820-?
Hone (Philip) 1827-34
Laverty (Henry) 1827-34
Leroy (Robert) 1827-35
Rogers (Henry) 1827-34
Schenck (Peter H.) 1833-35
Staples (Seth P. atty.) 1827-35
Stone (Joel) 1827-29
Wyckoff (F. S.) 1827-29

paste-up

Fig. 4b

Windfall Software

my daughters of course to exhibit there."[60] Laverty was the father of that
talented Ellen, whom Samuel Tooker had adopted. She was being polished
for a brilliant marriage. She and Sarah exchanged news at a party in 1829,
when Ellen was looking forward to a winter to be spent in Rome—yet
another reminder to Sarah of what she so much desired, in vain.[61]

For whatever reason, the Woolseys went to the Garden Street church
(no. 28 on the map).[62] It was much less swank than Trinity or Grace or
Cedar Street, but the fact had no effect on the circle of their friends.
Among the pew-holders of these other three congregations, just examined, it is noticeable how many belong particularly in Sarah's close
circle—registering in her letters to Carrington, not in the general family
correspondence—and how many can be found also, in the adjoining map,
in the street-lists for Greenwich, Washington, Courtland, and Warren.
That was the neighborhood in which she lived and walked about, paying
her visits as women who had no need to work generally enjoyed doing,
constantly. In her letters to Carrington, she expects to meet him in the
natural course of such outings with or without her mother or a friend on
lower Greenwich Street (no. 11 on the map), or Chambers, Pine, Garden,
or Wall Street (nos. 13, 26, 28, 31). Her mother by herself was less likely
to walk than take the family barouche (a handsome piece of carriage-work
at $250).

As anyone may learn from the experience of living in a small city, or
even in lower Manhattan fifty or seventy-five years ago, the flow of people
one passes in the street has no meaning; but they are not so overwhelmingly
numerous that one doesn't scan their faces to recognize those one knows,
and exchange a nod—or more. Who one looks at, or looks for, constitute
what may be called one's 'village': the socially manageable community to
which one responds and before which one acts out one's life. Everyone has
something of the sort, selected out of the whole urban population.

Sarah's village, I have so far suggested, was the creation of Sunday
services, at her favorite church or at any of several others, or the creation
of little visits to people's houses for tea or the like. A third way of meeting
people was of course through parties. Of these, the Woolseys offered their
share. Their wine bills show it; likewise, the number of servants they
kept; and, most clearly, in Sarah's reporting to a brother, "we had a small

party" including Cousin Charles Johnson, several ministers, a Sedgwick, the Sebors, the Neilsons, Verplancks and Coldens among others, "the said party, one of the pleasantest I ever knew where there were only 12 or 14 ladies. The quantity of beaux was however double."[63] One wonders what a "large" party would be. There are in fact some indications, quite remarkable: at the house of Laverty or Beer, famed for lavish hospitality, elaborate balls and gigantic banquets, on a scale to which the Woolseys also aspired, and might require help from caterers.[64] But the Woolseys also had house guests, sometimes for months, sometimes by the half dozen or more.[65] The house had a breakfast room eventually turned into a library, and at least one suite able to accommodate a couple with children and a nurse; so, ample room and staff for hospitality.

Young people at these parties brought each other up to date about marriage: who was interested, or engaged, or wed with whom—that was the subject above all discussed, though much more by girls and young women than by men. It was well understood that that was what balls were intended to promote, though a cynic might note, the year Sarah turned fifteen, that, despite their glamor and expense, "not a single marriage, of all the young ladies exposed for sale, at these entertainments has taken place this season. Indeed the young men are too profligate, the young ladies too extravagant to admit of marriages."[66]

These young cannot be overheard; but their letters can be read, rarely without some item of news on this front. They describe the conduct of wooers, broken engagements, the dishonorable or mismatched, and who was or was not an heiress. Lucky the man who got Miss Buchanan, bringing with her no less than $150,000 (though in the end she never said yes to anyone). The compiler of value, Moses Beach, published the figure. Lucky again, young William Samuel Johnson, who "gets the mass of his fortune by marriage with the daughter of 'Cardinal Woolsey,' as this eminent merchant used facetiously to be called 'on Change'. The 'Cardinal' was an extensive operator, in Connecticut banks, and became very rich."[67] That was how the world sized up the choice that Sarah's sister made—unless it was Mr. Woolsey's.

It was a commonplace in novels of the day, reflecting realities, that marriage should take account of realities. What a trial and sadness, then, to the loving father who could provide no great dowry! It was a cost or pain peculiar to New York; for, of any young lady one didn't know, "three of our big cities would ask each a different question: Boston saying, 'What is she?'; Philadelphia, 'Who is she?'; and New York's business mind demanding, 'What has she?'"[68]

Occasional voices were raised against the judging of all merit by the standards of Wall Street. Mrs. Sedgwick spoke out for that length of well-to-do ancestors and education in her own background, and for those tastes she herself preferred, which best entitled one to the rank of arbiter in the world.[69] Perhaps only those like her listened. Her contemporary, Mrs. Follen, observed more truly that "the greatest influence [in the city] on the whole is exercised by lawyers and by rich merchants."[70]

As illustration of the city's way of thinking, take a certain long letter from Woolsey to Theodore. It is of the right character, "solid and instructive, and turns upon business" (chap. 1, above, at n. 50). The occasion was his son's writing him to inform him of his engagement to Martha Elizabeth Salisbury, then in her teens. The two had been writing each other since at least the spring of 1830. By January next, she had become "ever yours," and before the year was out they were discussing where to build a house. It was high time that Mr. Woolsey should be brought into the picture; and so he was, and he wrote in response, offering worldly wisdom. It would have been understandable if he had thought a girl of Martha's tender age needed this, but he was actually writing to a man in his thirties, and no fool:[71]

> . . . I now proceed to reply to your letter. I do not know the lady you are attached to, if she is as amiable and good as you present we shall love her, if her friends are worthy we will esteem them, and if her mother is a liberal and unmanaging woman, we shall always treat her with the affection and kindness due to the parent of your wife. With regard to property I w[oul]d not have you in the selection of a partner make it a prime object, that w[oul]d be mercenary, but to disregard it, to make it an objection, or not to use it for the benefit of a family including a wife would in my opinion be eminently unwise. If a husband & wife have separately or together property and it is well managed it contributes more to happiness than you are aware

of. Without it or without a certain prospect of possessing it a prudent man will not marry. You probably will have a family, its support is to be derived from the united efforts and means of both parents, if you have income or property it must go for that purpose, if your wife has property there is the same obligation to devote it to the same object, unless her minority should prevent such an application of it. If there are no children the obligation to use for the benefit and the happiness of each other, the means that each may have a controul over is imperative; the withdrawal by the wife of her income from the common object to have it accumulate for a connection less near than her husband, or the omission of a husband to contribute so far as he can consistently with other duties to the comfort of a wife while they are living together, or to her maintenance after his death, are equally evidences of the destitution of affection and correct feeling.

You have an income from y[ou]r office of $1000 which is equal to a Capital of $16666 at 6 p.c., y[ou]r property and what you may ultimately receive (that income continuing) may add enough to that to make it equal to $4000, if the lady has even half that sum you will eventually be well off as to the means to raise up a family. If it should be urged that the ladies property be made over to Trustees to her use or to be at her disposal, the proposition implies a doubt of your capacity to manage it, or your faithfulness in the use of it. It must be managed by some person. Is not the husband or the father more interested than any other, and as likely to be careful and attentive in the management as any person? If the husband is in business which may risk her own estate, and a part or even all a wife's property is made over to Trustees for the benefit of the family, and for her benefit if there is no family, he to have the income or a fair portion of it if he survives her and they have no children, it is an arrangement which prudence w[oul]d justify and affection would not condemn.

I have expressed my views of the situations on which men who marry ladies of more or less property are placed; but nonage, with parents, and opinions of Guardians affect the case, and render the circumstances so different that general principles are not always applicable.

I regret very much that you were silent to me as to your feelings and views, and that your communications to your mother left her not at liberty to mention them to me, if I had known your wishes I could probably have prevented any embarrassment which may arise out of y[ou]r conversation with Mr S[alisbury] and I may still be able to do so after seeing you; if mean time it is necessary for you to decide on any point I hope you will consult Mr Winthrop or Mr Johnson after reading this letter to them. Their counsel w[oul]d be discreet and wise. But I am particularly desirous that you do not give way to your feelings of disinterestedness, or of aversion to what you mistakenly consider as mercenary, and be led to bind yourself by any promise that the property of the lady should go in any other way than the support of a family, or that if you survive her no benefit from it should accrue to you.

I will add that as soon as the difficulties which I have mentioned are removed, and my arms less confined than at present [in the wake of William Woolsey's failure], you may rely on my doing all that an affectionate parent can do for you, also that I will at once do all I conveniently can without embarrassing myself. I hope to see you in a few days if your health is preserved during the sickly period [of yellow fever in the summers]. It may be well for you to know that I have given to your brothers about $15300 each to Mary Ann & Laura $5000 each to your Sister Elizabeth about $7000 and to you $7500—to Sarah nothing.

Your mother unites in love . . .

Reading this, it is easy to see why Theodore should have been slow to inform his father about the state of his heart. He could foresee that his father would, in reply, rather address his head. In the head, his father, from his own earliest teens, had found the organ that properly directed action. He had never outgrown his juvenile faith in it. Why indeed should he? It had won him wealth and esteem, and a place in the world. He could not doubt the value of its teachings for Theodore's situation.

Being clear on that matter, and having shared just such thoughts on marriage arrangements as a son required, Woolsey readily took over the design and building of a house for the couple, too, which, after all, he was going to pay for—as he had in the previous year paid for a Yale professorship that Theodore would occupy—and by the summer of the next year was deep into the details of construction: for instance, ". . . You are mistaken in supposing the furring will take up only 4 inches, it takes more than 9 inches."[72] He was proud of his grasp of the things that counted. So he played the part of a good father, head of the family, director of *Woolsey & Co.*

Though he had given up directorships in commercial companies, he remained in board-positions or offices of the New York Hospital, Chamber of Commerce, Bible Society, and University of New York, and had re-opened an office on the Exchange, where he was reported "in exceeding good spirits"; organized a meeting of influential people and chaired it; had his name in the papers; was a force and figure known to all "on Change."[73] There, too, he could give advice and be listened to. He was seen as wise.

Reputations like his were naturally measured in conversation, an essential means of conducting their daily affairs which the merchant set carried on for a time in the main room, thirty foot square, of the Tontine Coffee House (no. 25 on the map), there chatting and making deals and drinking a great deal more than coffee, until 1827, when they moved to better quarters on Wall Street.[74] They had formed themselves into an association to monopolize the place, with initial subscriptions by such great names as Rufus King, Archibald Gracie, Gulian Verplanck, William Bayard, all figuring already at some point in my account. To look their best, they repaired to a barber in the basement, later remembered as "an oracle of news" from having shaved the most prominent members, Richard Varick or William Walton Woolsey, early in the day. He listened to them through the suds, ready then to pass on whatever they told him to his subsequent customers.

Once a week the select of this merchant group had a rich dinner at a hotel a little uptown, and, after it, as was no doubt often wise, they stayed the night. Woolsey belonged to this group.[75]

They were clubby to an extreme, always ready to join this, or join that, or to start a new club on top of the others they belonged to. While the general population of the city formed its ethnic, trades, and benevolent societies, in such numbers that their annual parade stretched out for miles,[76] the more public-spirited among businessmen for their part formed cultural societies like the Historical and benevolent ones for the relief of distress in various civic categories.[77] They cooperated, too, in public committees, like that which oversaw the execution of a beautiful statue of Alexander Hamilton, meeting for years and years and wrangling with the sculptors.[78] In this, Woolsey took a principal part. Finally, he and his set superadded more exclusive clubs. A relative, a partial namesake, started the Walton Club in his own house on Pearl Street; the semi-political Krout Club, noted for the high spirits of its evenings, was balanced by the sober Turtle Club; and Fenimore Cooper established a fortnightly Bread and Cheese Club in 1824.[79] Perhaps the most often mentioned in modern accounts was the Friendly Club, to which Woolsey belonged, his brother George, his relative through marriage Gilbert Aspinwall, his brother-in-law William Dunlap of some fame, the president of Columbia, William Johnson, the novelist Charles Brockden Brown, Chancellor James Kent, and others less eminent.[80]

The social instinct at work in these associations of every type, as should be clear, helps to explain Woolsey himself. It is for that reason that I give a page to the various places and points of the day at which business-men, professionals, and ministers took each others' measure. Woolsey's wide presence and memberships, which he sought out or welcomed, af-firmed his place among men whose approval he quite evidently wanted, whose opinions he valued and was glad to reflect. With them he spent countless evenings just as he spent his days in very much the same com-pany, attending to his affairs. They constituted *his* 'village', as distinct from Sarah's—though there was certainly much over-lap.

Woolsey's lay generally in a different part of town, to be seen on the map: Wall Street where ten of his circle can be identified at their offices, not their homes (no. 31 on the map); Pine Street and Pearl (nos. 26 and 30) with another thirty, these two streets being partly residential but important commercial areas; Broadway with many more; and scattered offices of friends on Williams, Maiden Lane, and points south, close to the docks and warehouses for convenience in dealing with supercargoes and shipmasters.[81] One could, and no doubt Woolsey did, know hundreds of faces;[82] one could find all the social satisfactions one required at work, if that was one's chosen focus. As it was, decidedly, for Woolsey.

He knew his village intimately, as in turn its members knew *him* well: fellow pew-holders, they were with him; committee colleagues; bank directors together; partners in contracts, or dinner companions, whose names were woven into the fabric of his life; and at the end of life, at funerals, they formed final associations as pall-bearers, enumerated in published lists.[83] In 1831, for instance, Woolsey, Chancellor Kent, John Pintard, and other friends carried the coffin of Richard Varick to the grave. Woolsey and the deceased had served together as directors of the Merchants' Bank; no doubt they had often met at the Brick church where Varick was a member.

Varick died an old man; and Woolsey by the lights of that time was an old man, too—in his mid-sixties. Separated from Sarah by the span of a long generation and passing his days among quite separate circles and concerns, he can have understood his daughter no better than his sons. She confesses to Theodore in private that, when her mother was away, she found it very lonely at the dinner table in the evening with no one for company but her father.[84] The two had little to talk about.

By this point, the early 1830s, the family had long been settled into the adjoining nos. 57, 59, and 60 of Greenwich Street, with Chancellor Kent almost next door (no. 69). William and his wife occupied one of these houses; the Baileys (William's in-laws) were up the street, the interrelated Olmstead-Sebor group linked by marriage to the Winthrops who were linked to the Woolseys lived there, and so on.[85] These were the people Sarah talks about with Carrington, a part of her life.

The clustering, all snug and family and convenient, was just as important to Woolsey for another reason: it defined the best part of town. He wanted the assurance of that, as did his neighbors, too, no doubt. Gossip among the rich declared what were in fact those "best" parts of the city, observing closely who lived where, what streets were "good". Greenwich counted.[86] The reputation of other streets, too, was canvassed and talked about: they were "rising", "aristocratic," "fashionable", or the hub of trade, like Pearl Street.[87] By one's address one was measured.

Measurement could be quantified: that a mere one per cent of the population owned forty per cent of the city's real property.[88] Or that Woolsey's carriage cost what many of his fellow citizens could only earn in a year. And so forth. Numbers, however, could not bring out the affective consequences of disparities in wealth. The few who were rich, jostled by the many, felt—as they have always felt—a secret keen pleasure in having and doing things beyond the reach of the many. They could assert the "Esquire" after their names; they could demand front seats at gatherings; they or their women-folk could declare their inferiors, the many, "not *visitable*"; persons not dressed richly enough could be denied entrance, as inadmissable, to the best events; or be denied even the right to buy a ticket to a ball, provided though they might be with the money it cost.[89] In so many ways did the few keep the many at bay, all, essentially on the basis of wealth, just as Mrs. Follen and so many other social critics and commentators of the time reported. They have been quoted enough, above.

As to the claims for anything wealth couldn't buy, as Mrs. Sedgwick asserted, Woolsey—whose schooling had been so brief and whose letters were marred by misspellings—need not distress himself too much.

Mrs. Follen is worth quoting on a related matter: how a rich man might look on the attempt by a poorer to marry his daughter.[90] She offers a scene in a novel, the setting, Boston, but it will do for New York, where the heroine's father, Mr. Weston, is exclaiming at a piece of outrageous conduct: that "a beggar, a bankrupt, presume to declare his love to my daughter [Amy]." "Dishonorable," he says. Amy defends her lover, who "saw his failure a reason for separating himself from me." She herself had prevented him; but this her father condemns as "defiance of female delicacy." She calls it "frankness," but to him it is "romantic nonsense." "Almost foaming with anger," he goes on,

> "I always thought that your ridiculous romantic notions would be your ruin; and I cannot think it very honorable in Mr. Selmar to take advantage of your folly, and to propose marriage to you, now that he has not a cent.'
>
> "There was nothing, I hear, dishonorable in his failure[she replies]. I was attached to him before his misfortune; why should I not be now?'

"I tell you [Mr. Weston says], this is all romance. You have been so educated that you cannot be happy without those luxuries which money alone can procure. . . . One thing alone I shall insist upon, Amy, if I do consent to this engagement; and that is, it shall be kept a profound secret, till Mr. Selmar has so far proceeded in business that he may appear a suitable match for my daughter."

The passage gives animation and focus to a great deal that has been said about the Woolsey world in the preceding pages: a world or 'village' in which, to begin with, every proper inhabitant must maintain appearances at all costs, protect reputation in every way possible, conform to prevailing values, play out accepted roles as father or mother, capitalist or *haut ton*, member of the community at large—at all times being alert to keep pretenders and predators at bay.

Mrs. Follen's scene she extends into a slightly later conversation between Mr. Selmar and Amy Weston. He is conscious, more than she, of appearances. To aspire to marry her—"people would think it very strange." At which, she explodes, "People would think! These are the magic words that govern the fashionable world." Indeed: they governed Woolsey's immediate angry reaction to the doubts raised about him in the newspapers; they did so again in the matter of William's failure, where he "reflected that I was supposed to be a man of some property and it would be deemed unkind if I did not give that aid to so near a connection which might enable him to go on with his business"—the words were quoted earlier. He spoke very much like Mr. Weston, anxious that his son-in-law "may *appear* a suitable match for my daughter."

As to how Woolsey's daughter had been "educated", whatever the direction of the process before she took over for herself, no one ever gave a thought to how she might earn a living. A woman perfectly brought up was expected to be perfectly useless. She was taught no trade, she could not travel alone; even on the street she must have a man's arm, a "protector". The word is not uncommon in such connections.[91]

But there is no sign of rebellion in Sarah—rather, acceptance of her condition, if her comments on class may be taken in that sense. She and her family like others of their set in New York or other big towns were quite at peace with the stratification of their 'village', which assigned to some women, visiting, and to others, daily labor.[92]

Accordingly, a man having a daughter as Woolsey did or Pintard or Fenimore Cooper—all of whose thoughts on their parental duty have been mentioned in the notes, at one point or another—had to secure a life for the girl above all worries about money. Woolsey had pulled it off with Sarah's older sisters: all, offered to the world with a promise of much money, all wed to young men judged to be of suitable prospects in the earning of still more. Woolsey relished arranging people's lives, witness his parenting toward Theodore, well into the latter's thirties. By accident, the course of it is well documented. No doubt he behaved in the same way with his sons-in-law-to-be, George Hoadly, William Johnson, and Francis Bayard Winthrop, assuring himself that they understood what was expected of them.

There had been just such an understanding amounting to a contract in Mr. Samuel Johnson's hand—Johnson the father of William who was at the time Laura Woolsey's intended. He wrote to reassure Woolsey about the essentials, pronouncing himself "highly gratified with an event which promises a beloved son so much rational happiness." Woolsey for his part could be assured that young Johnson was well into a good career as a lawyer and "may rationally hope to advance gradually to that rank & distinction in Society, which he aspires to reach, & which he ought to claim as the friend & protector of your amiable daughter."[93] "Rational" was opposed to "Romantic".

Such a letter, Carrington's father was not alive to write. A pity. If there was money enough in the young man's hands to allow a life of only limited or occasional earnings, as seems to have been the case, it would hardly suffice to support Sarah and himself in "the proper rank & distinction in Society." So he must work hard and make a lot. Could he do that? Did he really want to? Was he *serious* about getting money?

How had he begun his life? In travel. That could be borne; the best people occasionally did it, though few. Nathaniel Chauncey had made the choice, and we know how Woolsey viewed this: negatively. He said often, and taught his children to say, that their uncle was indeed (but no more than) "a gentleman of taste and leisure . . . Our friend Mr C. has seen much and learned much but I am apprehensive his fine faculties and great acquisitions will in his country be hid under a bushel . . . ; all the information and excellence of Mr Chauncey's character will never be applied to do anything more than read & travel . . . I am afraid he will not take up any serious employment. It seems like throwing away one's faculties, and all the opportunities given to us by a kind providence, when we neglect to do our part in carrying on the labours of the world."[94]

What a man ought rather to do was exactly what Woolsey did: apply himself tirelessly to business while reserving a part of his efforts, but not too much, for church and civic causes.

Instead, Carrington had appeared for a time a Nathaniel-Chauncey type. He had seemed to value culture for itself—"had a french manner."[95] Next thing you knew, he'd be kissing his friends on both cheeks, like a certain young enthusiast fresh back from Paris.[96] The proper merchants' unpersuaded view of European ways was described in the first chapter. I recall once again what a European said: "The first society of New York is formed by the merchants, shipowners, lawyers, physicians, and magistrates of the city. This is truly American: they do not amuse themselves by apeing European manners; among them, conversation is solid and instructive, and turns upon business. . . ."[97]

Recovered from his unAmericanisms, Carrington remained nevertheless suspect, so Woolsey was convinced; it was his "secret opinion of this young man. He can never himself make a good lawyer or a good man. He is too light and fickle." The words quoted are in fact uttered by a lawyer in his fifties who appears in a novel of the period; but how is art different from life, when Woolsey is quoted by Sarah? "He did not think you a business man"; ". . . trifling, light, just the person who never would succeed in life."[98]

Such being the character of the suitor, a proper father must prevent the marriage. The law punished only clergy who presided over unions in which the bride or groom was under-age, meaning under sixteen, or under eighteen, or twenty-one according to different states.[99] None of this brought any comfort to Woolsey. Sarah had long attained her majority. Nor was there comfort in common opinion among his peers, so far as it can be recovered from anecdote or fiction.[100] Generally, it supported a father's veto with less and less force and enthusiasm over the course of Woolsey's lifetime, and, by the period of Sarah's engagement, took for granted the word of a parent in a marriage as a sort of *congé d'élire*. It was, so to speak, *nice* if a match had parental approval; it would show "correct feeling," to borrow a descriptive phrase from Woolsey; and, within any proper family, relations should always be of that character; but the young these days. . . .

So Woolsey's powers were reduced to the purse. It proved, of course, quite enough, controlling not so much what suitor Sarah chose, as what manner of life she might thereafter enjoy. With her Carrington, it would be very different from what she was used to on Greenwich Street—unless her father should set them up like her brother William and Caroline or like her sister Laura and the other William. For them, Woolsey chose to buy a good share of happiness, as he had done also for Theodore and John; he could easily have done the same for Sarah. But he would not lose out to Carrington. Even after the latter had attained a position to meet his demands, the match was forbidden; even after his own death, Woolsey's will was to prevail, by denying Sarah a share in his estate.[101]

As her exchange with Carrington shows, she looked on an unmarried old age with regret, or some darker feeling still; and as she saw it, old age set in at thirty or so. Only a few years of marriageable youth remained to her, in the early 1830s. She responded without delay to her cousin's suit. For all anyone can say, old Woolsey had been right, and this second choice was best for her. She asks in passing, in a long, loving, and happy letter written to Charles Johnson in the summer of 1834, "do you remember I once told you nobody in my life had shown me half the kindness you have?"[102] The question is very revealing of her life within her family. From that, Charles offered escape, and Greenwich Street or its Connecticut rural equivalent—everything "suitable." He needed no Woolsey money, he never formed a firm. A good match in character as well: he and Sarah seem like two slightly odd ducks who belonged together.[103] But the same might have been said of herself and her first choice.

Let us, however, suppose her happily married; a mother several times; died in her sixties—*in Paris*.[104] Home at last!

And Carrington? He too (chap. 1 n. 1) found, only two years after he had reached the depths of his despair, another love; he too lived a long life, into his late seventies, always in New York.

If such an ending in the 1870s should be counted as a happy one, it shouldn't obscure the character of the little drama played out so many years prior, in the letter-book: for in this, Carrington can be seen terribly torn apart by the whole affair, and Sarah, too; and Woolsey was miserable in his estrangement from his daughter.

Here was feeling enough; but yet, only on a tiny scale, involving only three people and those, not of much importance. It might claim to be of interest only to the extent that the three exemplified forces of more general operation. But they did. They show an older generation and a younger in conflict at a time of change in prevailing values, and they allow a rough estimate of the force of attachment of each, to its choice: Woolsey, to a structure of power in the family, to an ideal of masculine virtue, to a purpose in living, that came from the past and centered in Pearl Street; and for this, he was willing to inflict great pain on his child and to endure some little in return. As to Sarah and Carrington, they must have a touch of the romantic in their lives. The choice was of the times, or a little ahead. Their assertion of it was modest; yet it set them apart, and they were made to pay for it. By such punishments, by such pains, every society, every village, controls the rate of its change.

Abbreviations

Barck = D. C. Barck, *Letters from John Pintard to His Daughter Eliza Noel Pintard Davidson 1816–1833*, 4 vols. (New York 1940) [identified by the editor's name so as to avoid confusion between a reference to the book, and to Pintard the person]

BP = Woolsey Family Business Papers by month, day, and year (the writer ordinarily specified only if there is more than one document of the same date; the year, always in the 1800s, so "4/12/28" is May 12, 1828)

FP = Woolsey Family Papers in the same form as above

L-b = Letter-book compiled by H. C. Beach, inventoried as of 1825–35, which I cite not by letter-number but by page of the book (shown in chapter 2 in square brackets)

Scoville = [J. A. Scoville] "Walter Barrett, Clerk," *The Old Merchants of New York City*, 5 vols. (New York 1863–1870; reprint 1968)

Sisters = R. MacMullen, *Sisters of the Brush. Their Family, Art, Life, and Letters 1797–1833* (New Haven 1997)

MacMullen first pages   2000/11/9 10:49 v5.9   p. 161   Windfall Software

Notes

Preface Notes

1. My Johnson-quotation comes from Boswell's *Life* at the date Apr. 6, 1775. The Woolsey Family collection, including letters by Sarah Woolsey, I use by permission of Manuscripts and Archives, Yale University. Among the people who have helped me in my visits to various institutions, I must thank W. R. Massa at Yale, T. Knoles of the American Antiquarian Society, and O. Tsapina of the Huntington Library; J. E. Silver and R. Heman at the Parish archives of Trinity Church in New York; the staff of the genealogical collection in the New York Public Library, of the library in the New York Historical Society, and of the Connecticut State Library in Hartford—not to mention other institutions inquired of by mail, and all, courteously responding.

2. In support of so general a point I can offer only assertions: my own, which don't count (e.g. *Historia* 40 [1991] p. 437), or L. B. Namier in *The Listener* half a century ago, republished in his *Personalities and Powers* (London 1955) p. 3: "Although we know that man's actions are mostly conditioned by factors other than reason, in practice we have to assume their rational character." Regarding political ideas, he continues, "what matters most is underlying emotions" (p. 4); and a generation later, John Keegan, *The Face of Battle* (New York 1976) p. 32, insisted "that some exploration of the combatants' emotions, if not the indulgence of our own, is essential, to the truthful writing of military history" (p. 32, cf. pp. 31–33 passim, 295ff.).

3. Idem, *The First World War* (London 1998) p. 154, quoting the two Russian novelists in substantiation; and the scene they paint is "unforgettable."

4. On the need both to allow oneself to be moved, and to employ moving language, in presenting an interpretation of the past, cf. MacMullen, *Past and Present* 88 (1980) pp. 3–16 passim.

MacMullen first pages   2000/11/9 10:49   v5.9   p. 163   Windfall Software

5. As archeologists protest against collectors who treat artifacts as treasure trove, without accompanying dig reports—. But it would be invidious here regarding American sociocultural history to pick out particular examples of serious inquiry which handle great masses of data, but all with a broad brush, and decontextualized.

6. In the Woolsey Family Papers collection, the earlier parts alone are of interest to me ("BP", "L-b", and "FP"), augmented by the three collections designated under Abbreviations as Scoville, Barck, and *Sisters*. The latter two represent slightly lower social strata than that of the Woolseys, though with a few mutual acquaintances. Beyond these four very voluminous sources for early nineteenth-century New York, I haven't come on another on anything like the same scale.

Chapter 1 Notes

1. M. M. Bagg, *The Pioneers of Utica: Being Sketches of Its Inhabitants* (Utica 1877) p. 409. H. Carrington Beach (1794–1873) was the son of a Johnstown NY doctor who died when the son was only two; and the boy's mother died when he was twenty, cf. Helen Beach, *The Descendants of Jacob Sebor 1709–1793 of Middletown, Connecticut* (Hartford? 1923) p. 81. This source, Beach's daughter, and another daughter Mary, had earlier combined to write *The Descendants of Thomas Beach of Milford, Connecticut* (Hartford 1912), where, pp. 7–18, 29, they supply further facts about their father's marriage in 1836 in New York to the daughter Mary Charlotte of Margaret Yates Sebor by her marriage to Henry Louis de Koving. Margaret née Sebor was cousin to her husband de Koving, and the Sebors were of that merchant family of New York that appears in chap. 3 n. 85, below: originally of Middletown, Connecticut, active in their importing firms by the 1790s in New York, and one of them, Jacob Sebor, a Tontine Coffee House shareholder; their sister Elizabeth married to John de Koven, father to Henry Louis de Koven. His son-in-law H. Carrington Beach gained an appointment as ensign, then lieutenant, in the New York state militia, 1821–22, cf. *Beach Family Magazine* 1 (1926) pp. 50f.; owned property in Dunkirk (N. Y.) in 1836f. and 1847, ibid p. 588; and had six children, cf. Helen Beach, op. cit. p. 18. His death is barely noted in New York's *Evening Post* (1/23/1873) and *Tribune* (1/24/1873).

2. William Cecil Woolsey and George A. Ward, on whom see FP 12/11/27; on the last-named, see Scoville 1 p. 217: Ward b. ca. 1790, settled in the city by 1816, serving a clerkship with John and Philip Hone's auction house, and eventually (Scoville gives a mistaken date) forming a partnership with William Woolsey Jr. and Beach. Scoville also explains, 3 p. 129, "in every auction house, one of the partners held the commission [or license from the state] in his individual name"; and, p. 240, "none but a Democrat could get appointed. Consequently, many wealthy auction firms had to give a partnership to someone who had political capital." More than that was needed, too, since, p. 241, Beach had to pay $7,768.58 for his commission.

3. FP 10/2/31, writing in response to his fiancée's willingness to believe the worst of Beach.

4. FP 12/11/27; Beach described by Bagg loc. cit. as "amiable and accomplished," i.e. cultivated.

5. L-b 16.

6. German language unrecognizable in New London in 1825, *Sisters* p. 521; unknown in Boston, too, in the 1820s, cf. H. M. Jones, *America and French Culture* (Chapel Hill 1927) p. 72; G. S. Wood, *The Radicalism of the American Revolution* (New York 1992) p. 271, a Grand Tour by the well known Abraham Bishop in the 1770s; Mrs. Sedgwick's beau-ideal back from Europe about 1800, cf. M. Kelley, *The Power of Her Sympathy. The Autobiography and Journal of Catharine Maria Sedgwick* (Boston 1993) p. 92; Josiah Salisbury, Theodore's father-in-law, for a two year sojourn intended at the start for theological study, but soon degenerating into mere civilization, 1801–02, cf. Box 55 of BP, "Family Memorials," privately printed genealogical work, pp. 73ff.; A. B. Faust, *The German Element in the United States* (Boston 1909) 2 p. 208, on a medical student of the 1790s to Germany; J. T. Krumpelmann, *Southern Scholars in Goethe's Germany* (Chapel Hill 1965) p. 2, on the first American PhD from Göttingen in 1800; [E. L. Follen], *The Works of Charles Follen with a Memoir of His Life* (Boston 1842) 1 p. 265, "many young Americans" are studying theology in his homeland, so Follen reports in 1829; H. A. Pochmann, *German Culture in America. Philosophical and Literary Influence 1600–1900* (Madison 1957) p. 60, on the publicizing role of a book (New York 1803) by Samuel Miller of the New York Friendly Club (a friend of Theodore Woolsey, cf. e.g. FP 1/11/27, 9/30/30), and, p. 62, of Joseph

Buckminster a few years later, his friend and executor being George Ticknor; pp. 63, 101, on the influence of "De l'Allemagne" (1799; English ed. in London 1813; New York, 1814) through 54 pages of the *New York Quarterly Review* of the latter year; and Washington Irving's visit of 1822–23, pp. 373ff. (he too being a Friendly Club member); Jones loc. cit., P. Matenko, *Ludwig Tieck and America* (Chapel Hill 1954) pp. 5, 8 (on Edward Robinson, cf. FP 12/11/27), 10, and P. G. Buchloh, *American Colony of Göttingen, Historical and Other Data* (Göttingen 1976) p. 22, all providing some picture of the American influx to Germany in the 1820s.

7. E.g., FP 4/22/28.

8. E. Y. Smith, "The descendants of William Edwards, colonist of Connecticut Colony, 1639," *New York Genealogical and Biographical Record* 72 (1941) pp. 124f.; Pochmann (cit., n. 6) p. 77; F. B. Dexter, *Biographical Sketches of the Graduates of Yale College* 6 (New Haven 1912) pp. 16ff., Henry Dwight's fiancée Elizabeth Salisbury after his death in 1832, in 1836 married Nathaniel Chauncey; and B. W. Dwight, *The History of the Descendants of John Dwight of Dedham, Mass.* (New York 1874) 1 p. 210.

9. FP 5/31/29, 7/1/29, and 12/7/29.

10. FP 4/22/22, a seminary friend to Theodore, "I saw your dear sister, and earnestly desire that she may with her idolized brother Theodore enjoy the consolation of religion"; quoted, FP 7/8/32; and a large number of letters Theodore wrote to her, e.g. one of fourteen pages, FP 10/8–10/27.

11. "Awake" in his and his friends' letters, FP 3/10/22, 4/9/22, 4/10/22, etc.; particular fervor of piety in their correspondence, FP 2/22/22, 8/17/22, 1/21/25, 7/17/25.

12. FP 10/7/32, Martha Salisbury; Sarah Chauncey Woolsey to Theodore, FP 12/31/22; on her church-going, 5/14/27 and 9/15/28; below, e.g. chap. 3 n. 48, on her father's involvement with his church, in which his son William had an active interest, FP 5/14/27; and Sarah's letter quoted, FP 1/14/29, with Mathews' dates of ministry, 1813–34, in J. Greenleaf, *A History of the Churches of All Denominations in the City of New York* (New York 1846) p. 19, cf. L-b 12/24/28 on attending a bible class; her letter FP 7/9/34 to her fiancé Charles; also FP 8/4/35.

13. See, e.g. J. F. Cooper, *Correspondence of James Fenimore-Cooper* (New Haven 1922) 1 pp. 112f., the author's letters, and 201, his wife writes, too;

Jones (cit., n. 6) pp. 279 n. 150 and 280 n. 151, on Fenimore Cooper, Irving, Emerson, Longfellow, Bryant, et al.; also Pochmann (cit., n. 6) pp. 362, 373ff., 410f.; on 1830, besides more famous reporters, Theodore's friend from Paris, FP 7/30/30; in 1838–39, Theodore Sedgwick, nephew of the novelist, in Dwight (cit., n. 8) 2 pp. 743f.; Sereno Dwight (son of the Yale president Timothy), ibid. 1 p. 204, and family letters about him, e.g. BP 10/1/24; overseas in 1823–28, Nathaniel Chauncey (1789–1865), cf. Dexter (cit., n. 8) 6 pp. 16ff., and such letters as FP 3/23/24 or 11/8/24; Charles Frederick Johnson, e.g. FP 3/25/28; George Muirison Woolsey (1772–1851) and his wife Abigail née Howland in Genoa, FP 11/19/29, etc.; their son Charles, FP 3/9/30; all nine children of the rich New York merchant, John McVickar, cf. M. Lamb, *History of the City of New York: Its Origin, Rise, and Progress* (New York 1877–80) 2 p. 520; Philip Hone, involved with Woolsey in 1826, BP 11/28/26, doubtless on many other boards and committees, traveling abroad in 1821 and 1836, *Dictionary of American Biography* 9 (1932) p. 192; Mrs. Sedgwick directly reporting through her *Letters from Abroad to Kindred at Home* (New York 1841) 1 pp. 188, 239, etc.

14. European travels by friends outside the family: Mr. Woolsey's old business partner Moses Rogers takes a trip to England, 12/29/21; later, FP 5/31/29, 9/30/29 with 10/19/29 and 3/31/30 (Van Ness and Sheldons and the latter again, FP 8/1/33), 11/19/29 (Howlands), 6/15/29 (young Ralston), and 2/28/30 (Theodore in Rome, meeting Peter Schermerhorn); of the same date, Sarah's sister Laura reports "the good clergyman Dr. Milnor goes to England," and another friend is in Italy; J. A. Yates in Rome, too, quoted, FP 6/6/29; and Sarah noting, FP 3/31/30, "a great many New Yorkers are going to France this spring," e.g. the George Richards family and Mrs. Charles Lewis; Jones (cit., n. 6) p. 279 n. 151, several pre-1832 travellers; the young Abeel brothers in Rome in 1832, cf. Barck 4 p. 29, and, on the family, 1 p. 162, 4 p. 29, known to the Pintards at least through joint activities, cf. H. C. Brown, "One of our oldest societies—New York Historical," *Valentine's Manual of the City of New York*, Ser. 2, 1 (1916–17) p. 61, known in *Sisters* in the 1820s, pp. 160, 212, and long listed in *Longworth's Directory* (Garritt B. Abeel, ironmonger, 1814–30).

15. Sarah to Theodore, FP 4/15/29.

16. FP 5/14/30, or again 11/30/31, with many other displays in parts of letters, FP passim, of languages learned by Theodore and his friends; and Sarah's smile, 4/15/29, quoted.

17. M. E. Dewey, ed., *Life and Letters of Catharine M. Sedgwick* (New York 1871) pp. 106 (1818), 139, 171 (1825), 213, etc. Cooper (cit., n. 13) 1 p. 201; with more on Opie, 202 (and no different among the English, cf. Betty Patterson Bonaparte to Lady Morgan in 1824, " . . . les détails de ménage" where "household matters" would have done just as well, in Jones p. 62 n. 82); or George Bancroft's confession in a letter, "many an unfortunate French or German phrase or sweet Italian is interceding for utterance" when he writes home, cf. O. W. Long, *Literary Pioneers. Early American Explorers of European Culture* (Cambridge 1935) p. 141. On Dunlap's adaptation of French plays and melodramas, 1797–1828, see Jones (cit., n. 6) p. 347.

18. [E. Bulwer Lytton], *Pelham; or, the Adventures of a Gentleman*, ed. 2 (New York 1828) 1 pp. 12f., &c; C. M. Sedgwick, *Clarence, or, a Tale of Our Own Times* (London 1830) 1 p. 82, 3 pp. 1, 6, 8, 12, &c, while in her own voice using a good bit of needless French (*éclaircissement* often, e.g. 2 p. 222; 3 p. 23, cf. 2 p. 272, *gaucherie*, 3 p. 206, &c) and occasionally putting French into the mouth of a character meant to be admired (e.g. 3 pp. 37, 155, 280f.). Those beneath the *haut ton* would of course know no French, 3 p. 103. For more French in the same style, cf. Mrs. Follen's *Sketches of Married Life*, ed. 2 (Boston 1839) p. 58, a satirically presented *belle*; or the anon. ("by a lady") *Familiar Letters on Subjects Interesting to the Minds and Hearts of Females* (Boston 1834) p. 16, the imagined writer addressing *ma chère amie*; or again, Theodore Sedwick Fay, *Hoboken: A Romance of New-York* (New York 1843) pp. 64f., 66, 68, pretentious French. Even the *Christian Examiner* in its editorial voice dropped in some French, satirically, quoted in Jones (cit., n. 6) p. 279.

19. Italian dropped in, Sedgwick 3 p. 196; Latin phrases, 1 pp. 268, 273 (*sub rosa* misused by an ignorant woman); 3 pp. 2ff., 25, 79, 93, &c.

20. Jones (cit., n. 6) pp. 269f., 277, 284f.; confirmation in *Sisters*, e.g. pp. 293, 298, 349 or Sedgwick, *Clarence* 3 p. 12.

21. Theodore Sedgwick Fay, *Norman Leslie* (New York 1841) 2 pp. 541f., the hero being joined by his friend, then by the heroine on the arm of her father.

22. Tutors for girls in their homes in the period ca. 1805–15, Cooper (cit., n. 13) 1 pp. 54f.; Jones (cit., n. 6) p. 168; M. Kelley, *Private Woman, Public Stage. Literary Domesticity in Nineteenth-Century America* (New York 1984) pp. 64, 69 (both French and Latin, for a Boston girl); a little later, 1833f., French and Italian learnt at home, cf. A. B. Warner, *Susan Warner ("Elizabeth Wetherell")* (New York 1909) pp. 112f. &c, and taught ancient languages by her father; the results generally scorned, *Familiar Letters* (cit., n. 18) p. 87; but enthusiasm for one Joseph Boeuf who perhaps, at the corner of Murray and Church, not only lived but taught, cf. the mention in Scoville 2 p. 34; for the mid-1820s, Barck 2 p. 174, a French and a Spanish teacher; and Margaret Fuller and a friend learn German in 1832, cf. Matenko (cit., n. 6) p. 65.

23. Scoville 1 pp. 338, 351.

24. FP 9/9/27.

25. Spanish and Italian, FP 2/15/24; an Italian teacher for further study, FP 10/30/27, cf. 11/14/27, "very busy learning Italian," and 12/31/27; but her teacher's illness ended the lessons, FP 3/14/28; continues on her own, prose and poetry, FP 1/14/29; requests books, 8/26/29, and gives thanks for them, 12/7/29; encouragement from Theodore who struggles with his Italian.

26. FP 11/8/24 (quoted); her schedule of French study, beginning with grammar, explained, FP 3/12/25, while Spanish remains her favorite; requests purchases of Spanish poetry books, FP 11/14/25; again, 7/26/26; drops Spanish phrases to John, FP 12/1/26; translates for her sister, FP 10/14/27, and drops some Spanish on Theodore, 9/8/32, "I thought I would put in one foreign word"; and scattered Spanish to Carrington Beach, e.g. L-b 79.

27. FP 2/4/26, two and a half pages in French, "ma mal Français"(!); writes and reads French, 8/17/26 to her brother John; drops French to him, 3/21/29; speaks to a French guest, FP 12/16/26 to John; shows many errors in written French, but has a teacher and does three and a half hours of work a day, 11/28/27, while asking Theodore whom she writes to, "comment

va le Français? et comment l'italique?" By December, she has another
teacher, FP 12/31/27; drops into French, to Theodore, FP 5/31/29; thanks
to Theodore for books sent, 1/9/30.

28. FP 3/31/30 to Theodore.

29. Cervantes in FP 2/15/24 and 3/12/25, part of the ideal library for Mrs.
Sedgwick along with Dante, *Clarence* 3 pp. 280f., taught to her in her
girlhood, cf. Kelley (cit., n. 6) p. 74; Spanish lyrics, FP 11/14/25, and other
books, FP 7/26/26 and L-b 112f. (1830).

30. FP 1/21/22, 11/14/25, and 1/14/29 on Dante; 8/26/29, Alfieri, Petrarca,
Metastasio, and Theodore's copy of Tasso, cf. FP 2/15/24, the poet also
favored by Margaret Fuller, cf. Matenko (cit., n. 6) p. 65, and by Susan
Warner, cf. Warner (cit., n. 22) pp. 133, 143, along with others making up
the Italian canon of the early 19th century in the U. S., cf. P. R. Baker, *The
Fortunate Pilgrims. Americans in Italy 1800–1860* (Cambridge 1964) p.
2: Alfieri, Metastasio, Ariosto, and Petrarca.

31. FP 2/15/24, Saint-Pierre's repute at the time appearing best in his selection
for a portrait by Rembrandt Peale, cf. *The Selected Papers of Charles
Willson Peale and His Family*, ed. L. B. Miller, 2, Pt. 2 (New Haven
1988) p. 1118; FP 8/26/29, Voltaire; L-b 118, Bossuet (read, too, by young
Warner); and French plays, the prodigiously prolific Scribe, L-b 65f., in
two volumes, other authors in four volumes, L-b 85, Racine in FP 2/4/26;
some approved for chapter-headings by Mrs. Sedgwick, e.g. *Clarence* 3 p.
109; less obvious writers, e.g. FP 10/16/32; and *Valérie*, L-b 55, 67.

32. FP 9/14/24; 1/21/22 and L-b 118, Scott; 4/15/29; L-b 110, Byron; 8/1/34;
L-b 118, Emerson; non-fiction, FP 1/21/22, 7/16/29 (naval history Mr.
Woolsey had been reading), L-b 118 and 124; Lady Mary Montague's
Letters, FP 7/29/29; Robert Hall's *Sermons* on the recommendation of
Charles Frederick Johnson, FP 7/9/34 and 8/1/34, Hall being active in an
English Bible Society, cf. his *Works* (G. & C. & H. Carvill, New York, n.d.)
2 pp. 357ff.; they were much admired by the city's educated class, cf. Barck
4 p. 57; Jeremy Taylor, FP 10/16/32; meets and obviously has read Mrs.
Sedgwick and Mrs. Sigourney, FP 12/24/33 and 9/8/32; Bulwer Lytton, L-
b 75, 86 (*Devereux*, 1829, and *Disowned*); FP 1/21/22, 5/30/27, Fenimore
Cooper; borrows popular books from a library, L-b 124.

33. Laura reads, e.g. FP 1/3/33, where, however, she calls a just-published book "a very old book" because it's set in a past time (and cf. "between you and I," FP 11/14/27); BP 9/3/33, quoted; Sarah reads, FP 9/26/27, 12/14/27, 1/28/30; Laura to Theodore 2/15/29; Mr. Woolsey's reading, quite active, FP 8/31/29.

34. FP 10/6/32, in the Salisbury family; Kelley (cit., n. 6) pp. 63, 73, Mrs. Sedgwick's childhood experience; also Susan Warner's, ibid. p. 89 and Warner (cit., n. 22) pp. 82ff., 113, and passim; F. R. Morse, ed., *Henry and Mary Lee: Letters and Journals . . . 1802–1860* (Boston 1926) p. 218, in Boston in 1814; and at meetings of the Friendly Club, Scoville 2 p. 335, to which Mr. Woolsey belonged; J. Q. Adams at Chancellor Kent's house in 1831, W. Kent, *Memoirs and Letters of James Kent, L. L. D* (Boston 1898) p. 251; and in novels, e.g. Mme. de Krüdener, *Valérie*, ed. M. Mercier (Paris 1974) p. 142, or George Watterston's *Glencarn* (Alexandria 1810) 2 p. 159.

35. FP 6/15/22 [thus, by the Yale-Archives dating, but actually 1820], to Theodore; further analytical or critical remarks in FP 8/17/26, 9/17/26 to Theodore on Disraeli's *Vivian Grey* (1826), model for *Pelham*, cf. R. A. Zipfer, *Edward Bulwer-Lytton and Germany* (Berne 1874) p. 53; FP 5/30/27 on a new Fenimore Cooper novel, *The Prairie*; a book of poetry criticism, FP 1/15/33 to Theodore.

36. FP 8/4/35; 1/15/33.

37. FP 9/17/24; in touch with Prof. Goodrich, whose book on Coleridge Sarah then reads, FP 12/25/30 with 1/15/33.

38. Theodore's poems, FP 1/1/23, 4/3/23, 2/15/24, 10/31/24, 3/14/26, 4/21/28, 4/15/30, 4/8/32, 10/26/32, 10/29/32, 12/12/32, 5/25/33, etc.; for a sense of New York as a home of amateur versifiers, cf. *Sisters* 195ff. and passim; Sarah's verse, e.g. FP 9/7/30.

39. "I recently read with much pleasure some of Racine's tragedies. At present I'm reading Stewart's philosophy of the soul, since I think I'm too gay, and that's why I have devoted myself to moral philosophy; and if that's not enough, I'll try what mathematics can do. I'm sure I'll accomplish my goal, at least by my old age." The quotation from FP 2/4/26, Dugald Stewart studied also by Susan Warner, cf. Warner (cit., n. 22) p. 166; Mr. Woolsey's amusement at the excesses of the Lafayette reception and a foreigner's bad

English in FP 10/23/24 and 7/16/29; again, 6/8/32, at things going wrong at a wedding party.

40. E.g., humorous treatment of a wagon on a trip, FP9/14/24, "it had no springs and was all aft"; humorous verse, FP 9/7/30; outrageous comparison of a baby to a racoon, FP 8/1/34.

41. Lectures, the 1826 series, see Scoville 2 p. 335 on McVickar et al. in the Friendly Club; M. J. Lamb, *History of the City of New York: Its Origin, Rise, and Progress* (New York 1877–80) 2 p. 706, and FP 3/14/28 and in a letter to Theodore dated only to 1833 (so, in the Yale Archives, at the end of that year), where she reports also on art study; girls taught to draw, Dwight, *Travels* (cit. below, n. 46) 1 p. 474, and *Sisters* pp. 227ff., 269f. (Ellen Tooker's lessons); Sarah attends an art exhibition, FP 1/15/33; 11/14/28, opera, *Der Freischütz* being the first of this art (in the early 1820s) to have been exhibited, cf. C. H. Haswell, *Reminiscences of an Octogenarian of the City of New York* (New York 1896) pp. 150, 223 (1827), the opera's popularity in *Sisters* p. 388; prevalence of music in the polishing of young ladies, cf. e.g. Dwight, loc. cit., or *Familiar Letters* (cit., n. 18) p. 87. The male sex of the city generally paid music little attention; but there were exceptions like Pintard, in Barck 2 p. 185, friends with Edward Riley, or Charles Peale also interested in music, partly through instrument-invention, cf. his consultation with Riley, *Peale Papers* (cit., n. 31) 2 Pt. 2, pp. 886f., 915, and V. L. Redway, *Music Directory of Early New York. A File of Musicians, Music Publishers* . . . (New York 1941) pp. 51, 76. Peale, however, was curious about *everything*. He and Pintard were, incidentally, acquainted, *Peale Papers* 3 (New Haven 1991) pp. 508, 525, 529.

42. As judged by a visiting Englishman, FP 4/5/22 and FP 3/14/28, quoted.

43. Two letters of the same date, FP 12/25/29; L-b 67.

44. FP 4/15/29, on Catherine Bailey Woolsey; 7/8/32, quoted; Martha's snubs, FP 1/15/33 and 12/24/33; and notice Sarah's disappearance from the family correspondence from the fall of 1832 for about a year, with absence from passages where one would expect her, e.g. 7/19/33 or 9/13/33.

45. FP 9/15/28.

46. Barck 1 p. 12; further specifying of intellectuality in women as unusual though not repellent, 2 pp. 88, 336; Sedgwick, *Clarence* 3 p. 106; and

such strictures of ignorance that prevented the proper education of young women as Timothy Dwight's *Travels in New-England and New-York* 1 (London 1821) p. 174, describing Boston around the time of Sarah's birth, quite in accord with the 1830s, cf. *Familiar Letters* (cit., n. 18) p. 87, or [S. Knapp,] *Extracts from a Journal of Travels in North America . . . by Ali Bey* (Boston 1818) pp. 32, 47, and passim, or with the description of the dreaded "bleu" in Philadelphia of the 1820s in S. J. Hale, *Sketches of American Character*, ed. 6 (Boston 1838) pp. 142f., the gentlemen there "ridiculing her pedantry, generally hated her person . . . , disgusted with the affectation of literature in the *bleu* . . . , sickened by the affectation of sentiment and sensibility in the *belle*; and could not but acknowledge that though learning might make a woman excessively disagreeable, yet she might be excessively disagreeable without it. . . ." For other scenes in fiction to the same effect, reflecting the same dislike and ridicule of blue-stockings, see e.g., G. Watterston, *Glencarn* (Alexandria 1810) 2 p. 189, the detestable Rodolpho, "a perfect model of American foppery. His manners were fashioned *a la mode de Paris*, and his style of observation borrowed from the British school of gallantry," or again, in Philadelphia, 1 pp. 31f., the hero warned, "take care to display no learning or sentiment, for the moment it is discovered, you are one of that cast, your reputation is lost forever"; or a selection from the early 19th century in H. R. Brown, *The Sentimental Novel in America, 1789–1860* (Durham 1940) pp. 80ff.

47. Quoted are Levasseur, Lafayette's secretary on the trip of 1824, 1 p. 120, in Jones (cit., n. 6) p. 270, and Betty Patterson Bonaparte in the same year from Baltimore, ibid. 62 n. 82; on New York's "literary circles (if there are any such)," Sarah to Nathaniel Chauncey, FP 3/14/28.

48. FP 2/23/25; Kent (cit., n. 34) p. 245, Klopstock rated highly by Kent's friend J. Q. Adams, cf. Follen, *Sketches* (cit., n. 18) 1 pp. 305f., along with Goethe and Schiller whom Kent names with Klopstock (so perhaps he only parroted Adams?)—he was "except for his odes, out of fashion here" in Germany, so Ticknor reported in 1815, cf. Long (cit., n. 17) p. 18; and rich businessmen collect art, e.g. Rufus Prime in Scoville 1 p. 68, or Luman Reed (1785–1836, prominent dry-goods merchant on Greenwich Street and patron of artists like Thomas Cole in the early 1830s); also Henry Laverty, big Pearl-Street dry goods jobber, hanging his adopted daughter's

art (Ellen Tooker) in his grand parlor, M. Y. Beach, *Wealth and Pedigree of the Wealthy Citizens of New York City*, ed. 3 (New York 1842) p. 17.

49. On Strong the father, BP 9/21/25; on the son at Columbia with such intellectually energetic friends as John MacMullen jr., see A. Nevins and M. H. Thomas, eds., *The Diary of George Templeton Strong, 1: Young Man in New York, 1835–49* (New York 1952) pp. 2, 6, 14, 37, and passim; on Hone, see B. Tuckerman, ed., *The Diary of Philip Hone 1828–1851* (New York 1889) p. 44, Hone noting "a vein of sadness pervades all his [Bryant's] writings, which is occasionally lighted up by soft and beautiful images. It is sad and melancholy, but never harsh or gloomy." On Hone's cultivation and energy in cultural institutions, see Lamb (cit., n. 41) pp. 704f.; Barck 1 p. 141; and (p. 47) Pintard is pleased to list among his many civic connections and responsibilities his offices held in the American Academy of Art, Historical Society, and Literary and Philosophical Society. On the Bread and Cheese Club, cf. Lamb 2 p. 706, noting (p. 707) that Verplanck with Bryant were also members of the Sketch Club of the 1820s. Out of this, for the same mix of people, some in business, some in the arts and books, the Century Association was born in the 1840s, with that same Verplanck a member, cf. A. Nevins in *The Century 1847–1946* (New York 1947) pp. 3f.; in the next decade Henry Winthrop (cf. FP 9/8/32), William Aspinwall (FP 9/11/27), and John MacMullen jr. (for a time, Librarian of the Society Library, then of the Century). And what riches of reading lay in the mind of a leading lawyer, father of George Templeton Strong; but how rare he was, too!

50. Betty Bonaparte on Baltimore quoted again from Jones (cf. n. 6) p. 62 n. 82; Murat, quoted ibid. p. 277; "our men are sufficiently money-making," said Sarah Hale (whose *Sketches* are quoted, above), in N. F. Cott, *The Bonds of Womanhood. "Woman's Sphere" in New England, 1780–1835* (New Haven 1977) p. 68.

51. T. Dwight (cit., n. 46) 1 pp. 476ff.; and Knapp (cit., n. 46) p. 34, quoted.

52. Barck 3 p. 189, with a touch of editorial updating.

53. Compare the cultural jingoism expressed by, e.g., Charles J. Ingersoll in his "Discourse concerning the influence of America on the mind, delivered to the American Philosophical Society" (Philadelphia 1823) pp. 13ff., or presented in typical discussions of literature in a novel, Watterston's Glen-

carn (cit., n. 34) 1 pp. 91f., 2 pp. 189f., 207f., against Fenimore Cooper, in Cooper (cit., n. 13) 1 p. 238, quoted, and matched by the ideas of universal vice in Paris held by his friend William Jay, pp. 112f.; Rembrandt Peale in 1808 to his wife, who "will be surprised to hear that ladies [in Paris] . . . dress with as much modesty as ours, & in the middling & lower classes a great deal more—and that they are as decent & correct in their deportment & manners as we are," *Peale Papers* (cit., n. 31) 2 Pt. 2 p. 1105; Mrs. Sedgwick in *Clarence* (1830) 3 p. 285, "the more polished and more corrupt circles of Europe"; her *Letters from Abroad to Kindred at Home* (New York 1841) 1 p. 161, "you will be astonished at the laxity of the Sabbath" in Germany, and, seen in the Milan opera, "forty to fifty dancing girls . . . all trained for the ballet, *and for what besides?*"

54. FP 9/11/27 to Theodore in Paris; cf. also Nathaniel Chauncey's views, FP 9/21/27; Mr. Woolsey warns his son against consorting with Catholics, whose views might rub off, FP11/10/27; disgust at nakedness in art, Rembrandt Peale, loc. cit. with his father's expression of shock, *Peale Papers* 3 (1991) pp. 493, 499; also Scoville 1 p. 62 and Sisters pp. 304f., 320; expectation of dishonesty, FP 11/20/28; elaborate disgust expressed by Charles Frederick Johnson at Paris, "the vilest place in Christendom," FP 3/9/29.

55. Among critics, none stronger than Timothy Dwight in his *Travels*, cit.; Knapp (cit., n. 46) p. 32; Julia Ward Howe's warning as a teenager from what she had been taught at home, cf. Warner (cit., n. 22) p. 133, Susan Warner's journal for 2/22/34; but also, e.g., Morse (cit., n. 34) p. 218, a young woman anticipates reproach for reading Maria Edgeworth (by no means the worst of the genre); H. R. Brown (cit., n. 46) pp. 3–9, many illustrations; T. Martin, *The Instructed Vision: Scottish Common Sense and the Origins of American Fiction* (Bloomington 1961) pp. 61, 74f., 79f., 82f.; M. D. Bell, *The Development of the American Romance: The Sacrifice of Relation* (Chicago 1980) pp. 10f., 13, 28; and C. N. Davidson, *Revolution and the Word. The Rise of the Novel in America* (New York 1986) pp. 40f., 277 n. 11.

56. The quotations are from the second edition (New York 1828) 1 pp. 12, 90 (oysters . . .), 32 ("remarkable" in a later edition, "obnoxious" in the earlier), 184 ("ambitious"); and influence of Disraeli, above, n. 35; an artificial character assumed, the self re-made, to be seen in Goethe himself,

cf. M. Peckham, *The Birth of Romanticism 1790–1815* (Greenwood 1986) pp. 49f. and Zipfer (cit., n. 35) p. 53.

57. Pelham 2 p. 88; Zipfer pp. 35, 39, quoted; J. L. Campbell, *Edward Bulwer-Lytton* (Boston 1986) p. 28; and on the vast vogue for Werther, see e.g. H. R. Brown (cit., n. 46) pp. 155–65.

58. Isaac Mitchell, *The Asylum; or Alonzo and Melissa. An American Tale Founded on Fact* (Poughkeepsie 1811), the frontispiece; Valérie (cit., n. 34) pp. 104ff., 143.

59. "Sensibility" at the heart of many characters and scenes in early 19th century American novels, cf. e.g. Bell (cit., n. 55) pp. 26ff.; C. Mulvey, *Transatlantic Manners. Social Patterns in Nineteenth-Century Anglo-American Travel Literature* (Cambridge [UK] 1990) pp. 65f.; sensibility especially the property of women, cf. e.g. Cott (cit., n. 50) p. 161 and K. Halttunen, *Confidence Men and Painted Women. A Study of Middle-Class Culture in America, 1830–1870* (New Haven 1982) pp. 56f.; "melancholy", in Vincent's comments on the literature of the time, quoted above, and above, n. 49, on Bryant; "delicacy" above, quoted from Mrs. Follen's novel. Sterne is imitated by Bulwer Lytton, e.g. the Uncle-Tobyesque figure Uncle William, in *Devereux. A Tale* (London 1829), or in *Sisters* pp. 35ff., 198f., or again in Watterston's *Glencarn* 2 p. 159, Sophia reads aloud to the man she loves "the pathetic story of Maria, by Sterne. As she proceeded her voice became tremulous . . . rushed out of the room in tears . . . ," and later, "pensive and melancholy," she is addressed by the hero, "You have been weeping, Sophia! I fear your sensibility is too acute. . . ." For the illustration, see *Sisters* p. 198 and Plate 7.16.

60. *Familiar Letters* (cit., n. 18) p. 62; above, n. 46, for other illustrations of the negative view, in Sarah Hale's or George Watterston's fiction.

Chapter 2 Notes

1. Sarah's three brothers were all alive, but she is evidently excluding Theodore by her "both". He was at this time in Europe.

2. On "friend", see e.g. John to his father, BP 7/10/33; Timothy Dwight to Woolsey, BP 1/7/33; or Woolsey to Theodore, FP 3/25/33. On "confidence", cf. K. Halttunen, *Confidence Men and Painted Women. A Study of Middle-Class Culture in America, 1830–1870* (New Haven 1982) pp.

119f., "Mutual sincerity was regarded as the substance of the romantic contract" (seen, however, in social contexts different from Sarah's).

3. In E. Bulwer Lytton, *Pelham; or, the Adventures of a Gentleman*, ed. 2 (London 1828) 2 p. 64, the hand "should never be utterly <u>ringless</u> . . . I know nothing in which the good sense of a gentleman is more finely developed than in his rings;" "Mais, tenez, la voila cet anneau que vous m'avez donné," and so on, in A. E. Scribe and G. Delavigne, *La somnambule* (in *Répertoire du théâtre de Madame* [Paris 1828]) pp. 57, 76f., or in the 1819 edition; below, L-b 66.

4. R. L. Bushman, *The Refinement of America. Persons, Houses, Cities* (New York 1992) p. 288.

5. Parts of novels carried forward in epistolary form, e.g. C. M. Sedgwick, *Clarence, or, a Tale of Our Own Times* (London 1830) 1 pp. 181–203 and elsewhere, with others in H. R. Brown, *The Sentimental Novel in America, 1789–1860* (Durham 1940) p. 69 n. 86, and statistics on the gigantic proportion of wholly epistolary novels within fiction of the closing 18th century, pp. 15, 22.

6. Barck 3 p. 189; and much on the elaborate style and literary posturing to be found in American fiction of the nearly 19th century, in Brown (cit., above) pp. 56, 58f.

7. Mary Denison appears in the family correspondence, staying five weeks in the house, FP 1/10?-15th/22; mentioned, e.g. Sarah to Theodore, 4/5/22, but drops out after 1822; a friend of Theodore's friend Twining, 1/25/23.

8. On the family (but I have not identified the young woman's first name), see Sarah to Theodore, FP 8/1/33, and on the parents, Sarah to Theodore, FP 4/5/22, and below, chap. 3 n. 85: relatives by marriage.

9. Margaret Aspinwall, of a family close and important to the Woolseys, as appears at many points, e.g. chap. 3 nn. 4, 77, and the map of the city (fig. 4).

10. "Farewell, my friend, may Heaven keep you safe for me" (though readers may need no help with Sarah's ventures into French, Spanish, or Italian—I put in a translation only here and there).

11. On Sally Woolsey's health, referred to with anxiety in a majority (!) of all references to her by her husband to her brothers, or in their letters to him,

see e.g. FP 1/14/22, 7/25/22 (trips for her improvement), 1/17/23, 3/21/23, 9/15/28, 4/21/32, 6/10/33 (can't travel); Sarah's illnesses from FP 8/17/26, 9/26/27 (sent to Saratoga Springs in preceding months), 9/28/27 (fainting), 4/21/32, 7/8/32, and so to 8/1/33 (cough, phlegm, &c).

12. Brown (cit., n. 5) pp. 125f.

13. R. Chartier et al., *Correspondence. Models of Letter-Writing from the Middle Ages to the Nineteenth Century*, trans. C. Woodall (Cambridge 1997) pp. 99f.; on the same testing in romances, K. Lystra, *Searching the Heart. Women, Men and Romantic Love in Nineteenth Century America* (New York 1989) pp. 157f.

14. Presumably her friend Mary Silliman, cf. FP 4/5/22, doubtless the "Miss" of FP 1/10–15th/22, 1/21/22, and 11/14/28; but FP undated of 1833 finds her at art classes with Harriet and Elizabeth Silliman.

15. Emily Aspinwall later married Edward Woolsey, cf. chap. 3 n. 4.

16. The Coits in Trinity church, chap. 3, below, at n. 55.

17. For "Mr. Bloodgood" the best possibility is a son of Francis A., the father prominent in Utica, cultivated, a Union College graduate, his son likewise, who "acquired some reputation as a man of letters," cf. M. M. Bagg, *The Pioneers of Utica: Being Sketches of Its Inhabitants and Its Institutions* (Utica 1877) p. 65. The father settled in Ithaca in 1823, where a Thomas Bloodgood was in business ten years later, BP 2/20/33, cf. *New York Daily Advertiser* 8/30/21, he with Francis Cooper and Frederick De Peyster is a director of a Wall Street insurance company.

18. Genealogical material toward the end of the Woolsey Business Papers shows a daughter of Moses Rogers marrying Samuel Miles Hopkins, a lawyer; also M. J. Lamb, *History of the City of New York: Its Origins, Rise, and Progress* (New York 1877–80) 2 p. 735 n. 1. Hopkins' daughter Mary married William G. Verplanck while the son Woolsey Rogers Hopkins married the widow of Woolsey's grandson (! the grandson being the son of William Cecil Woolsey), cf. B. W. Dwight, *The History of the Descendants of John Dwight of Dedham, Mass.* (New York 1874) 2 p. 1096.

19. Dr. Hodge of Philadelphia, who recurs at L-b 68, had married Margaret Aspinwall, Scoville 2 p. 338 (Margaret, daughter of John who married into the Howland family). He figures later as a theological controversialist, cf.

H. A. Pochmann, *German Culture in America. Philosophical and Literary Influences 1600–1900* (Madison 1957) p. 110.

20. George Pumpelly, another Philadelphian, FP 1/8/31, classmate of Theodore at Yale, FP 3/17/31, whose visits to New York register in the correspondence in the early 1830s.

21. James Kent, whom the family knew through Woolsey's connections with him on the Athenaeum board and Friendly Club, cf. FP 2/23/25 and chap. 3 n. 80.

22. She had since January been attending Dr. Mathews' bible-study classes, FP 1/14/29.

23. Louis Peugnet, FP 12/25/29.

24. Among all her Dwight kin, this is surely Henry.

25. Mrs. Van Beuren, sister to Miss Aspinwall, FP 7/26/26; other mentions of the family, FP 1/10?-15th/22, 5/18/33; and Dwight (cit., n. 18) 1 p. 252, John Van Beuren married Elizabeth Aspinwall, and their daughter Sarah married the son of Woolsey's daughter Mary Ann (who had married, first, Jared Scarborough).

26. The Wallace daughter, cf. FP 11/14/28, 1/14/29 (staying at the Woolsey house); daughter, I assume, of John and Susan Binney Wallace, Barck 2 pp. 88, 90, 336.

27. John Cadwallader married Mary Binney in this month, for whom Sarah was bridesmaid, cf. Laura to Theodore FP 9/15/28, Sarah to Theodore, 11/14/28. James Bayard in fact married someone else a few years later, FP 12/4/34.

28. Susan Johnson, Sarah's niece.

29. Woolsey Rogers Hopkins, son of Samuel and Sarah (above, n. 18), married Fanny Sheldon after her first husband's death (he, the son of William Woolsey, Sarah's brother). It is this Hopkins connection that most naturally explains the encounter; and "Mr. Sheldon" would be Fanny's father. Another male Sheldon just married appears in FP 3/14/28 (Sarah to Nathaniel) and travels to Europe, FP 9/30/29 and 10/19/29; and a Henry Sheldon is a friend of Miss Aspinwall's, FP 9/28/28. These are the possibilities, in addition to Frederick Sheldon, below.

30. Sarah Aspinwall appears in FP 3/30/22, 12/5/22, 6/14/28 (along with Margaret McWhorter), and 7/16/29 as a friend of Laura's, but also of Sarah Woolsey's, cf. Sarah to Theodore FP 4/5/22, 5/31/29, 10/16/32, and of John Woolsey's, 7/9/22.

31. Mrs. Rogers, sister to Mrs. John Winthrop, appears often, below.

32. Samuel Ralston's death reported, FP 5/31/29; lamented by (father?) Ashbal, Sarah to Theodore, FP 6/15/29; Sarah Ralston pays a visit, FP 4/21/32; and Robert Ralston writes to Theodore, FP 4/27/27, cf. his interest in evangelism, C. Sellers, *The Market Revolution: Jacksonian America, 1815–1846* (New York 1991) p. 213.

33. John Pintard's daughter was a friend of a Miss Van Ness (Barck 3 p. 89, of 1829), a daughter(?) of the lawyer, eventually judge William Van Ness, cf. Scoville 1 p. 338 and J. J. Horton, *James Kent. A Study in Conservatism 1763–1847* (New York 1939) p. 245.

34. Benjamin Curtis, chum of Sarah's, a friend of Theodore's as well, FP 11/14/28, 4/15/29, 8/31/29, 9/30/29 ("smitten" with Miss Van Ness), writing to Theodore from Europe where he pursues Miss Van Ness, 7/30/30, still abroad in 12/18/32, etc.

35. Gerald Lathrop or a kinsman? (pew-holder in Trinity church, cf. below, chap. 3 at n. 55).

36. A Charleston family being entertained in New York; friends of the Winthrops as well, cf. BP 7/11/33.

37. FP 12/10/32.

38. Burns enjoyed great popularity, beyond his most familiar poem of 1797, cf. Barck 1 p. 159, 3 p. 264, and his verse to head chapters in T. S. Fay, *Norman Leslie: A Tale of the Present Times* (New York 1835) 1 chap. XI, 2 chap. III; C. Follen, *Sketches of Married Life*, ed. 2 (Boston 1839) p. 94; and Sedgwick (cit., n. 5) 3 p. 81, the heroine "Gertrude loved all the poets—the glorious company; but she preferred the touching simplicity, the penetrating tenderness of Burns."

39. Wife to John Schroeder, assistant rector at Trinity church since 1824.

40. Robert Charles was a young man who occurs in other social contexts, below, and in other parts of the family correspondence, without supplying a clue to his identity.

41. With some uncertainty about which Howland is which, I suggest Mrs. Samuel Howland is meant, here, whose husband was connected with Woolsey in many ways, cf. chap. 3 at nn. 4f. or FP 3/14/28, Laura and Sarah to Theodore; in social ways, FP 11/29/28, 11/19/29; the son Gardner in FP 1/10?-15th/22 or 6/15/29.

42. Perhaps Mrs. Joseph W. Meert (his business on Front Street, cf. fig. 4).

43. On Cadle, see chap. 3 at nn. 15, 52.

44. *Woolsey, Ward & Beach* closed its doors toward the end of 1830, so Carrington was out of work.

45. Sarah to Nathaniel Chauncey, FP 9/26/27.

46. C. M. Sedgwick, *Letters from Abroad to Kindred at Home* (New York 1841) 1 p. 31; cf. below, chap. 3 n. 59.

47. The blank that Sarah leaves can be filled in, cf. below, chap. 3 at n. 31.

48. Mary of the forty-ninth letter.

49. Mrs. John Bullus on Broadway, see fig. 4, below.

50. A likely connection lies through William Cecil Woolsey's father- and mother-in-law, Theodorus and Rebecca Talmadge Bailey, cf. Dwight (cit., n. 18) 1 p. 255.

51. His name appears in chap. 3 n. 6 and elsewhere, and on Mercer and Bond Streets and Broadway (fig. 4): a long-time business associate of Woolsey.

52. He figures in BP 12/10/23, of the family often referred to.

53. Leonard Bacon was an old seminary friend and long-time intimate of Theodore's, married since 1824.

54. Mrs. Hoffman may be sought among the family of Helena who married Moses Rogers' son, Benjamin. The details are in the genealogical material toward the end of the Woolsey Business Papers.

55. John Cadwallader would marry Mary Binney, so, Laura to Theodore, 9/15/28, Sarah to Theodore, 11/14/28; and the family saw the Woolseys and their kin.

56. Elizabeth Dwight (1806–33), daughter of Timothy Dwight (who married Mary Edwards) and grand-daughter of the Yale president, married Samuel Warner Kirkland, cf. Dwight (cit., n. 18) 1 pp. 261f.

57. FP 7/8/32.

58. FP 9/17/26, 5/31/27, 9/13/27, and Alexander Twining to Theodore, 2/26/29; Miss Devereux, a sister (?), also a friend, 5/31/29, 11/5/32, Sarah to Martha Salisbury, 11/?/34, etc.; and other members of the family mentioned, Thomas, "Mr. B.", and John Devereux.

59. FP 10/16/32.

60. John Staples, mentioned as engaged in 1829, Laura to Theodore FP 12/29/29, had been a business partner with William Johnson. It will be his wife who is mentioned here.

61. FP 3/23/33.

62. [Samuel Knapp,] *Extracts from a Journal of Travels in North America . . . by Ali Bey* (Boston 1818) pp. 47, 50, girls of fifteen or sixteen are "looking forward to matrimony as at once their goal and asylum" and "after twenty-five they are regarded as confirmed old-maids"; B. Tuckerman, ed., *The Diary of Philip Hone 1828–1851* (New York 1889) p. 178, "the bride is very young, only seventeen years old"; and very noteworthy in a letter is a girl's engagement at the age of fourteen, Woolsey to Chauncey, FP 10/23/24.

63. FP 7/9/34 is Sarah's first surviving letter to Charles, extremely long and brimming over with confidence in the relationship; nothing more till mentions of him in hers to Martha Salisbury Woolsey, FP 1/21/35; then details of the wedding explained by Laura to Martha, FP 4/6/35; and Sarah on her wedding trip, 8/4/35; etc., happily ever after.

Chapter 3 Notes

1. M. Y. Beach, *Wealth and Pedigree of the Wealthy Citizens of New York City*, ed. 3 (New York 1842) p. 16, Woolsey termed "The Cardinal." The family later traced back the connection, which was not direct.

2. Some dates in the anon. finding aid to the Woolsey Family Papers in the Yale University Archives; Scoville 1 pp. 102f., 107, with Walton House on Pearl Street, the family pew in Trinity Church, and Walton a founding member of the Marine Society; 2 pp. 379ff.=Chapter XXXVIII on the Woolseys; 2 pp. 308f. on Moses Rogers (1750–1825), of *Rogers & Woolsey*; pp. 317f. on Sarah Woolsey the elder (1750–1816) marrying Rogers in 1773; B. W. Dwight, *The History of the Descendants of John Dwight of*

Dedham, Mass. (New York 1874) 1 pp. 167, 248f., Woolsey's marriages to Elizabeth Dwight (1772–1813) and then to Sarah Chauncey (1780–1856), and Timothy Dwight's marriage to Mary Woolsey (1754–1845), Dwight later Yale president; other kin lines, 2 pp. 1091ff.; and a little more in E. Y. Smith, "The descendants of William Edwards, colonist of Conn. Colony, 1639," *New York Genealogical and Biographical Record* 72 (1941) pp. 124ff., 320ff.

3. Besides these presidencies—Edwards' at the end of his life, 1758–59, his son's in 1799–1801—there is the Rev. Sereno Edwards Dwight, son of Timothy, president of Hamilton college in 1833–35, cf. Dwight (cit., n. 2) 1 p. 203. Woolsey through his uncle's daughter, married to James Hillhouse, was also related to that prominent New Haven family, members of which turn up in the correspondence, e.g. FP 9/4/34; and he "was at one time in the firm of *Dwight, Palmer & Co.*, as a secret partner. The senior was one of his New Haven relatives by marriage"—so, Scoville 2 p. 386.

4. Dwight (cit., n. 2) 2 p. 1101 and Scoville at 2 p. 385 tie Emily Aspinwall to a Woolsey; and Scoville at 1 pp. 302, 306, and 2 pp. 337f., gives the highlights of the Howland rise, from Gardner Greene Howland's start as a clerk with the Le Roy firm and later business connections (esp. to Aspinwalls), into the 1830s' emergence of the firm of (William) *Howland & Aspinwall*; cf. also Beach (cit., n. 1) p. 1. For the newspaper ads, see e.g. the 1820 issues of 8/14 and 8/23.

5. Scoville 2 pp. 317ff., 381; John Pintard a cousin of sorts to William Bayard, as was Rev. Lewis Bayard Pintard, see Barck 1 pp. xf., 78; J. Cornell and J. C. Pumpelly, *American Families of Historic Lineage* (New York, n. d.) 3 pp. 24f.; Dwight (cit., n. 2) 2 p. 1097; E. Y. Smith, "Residents on West Side of Greenwich Street (Early Nineteenth Century)" (typescript 1940, New York Historical Society, unpaginated) at #4, Nehemiah Rogers, and at #64, Gardner G. Howland; and M. J. Lamb, *History of the City of New York: Its Origins, Rise, and Progress* (New York 1877–80) 2 p. 375 n. 1.

6. Scoville 2 pp. 310, 313 (Archibald's daughters Sally and Eliza marry the two sons, James G. and Charles, of Rufus King, he of great fame and wealth, with Charles eventually becoming president of Columbia, and, ibid. vol. 1 p. 10, James becoming partner first in *King & Gracie*, then in *Prime, Ward & Co.* ; 3 p. 86; 4 pp. 148f. (Archibald Gracie head of *New York Insurance*, with William Neilson and Henry Wyckoff as directors; son

Robert marries Susan daughter of Neilson). Beach (cit., n. 1) p. 24 adds that Nathaniel Prime, founder of the firm, was set up in business by Rufus King; and as to Smyth Rogers, friend of John Pintard, see Barck 3 p. 50.

7. Woolsey as a clerk, Smith (cit., n. 2) p. 323; aspirants, Scoville 1 pp. 56f.; 2 pp. 12f., 102; and passim; on Murray's *Reader*, see *Sisters* p. 191; on "Daboll" for numbers, ibid. p. 493.

8. E.g., BP 6/29/21, 5/13/23, etc.

9. E.g., BP 9/6/20 and 2/2/21, John Woolsey in the South as Woolsey's agent dealing with customers; also William Woolsey active for his father from down South, e.g. BP 11/29/25, 12/19/34, etc.; BP 10/1/20 or 10/1/20, Samuel William Johnson using his son as his agent; Theodore Woolsey invited to law training in Philadelphia by Charles Chauncey, BP 10/14/20, 11/11/20, 11/16/20, etc., where Theodore finds among other trainees a relative, William Dwight; BP 8/7/23, Woolsey's brother from England sends a son, Charles William, to Woolsey to be trained; John Scarborough a Woolsey agent, too, he being a kinsman through Woolsey's eldest daughter's marriage, BP 4/28/21, etc.; and the Scarborough grandson placed in an apprenticeship in New Haven, FP 5/8/30. Compare Elbridge Gerry, Jr., to Catherine Coles Payne, 10/17/13, on his seeking a law apprenticeship with his brother-in-law (the papers in the Huntington Library); or compare the situation conceived in T. S. Fay's novel, *Hoboken: A Romance of New York* (New York 1843) p. 139, a trusted clerk and a son are handed over the business by the father.

10. E.g. William Gracie in Jamaica, BP 2/16/32, or examples galore in Scofield 2 pp. 61, 214, etc.; C. Sellers, *The Market Revolution: Jacksonian America, 1815–1846* (New York 1991) p. 22; G. S. Wood, *The Radicalism of the American Revolution* (New York 1992) p. 48.

11. BP 12/10/1799, with later indications of real-estate concerns in the correspondence, passim.

12. Scoville 2 pp. 240, 265, 381.

13. J. F. Watson, *Annals and Occurrences of New York City and State in the Olden Time* (Philadelphia 1846) p. 189, population showing a roughly 60% increase by decade, 1810–1820–1830; K. A. Scherzer, *The Unbounded Community. Neighborhood Life and Social Structure in New York City, 1830–1875* (Durham 1992) p. 27; B. Still, "New York City in 1824. A

newly discovered description," *New York Historical Society Quarterly* 46 (1962) p. 137. Lamb (cit., n. 5) 2 p. 437 quotes an estimate of 800,000 as the market accessible through New York's harbor and houses even by the 1790s.

14. "Memorial presented by Board of Trade to Presidents & Directors of all the Banks in this City," BP 3/8/34. Similar vaunts are often cited, e.g. of Fenimore Cooper in his *Notions of the Americans*, Letter VIII, sent to the publisher in 1828, in P. Gould, *Covenant and Republic: Historical Romance and the Politics of Puritanism* (Cambridge 1996) p. 138.

15. I draw examples conveniently from Scoville 2 pp. 320f., 335 (Aspinwall, from 1830 to the '40s); Cadle, 5 p. 53; tea by Astor, 1 p. 91; sugar by Roosevelt, 1 p. 270; sails by Warren, 4 p. 166; J. J. Phelps or Willet Hicks as instances of fortunes made in dry goods, 1 pp. 113, 138f.; Tooker, 2 pp. 365f., adopting the daughter Ellen of his brother-in-law, the great Henry Laverty, see *Sisters* pp. 186, 269f., and passim; his partner's daughter marries another grocer, Scoville 2 p. 377; John MacMullen, for decades on Greenwich Street and able to offer $11,000 for a house lot he already rented from the church, as its records show; Reed or Peter Embury also on Greenwich, Scoville 1 pp. 92, 204f.; and to end with, Isaac Clason whose wealth was founded in the grocery business and who could offer a half million dollars to a good cause, a loan to the U. S. government in 1814, 1 p. 365. It was such exemplars of the trade that led to the suggestion that a New York grocer be included, where none happened to be named, as a director of the Second Bank of the United States, cf. M. E. Brown, *The Second Bank of the United States and Ohio (1803–1860)* (Lewiston 1998) p. 85.

16. Wood (cit., n. 10) pp. 316ff. with notes.

17. E.g., BP 12/11/20, 3/3/21, 1/12/33, 8/8/33.

18. BP 3/8/23, cf. 5/14/23, where George assures his brother that he never doubted his veracity.

19. BP 9/13/20, 9/17/20, 9/19/20, 9/21/20, 10/3/20; cf. the exclamation in 1824 against a world in which the debtor was "degraded and stripped even to the last cow that gives sustenance to his family, to meet the demands of his creditors," quoted from Sellers (cit., n. 10) p. 162.

20. BP 4/7/35, Tappan's great wealth, in the previous decade, reflected in Barck 3 pp. 25, 80, 192; worth $400,000 in 1834, Scoville 1 p. 235, and in the end retired rich, p. 237.

21. C. M. Sedgwick, *Clarence, or, a Tale of Our Own Times* (London 1830) 1 p. 66, cf. p. 182 referring to the same phenomenon as an ordinary fact of life, "families breaking up, and merchants breaking down"; or again, 3 p. 3, "the rich house of his father, Daisy & Co., did what most others, rich and poor, do in our city—failed"; and the last quotation from A. Greene, *The Perils of Pearl Street, Including a Taste of the Dangers of Wall Street by a Late Merchant* (New York 1834) p. 7, with failures described, pp. 32, 138.

22. Barck 2 p. 195, cf. p. 207, "disasters that have prostrated so many both in your city [New Orleans] and this [New York]," with more of the same, pp. 209, registering (p. 285) in his most invulnerable-appearing friends in July of 1826, then striking another (Frederick De Peyster), 3 p. 2, in January of 1828; cf., on one of these years, 1826, I. N. P. Stokes, *The Iconography of Manhattan Island 1498–1909* (New York 1915–28) 5 p. 1653; and earlier (1819) a mention of a similar downfall of a secure-seeming family "belonging to the 'first circle' of society in New York," quoted in M. Kelley, *Private Woman, Public Stage. Literary Domesticity in Nineteenth-Century America* (New York 1984) p. vii, with more on the Panic of that year in Sellers (cit., n. 10) p. 137, and E. S. Kaplan, *The Bank of the United States and the American Economy* (Westport 1999) pp. 67ff.; and Beach (cit., n. 1) p. 7, Levi Coit's son fails and quits the city.

23. Scoville 1 p. 128, who invites in successive volumes of his work correction or additional material from his readers, which he then includes, gives proof of being in touch with a body of good information beyond his own, and responsible to it (e.g. at 4 p. 176); and cites among business failures a number of major players in the game, 1 pp. 162 (a Le Roy), 306 ("hundreds of houses" in 1826); 4 pp. 78f. (in Philadelphia in 1828); 5 p. 35; adding in his novel, *Clarence Bolton: a New York Story, with Society in All Its Phases* (New York 1852) p. 85, a general assessment of the very high likelihood of bankruptcy, in line with what he says in his memoirs, 1 p. 317, that a veteran of the New York mercantile world rated the successes among the merchants at seven in a hundred, and "hundreds of untold thousands have been bankrupts." Further, C. H. Haswell, *Reminiscences*

of an Octogenarian of the City of New York (1816 to 1860) (New York 1896) p. 183, a rash of failures in 1826; Barck 2 p. 90, others in 1821, and, in 1825, the passage cited from 2 p. 195.

24. De Peysters, FP 4/5/22; Coits, L-b 62; these two names, in the preceding note; BP 6/29/21; FP 10/23/24 and 11/25/24 (Hollingsworth and Dillingham, friends of the Woolseys and Dwights); 7/14/32, 7/17/32, 9/1/32, 1/30/33, and 1/31/34, the last, quoted, on Warren (above, n. 15), "failed today, this the most unlooked for, of any that has occurred."

25. E.g., BP 1/1/32, 1/3/34; FP 2/22/25, 1/30/29, 6/30/29, or 12/24/33.

26. Above, n. 3; involvement with Elihu and Charles Chauncey and Timothy Dwight, where Elihu's name must never emerge, and the district attorney's office threatened, cf. BP 8/15/21 and many subsequent letters of August through December 1821, Woolsey advising and handling the printing of anonymous attacks, BP12/21/21; and stockholders' names have been changed, 12/29/21; the immediate cause being the exchange of letters by "Plain Truth" and others in the *New York Daily Advertiser* of 1821, July 24, Aug. 4, 11, 14, 16, 18, 21, 23, Sept. 25, 27, and Oct. 2, 3, 8, and 10, making public charges of bad faith, destabilizing of share prices, and violation of the bank charter for personal gain by "speculators," while the deeper cause was Elihu Chauncey's involvement in the business of the Second Bank of the United States, cf. some indication in Kaplan (cit., n. 22) p. 80.

27. Scoville 2 p. 88; cf. the finding by J. Appleby, *Inheriting the Revolution. The First Generation of Americans* (Cambridge 2000) p. 164, that even in their diaries, Americans "rarely confided their feelings" or much of anything else but the outline of daily doings, as I have certainly found to be true among all classes.

28. BP 12/27/25, son Charles having taken $4,000 from the House to speculate with the money on his own account; more, BP 1/12/27.

29. BP 3/12/34, the writer has a son Edward, identifying the father through FP 12/25/29 or 7/15/30; cf. BP 8/1/25, George to his brother, early difficulties. Woolsey children like Theodore visit and mention their Woolsey uncle and aunt from time to time.

30. FP 10/14/27, 10/30/27, 12/11/27. Dwight (cit., n. 2) 1 p. 255 wrongly dates the start of the firm to 1829; it "did a very heavy business for a few years,

and in 1830 they dissolved," Scoville 1 p. 218 (for 1830, read 1831, see note 31).

31. FP 7/8/32; "only think," writes Sarah, "he [William] entered that firm with a pretty property, 18 months ago, and now is literaly plucked," FP 7/8/32). Benjamin Poor, merchant at 161 Pearl Street, turns up in *Longworth's American Almanac, New-York Register, and City Directory* in the twenties and early thirties, where also *Woolsey, Poor & Convers* did business in 1831–32. *Woolsey, Ward & Beach* had done business on Pearl corner of Pine in 1829–30–31.

32. FP 8/15/33.

33. Scoville 2 p. 384; Dwight (cit., n. 2) 1 p. 250, with an error of dates; B. M. Kelley, *Yale. A History* (New Haven 1974) p. 150; and a great deal of normal business correspondence of Hoadly with the Woolseys, mostly with Mr. Woolsey himself, e.g. BP 10/2/20, with no hint of difficulties until BP 7/28/25, tracing the problems back to 1823; then BP 10/4/25.

34. BP 12/1/25; bank publicity of May 1826 signed by HC and HD (perhaps a Chauncey and a Dwight?); BP 1/5/26 (Strong's publicity release), 8/1/26, 9/25/26, June 1828 (copy of an arrest warrant for Hoadly, charging him with actions going back to 1817); his imprisonment, FP 6/14/28, cf. 7/14/28 (was he really guilty, or deceived? the Woolsey family wonders), 8/27/28 (his trial and conviction), and 9/25/28 (Winthrop to Theodore, quoted).

35. FP 6/16/33.

36. D. A. Ringe, "New York and New England: Irving's criticism of American society," *American Literature* 38 (1967) pp. 458f., 466f. (criticism of commercialism), cf. [S. Knapp,] *Extracts from a Journal of Travels in North America . . . by Ali Bey* (Boston 1818) pp. 85f. (of Boston); Gould (cit., n. 14) pp. 49f.; Sellers (cit., n. 10) p. 153, esp. p. 22, "And because credit was the lifeblood of commerce in this capital-hungry economy [post-1790], success depended upon trust among merchants"; Wood (cit., n. 10) pp. 254f., 325f.; but not to be forgotten, in marveling at a new American pursuit of money, is Dr. Johnson, *The Idler* No. 73 (September 1759), "a nation like ours, in which commerce has kindled an universal emulation of wealth, and in which money receives all the honours which are the proper right of knowledge and virtue."

37. Barck 1 p. 267; 2 p. 270.

38. Greene (cit., n. 21) p. 93; cf. Joel Hawes' *Lectures Addressed to the Young Men of Hartford and New Haven* (1828) p. 112, quoted in K. Halttunen, *Confidence Men and Painted Women. A Study of Middle-Class Culture in America, 1830–1870* (New Haven 1982): reputation "makes friends; it creates funds; it draws around him [the young man] patronage and support; it opens him a sure and easy way to wealth, to honor and happiness."

39. Beach (cit., n. 1) p. 1. The need felt for this work shows in the fact that a third edition (1842), which I use, came out in the same year as the first two and a fourth.

40. Fay (cit., n. 9) p. 139.

41. BP 6/8/22, "very industrious &c when assigned his task in a subordinate station"; FP 9/15/28; and a young nephew of Fenimore Cooper reports on "the brother of a silk merchant in New York in easy circumstances, but as far as I can learn poor himself. He was in Cooperstown before his marriage, when I heard reports about him of an unfavorable character," J. F. Cooper, *Correspondence of James Fenimore-Cooper* (New Haven 1922) 1 p. 236, of 1831.

42. Subscriptions, e.g. B. Tuckerman, ed., *The Diary of Philip Hone 1828–1851* (New York 1889) p. 73, contributors of $500 to the Marine Pavilion in 1833 including Philip and Isaac Hone, Nathaniel (founder of *Prime, Ward & Co.*) and Rufus Prime, John Haggerty, S. S. Howland, Isaac Carow, Isaac Jones, and Henry Laverty; Scoville 1 pp. 329ff., subscribers in 1813 to a war loan, John Howland giving $500,000, John Bullus $10,000, Samuel Tooker $20,000, William Van Ness $20,000, W. P. Van Ness $25,000; but provision needed for men like William Edgard "who gave the best dinners and best wines, but never performed a single act of benevolent duty," cf. Barck 1 p. 343.

43. Scoville 1 pp. 235ff.; cf. 4 p. 195, other merchants with information to match Arthur Tappan's.

44. Scoville 1 p. 155, instancing some names; p. 167, another person "is like most of our old school merchants, pious. He is a prominent member of the Episcopal church."

45. Sellers (cit., n. 10) pp. 29f., 209; D. W. Howe, "The market revolution and the shaping of identity in Whig-Jacksonian America," *The Market*

Revolution. Social, Political, and Religious Expressions, 1800–1880, eds.
M. Stokes and S. Conway (Charlottesville 1996) pp. 261ff.; an indication of
the ubiquity of religious publications in H. M. Jones, *America and French
Culture* (Chapel Hill 1927) pp. 63, 69ff. (tables of types of publication in
1835).

46. Sellers pp. 210f.

47. FP 7/8/32.

48. High patrons of the Society, Barck 1 p. 191; p. 289, Milnor; 3 p. 80, A.
    Tappan gives $5,000; FP 1/7/22, Dwight and Carow, FP 1/3/23, Dwight
    to Woolsey on ABS business, and FP passim on Woolsey's activities as
    treasurer. Succeeding Woolsey in the post was a well known merchant,
    John Adams, cf. Scoville 3 pp. 23, 29, and Barck 4 pp. 11f.

49. Theodore's religious musings and convictions in, e.g., FP 2/22/22, 4/24/22,
    8/17/22; many letters of friends to him; others interested in notable
    preachers, e.g. Papers of Lewis Tappan, Notebook, on microfilm, the
    page for 1828 (visits the Brick Church); A. Nevins and M. H. Thomas,
    eds., *The Diary of George Templeton Strong, 1: Young Man in New York
    1835–1849* (New York 1952) p. 27; Barck 2 p. 39; Charles Chauncey to
    Sarah, FP 1/13/23; Sarah to Theodore, 5/14/27; Theodore's fiancée to him,
    11/5/32 or 11/24/32.

50. His father to Theodore, 1/18/23.

51. Rev. Johnson, cf. Dwight (cit., n. 2) 1 p. 256; Rev. Mathews, cf. Lamb (cit.,
    n. 6) 2 p. 710 and FP 3/29/25; Scoville 4 p. 116, a Trinity Church minister
    on Greenwich St.; Rev. Dr. John N. Abeel of a well known merchant family
    (chap. 1, above, n. 14), vastly rich (Barck 4 p. 123), colleague with Pintard
    in the Historical Society, cf. H. C. Brown, "One of our oldest societies,"
    Valentine's Manual of the City of New York, Ser. 2, 1 (1916–17) p. 61,
    Abeel resident on Water Street, Milnor on Beekman, or Mathews on
    Liberty, then on Broad, cf. *Longworth's Directory* for the 'teens to early
    30s; Barck 3 p. 124 (no dancing in Rev. John Schroeder's and Bishop James
    Onderdonck's company); 1 p. 94, quoted, Pintard first explaining, "Henry
    Ward Beecher . . . would be a small party in Plymouth Church, but for his
    wealthy mercantile congregation."

52. H. W. Jessup, *History of the Fifth Avenue Presbyterian Church of New
    York City, New York, from 1808 to 1908* (New York 1909) p. 7; Scoville

3 pp. 26f., 29 (elder, 1815–55)—but I can say little about the church of the time, being informed that its records begin only from a later date (my thanks to help from the Archivist, E. W. Roberson); Barck 1 p. 47; ibid. p. 283, among other relations in the church, "our kinsman" Lewis Bayard Pintard, officiating at St. Paul's; Trinity Church vestrymen, Scoville 4 p. 166 (Warren), Jessup p. 34 (Howland), M. Dix, *A History of the Parish of Trinity Church in the City of New York*, Part IV (New York 1906) pp. 41, 123, 135, 579 (Cadle through Le Roy, as mentioned in my text); Carow, in H. Anstice, *History of St. George's Church in the City of New York 1752–1811–1911* (New York 1911) p. 53; and Moses Rogers in Dwight (cit., n. 2) 2 p. 1095. On Schroeder, see Dix, Part III (New York 1905) p. 405.

53. A guest in one's pew, Philip Hone's, cf. Tuckerman (cit., n. 42) p. 62; Barck 1 p. 351, Pintard at Grace Church, and 2 p. 35; J. Greenleaf, *A History of the Churches of All Denominations in the City of New York from the First Settlement to the Year 1846* (New York 1846) pp. 62–64; Anstice p. 121, Milnor and the ABS.

54. Barck 2 pp. 231, 236, 270 (quoted); a humble clerk gets $250 to $300, Scoville 1 pp. 238, 320; idem, *Clarence Bolton: a New York Story, with Society in All Its Phases* (New York 1852) p. 57.

55. Jessup (cit., n. 52) pp. 12, 216–26; L-b 62, 164 (Mrs. Staples, cf. Jessup p. 225); Ludlows, in Jessup pp. 219, 225, and FP 4/5/22, 4/22/22 (with 12/29/29, 6/16/33, Rev. H. Ludlow a chum of Theodore's); Lamb (cit., n. 5) 2 p. 446 n. 1 on Ludlow connections with Verplancks etc.; Jessup p. 219, Johnsons; and the other names, Jessup pp. 12, 217f., 222, with FP 11/17/29 (Le Roy) and BP 12/27/30 (Wyckoff) and 1/5/26 (Benjamin Strong).

56. Scoville 5 p. 2, instancing affairs on Pearl Street; clerks, 1 pp. 50f.; an instance, 4 pp. 107f., Emma Beers teaching Sunday school in Trinity, she, sister to the rich Cyrenius, kin through marriage to Benjamin Curtis.

57. With my thanks to R. Heman, Archivist, and J. E. Silver, Historian of the Parish of Trinity Church in the City of New York, I have been able to find relevant material in the *Trinity Church Pew-Book 1806–1814*, the *Records of the Pews 1817–21, St. John's and St. Paul's Chapel*, and *Trinity Church* itself, *Pews in Trinity Church 1822–1828*, the *Pew Book for Trinity Church 1828–1864*, noting Ralph and Sarah Hodge each with their own pew and John MacMullen in 1820–21 as a two-pew holder, who was married to

Lucy Civill in the church in 1807, *Register of Marriages. Trinity Parish New York* 1 p. 315, with others of the family married and buried there.

58. Thomas, Carey, Charles, Gabriel, and Daniel Ludlow (or widow or heirs) in 1816 through 1834; Rufus King in 1806 and sons John and Charles by 1817; William Walton a pew holder, Scoville 1 p. 106; trustees, in Dix (cit., n. 52) p. 182. On the ground floor there were 80 pews in the nave, 15 in each side aisle, more in the balcony.

59. Scoville 2 pp. 137, 142. One daughter married a vestryman, the others, equally well.

60. *Sisters* p. 272 (of 1823).

61. FP 4/15/29.

62. BP 5/14 or 15/23, bill for the "barrouch"; Greenleaf (cit., n. 53) p. 19, on Mathews at the Garden Street church 1813–34; Woolsey attendance, e.g. FP 11/5/32; and many Woolsey mentions of or communications with Mathews.

63. The Woolsey house "the abode of good old fashioned New York hospitality," Scoville 2 p. 384; wine bills, e.g. BP 1/22/28 or FP 5/23/26; Theodore speaks of having in his own more modest establishment "plenty of servants," BP 12/26/33 and 9/8/34 and 9/27/34, references to his "Caesar," an Afro-American servant, cf. his parents' Afro-American servant, I presume one of many, L-b 144; Sarah's "small party" of perhaps forty guests, FP 4/5/22.

64. FP 1/10?-15/22, Sarah to brother John about a ball, or 1/28/30; 12/29/29, Laura writing, "Papa is busy with a dinner party tomorrow which also employs Mama & Sarah, one after the old fashion grand by Alderman Wyckhoff & Hone & which you can imagine if you ever attended one." Compare the extemporized party by Alderman Cowdrey for eighty, celebrating his election, with a second party for 150 immediately following, *Sisters* pp. 298f. For grand parties, the caterers, chefs, confectioners &c most in vogue were hired, cf. FP 1/14/29, Sarah to Theodore, that the Chamber of Commerce has hired "the prince of pastry cooks"; Tuckerman (cit., n. 42) p. 8, Simon the chef famous for years died in 1828; p. 89, a ball calling on all the "artistes"; Scoville 1 p. 397 (Laverty) and Barck 2 p. 319 (Joseph Beers, 1826).

65. E.g. FP 12/31/22, 1/14/29, 12/25/29, 9/13/32 ("only ten" guests in the house).

66. For comparison, there is of course a great deal of family correspondence, some, published, e.g. Cooper (cit., n. 41) 1 pp. 117 (1827), 236, or Eliza Southgate, *A Girl's Life Eighty Years Ago* (New York 1887), passim; but among the Woolseys, see Mary Ann Hoadly, FP 1/26/22; Laura, FP 9/28/27, 12/28/29; Martha Salisbury, FP3/23/33; Sarah's letters, e g. 1/10?–15th/22, 4/5/22, 7/26/26, 9/28/28, or (to Theodore) 4/30/34, "the whole world are engaged." Quoted is Pintard (1819), in Barck 1 p. 174.

67. FP 2/15/29, Laura to Theodore about her new sister-in-law, not rich; Beach (cit., n. 1) p. 5, the daughters of Thomas Buchanan, on whom, see Scoville 1 p. 349, 2 pp. 35, 46, 269 (Jane and Frances, dying unmarried); also, quoted, Beach p. 16.

68. See, e.g. Sedgwick (cit., n. 21) 3 p. 1; Knapp (cit., n. 36) p. 50, to win admirers, girls need "above all, wealth"; quoted, Pintard again, Barck 1 p. 250, "my humble Lily of the Valley [daughter Louise] is born to blush unseen, for partners are only to be found among the gay & venal"; "for such is the state of society here, that a young lady, without money, has a hopeless prospect of settlement" (p. 288, 1820). The comparison of the three cities in A. B. Warner, *Susan Warner ("Elizabeth Wetherell")* (New York 1909) p. 1 (of what was proverbial in the 1830s).

69. Sedgwick (cit., n. 21) 1 p. 65, "the most elevated class" contrasted with "the aristocracy of wealth"; p. 206, "refined taste" contrasted with "the power of wealth"; speech errors characterize the vulgar, 3 pp. 102f.; high cultivation, 3 pp. 280ff.; and often distinguishes the class of person she meets, e.g., one with "the air noble," or scornful of "the inferior orders" on her travels, see her *Letters from Abroad to Kindred at Home* (New York 1841) 1 pp. 147, 188; her pride of ancestry and sense of entitlement to be above others, M. Kelley, ed., *The Power of Her Sympathy. The Autobiography and Journal of Catharine Maria Sedgwick* (Boston 1993) pp. 45ff., 52f., 64. A father who went to Yale and a woman's own education in languages, geography, &c, and more than "paltry accomplishments" in music, will mark one off from "low people [who] have great wealth," so says *Familiar Letters on Subjects Interesting to the Minds and Hearts of Females, by a Lady* (Boston 1834) pp. 16, 78, 87; and Philip Hone looks down on "people who are neither distinguished nor fine, but rich, and that, in their opinion, entitles

them to more consideration than either," cf. Tuckerman (cit., n. 42) p. 34; but Scoville, *Bolton* (cit., n. 23) p. 10, declares wealth will open all doors.

70. C. Follen, *Sketches of Married Life*, ed. 2 (Boston 1839) 1 p. 168.

71. FP 5/20/30 from Martha appears to be her first letter to Theodore, thereafter some in June, etc.; "ever yours" by FP 1/21/31; discussion of a house-lot to purchase at some point in 1831 (FP 1831, undated); FP 7/8/32, Woolsey's long letter to Theodore; and FP 7/11/32, where his mother "regretted that you had not spoken to your Father as was your intention, when you requested me not to do it."

72. After Theodore's vain search for a professorship at other institutions, beginning in the fall of 1830, FP 9/28/30, etc., Woolsey intervenes to set up a professorship at Yale, to be defined by Theodore's long suit, languages, see FP 6/17/31, 8/8/31, etc., ending with a virtual contract written by Woolsey, FP 1/1/32; on the house, FP 11/16?/32, 11/24/32, etc., into details, 3/25/33 (quoted).

73. Scoville 2 pp. 381, Chamber of Commerce, 383 (hospital); on NYU, cf. Dwight (cit., n. 2) 1 p. 249, FP 10/26/33, and 11/19/33, offer of a professorship to a friend by Theodore, no doubt counting on his father to get it; FP 2/10/32, Sarah to Theodore, "good spirits."

74. T. S. Fay, *Views of the City of New York and Its Environs* (New York 1831) pp. 25, 34; Haswell (cit., n. 23) p. 12; Lamb (cit., n. 5) p. 383; Stokes (cit., n. 22) 1 pp. 453f., 5 p. 1279, etc.; and Scoville 1 p. 19, 2 pp. 55ff., 64 (barber, Varick's and Woolsey's names specified among his customers; but this one only to 1808), and 387 (the bar active).

75. Scoville 2 p. 386.

76. Scoville 2 pp. 330f., the St. Andrews', and elsewhere, passim, St. George's, St. Tammany's, and Military Societies, the Columbian Order, etc.

77. Tuckerman (cit., n. 42) p. v notes Philip Hone in the Literary and Philosophical Society; John N. Abeel and John Pintard were among the founders of the Historical Society, cf. Brown (cit., n. 51) p. 61; and Pintard brought together a Literary Club, Barck 1 p. 141; Scoville 2 p. 318 cites Moses Rogers in the Marine Society, the Society to Relieve Distressed Prisoners, and the Society for the Manumission of Slaves, with Woolsey a member of the last; Woolsey was signed into the Society for the Reformation of

Juvenile Delinquents by its president, Cadwallader Colden, BP 5/6/24; Richard Varick, William Bayard, Archibald Gracie, John Aspinwall, John Pintard, and many other names familiar in this study, enrolled in the Free School Society, cf. H. C. Brown, "Beginnings of free public education," *Valentine's Manual of the City of New York*, Ser. 2, 1 (1916–17) pp. 85f.; Pintard belonged to the Corporation of the Sailors' Snug Harbor, Barck 1 p. 47; there was the Seaman's Fund, Tuckerman (cit., n. 42) p. v; Barck 2 p. 199 and 3 p. 197, on the miles of parade by Firemen, Carmen, Butchers, etc. Cf., in general, Wood (cit., n. 10) p. 328.

78. BP 12/27/30 indicates some of the membership: James Olmstead, William Dunlap, Henry Wyckoff, Isaac Carow, Woolsey, and others; and the documents in the case later are many, the statue itself being destroyed not long after it was finally in place.

79. Scoville 1 p. 62; Barck 2 pp. 6f. with Lamb (cit., n. 5) 2 pp. 513f.; p. 706, Bread and Cheese; further, Lamb 2 p. 706, noting members Gulian Crommeline Verplanck, Philip Hone, and (p. 710) the [Philip] Hone Club and the Union Club; and Fenimore Cooper later (1827) joined "a gentlemen's social club called 'The Lunch,'" cf. Stokes (cit., n. 22) 5 p. 1664.

80. Friendly Club: Lamb 2 p. 519; J. T. Horton, *James Kent. A Study in Conservatism 1763–1847* (New York 1939) p. 116; Scoville 2 pp. 335f.; and, setting the meetings not in members' houses in rotation, but weekly at a certain bookstore, J. Appleby, *Inheriting the Revolution. The First Generation of Americans* (Cambridge 2000) p. 182. The relation of Dunlap to the Woolseys is spelled out in Scoville 2 p. 380: Dunlap married Elizabeth Woolsey daughter of Benjamin and sister of our Woolsey (William Walton). Dunlap appears often in the correspondence, e.g. BP 7/11/22, an I. O. U.; 5/11/32, another request to Woolsey to borrow money. The Sketch Club wasn't established until 1829, Stokes (cit., n. 22) 5 p. 1686.

81. I draw the addresses from *Longworth's Directory* for the years in which Sarah and Carrington were engaged. Her letters to him mention close to forty New York family names (and often more than one member within a family), with a score more in correspondence with Theodore or other family members. It will be clear that I have listed both business and residential addresses, so that many names occur twice; and it is not closely

accurate, since there was so much moving around of both, at the time, as was often remarked on in the period.

82. "In 1830 a New Yorker of no very extended acquaintance could tell the names of all the principal merchants, and where they lived," says Scoville on his opening page, and quite believably; cf. 4 p. 190, "business people all knew each other. If not by name, they would know each other by sight. Even now [forty years later], I suppose, I can pick out hundreds of people."

83. Scoville 3 p. 284 lists pallbearers for one great merchant; Barck 1 p. 86 gives the list of another funeral, and (3 p. 267) for Varick, with Tuckerman (cit., n. 42) p. 34. For his association with Woolsey, see also Scoville 5 p. 62 and Jessup (cit., n. 52) p. 219.

84. Sarah to Theodore, undated, FP 1833, and earlier expressions of longing for more company at home.

85. Elizabeth Winthrop, daughter of John Still Winthrop, married Jacob Sebor, cf. [R. C. Winthrop], *A Short Account of the Winthrop Family* (Cambridge 1887) pp. 12f.; she was his second wife, after a Wyckoff daughter, Scoville 1 p. 122; son William at no. 57, 1831–34, and Woolsey *père* at no. 59, in *Longworth's* for 1833–39 (his death), but, less reliably, at no. 61, cf. E. Y. Smith, "Residents on West Side of Greenwich Street (Early Nineteenth Century)," typescript 1940, N. Y. Historical Society, unpaginated, under #61; the family had been on the street since at least 1822, FP 4/22/22; it was losing value by the 1840s, Scoville loc. cit. and George T. Strong, who was born there in 1820, quoted in K. A. Scherzer, *The Unbounded Community. Neighborhood Life and Social Structure in New York City, 1830–1875* (Durham 1992) p. 23.

86. When Harry Sedgwick moved into town (he, publicist and editor to his sister the novelist), it was on Greenwich that he bought, cf. M. E. Dewey, ed., *Life and Letters of Catherine M. Sedgwick* (New York 1871) p. 104; "all the wealth and fashion was in that quarter" in 1810, so, Scoville 2 p. 315; "a rich neighborhood," 4 p. 116.

87. A sort of proto-Baedeker published in 1828, labeling some streets as "fashionable" or not, cf. Stokes (cit., n. 22) 1 p. 1673; Broad Street, Scoville, *Bolton* cit., n. 13, p. 56: idem 1 pp. 328, Park Place, "aristocratic quarter," and p. 22, Pearl Street "most aristocratic," with Barck 4 p. 90, Pearl Street "this great Bazar of our dry goods trade."

88. Sellers (cit., n. 10) p. 238, of the year 1828.

89. Sedgwick (cit., n. 21) 2 p. 38, a Good Person addresses a letter to another as "esquire", cf. *Sisters* p. 380 of 1826, or FP 7/12/32, John Woolsey careful to "Esquire" his father; another correspondent properly careful, FP 4/25/35; seating, Sedgwick 3 pp. 13, 124, cf. *Sisters* p. 208 (1821); "*visitable,*" Sedgwick 3 pp. 102f., her italics; "no one was alowed to put their heads inside the house unless in full ball dress," *Sisters* p. 293, cf. pp. 160, 186, etc., for inability to accept invitations in a dress too poor; ibid. p. 293 and Haswell (cit., n. 24) pp. 150f., a mere barber may not attend a ball; C. Mulvey, *Transatlantic Manners. Social Patterns in Nineteenth Century Anglo-American Travel Literature* (Cambridge [UK] 1990) pp. 12, 66; Halttunen (cit., n. 42) pp. 62f., 96, ascribing to the middle class, on which alone she intends to focus, the same aggressive insistence on "fashion" and position that I find among the upper class. But in fact she is sometimes speaking about the upper class.

90. Follen (cit., n. 70) pp. 20ff., with Mr. Selmar's remarks to be quoted in the next paragraph.

91. An upper-class young woman must discard "foolish pride" about working, for "it is always honorable to earn a livelihood," says Fenimore Cooper to a niece, Cooper (cit., n. 41) 1 p. 248f. (1831), where he also makes plain that he intends to dower and marry off his own daughters; for "protectors," cf. e.g. L-b 182 or FP 12/24/33, or "trusted guardian," L-b 40; N. F. Cott, *The Bonds of Womanhood. "Woman's Sphere" in New England, 1780–1835* (New Haven 1977) p. 53, noting the exceptional concern in one woman's letters, cf. F. R. Morse, ed., *Henry and Mary Lee: Letters and Journals . . . 1802–1860* (Boston 1926) p. 205 (1813); Wood (cit., n. 10) p. 343; and E. Foner, "Free labor and nineteenth-century political ideology," *The Market Revolution in America. Social, Political, and Religious Expressions, 1800–1880,* eds. M. Stokes and S. Conway (Charlottesville 1996) p. 113.

92. See the treatments of women referred to in the previous note; Sarah contemptuous of "the vulgar classes" and their silly ideas, FP 3/12/25; and "menials" and "gentlemen" distinguished, in the bank, by Chauncey to Woolsey, BP 8/30/21.

93. FP 7/19/22.

94. Woolsey to Theodore, FP 10/31/28; Laura to Theodore, 9/15/28 and
    6/15/29; and Woolsey again, 10/29/29, flowed together, to which views
    Martha Salisbury supplies an echo in due course, FP 3/17/32. For Wool-
    sey's views generally on usefulness, see also FP 1/18/23.

95. L-b 62.

96. As George Bancroft upon returning from Paris kissed his friend Andrew
    Norton, a greeting received with long-cherished outrage, cf. O. W. Long,
    Literary Pioneers. Early American Explorers of European Culture (Cam-
    bridge 1935) pp. 140f.

97. So, Murat in 1824, quoted from Jones (cit., n. 45) p. 277.

98. Fay (cit., n. 9) p. 139; L-b 53, 108.

99. Worley v. Walling, I Har. & John. 208 (Md. 1801), where the father claimed
    no right to prevent the marriage, though he might reward a daughter's
    obedience; Ellis v. Hull, 2 Aiken 41 (Vt. 1826), where the bride must be
    eighteen but the law falls only on the minister officiating; U. S. v. Mc-
    Cormick, 26 Fed. Cas. 1059 (D. C. 1802), where the bride must be sixteen;
    Stansbury v. Bertron, 7 W. & S. 362 (Pa. 1844), where again the law falls
    only on the minister, if the bride is under twenty-one; and Donahue v.
    Dougherty, 5 Rawle 124, 127–128 (Pa. 1835), where the minister is at fault
    if the bridegroom is a minor and the father gives no consent. M. Gross-
    berg, *Governing the Hearth: Law and the Family in Nineteenth-Century
    America* (Chapel Hill 1985) pp. 330f. cites but somewhat misrepresents
    the law, while offering valuable discussion elsewhere, pp. 26f., 66f., 74,
    106f.

100. In fiction, parental consent to a marriage figures only if it is withheld for
     reasons the novelist presents as wrong, cf. e.g. Sedgwick (cit., n. 21) 1
     pp. 243f., 3 p. 34 (the girl, only 16); or Susanna Rowson in her immensely
     popular *Charlotte* (Philadelphia 1794) 1 p. 36 espousing parental consent-
     rights, but for teen-age girls. The picture recoverable in letter-manuals
     favors free choice and attraction, cf. R. Chartier et al., *Correspondence.
     Models of Letter-Writing from the Middle Ages to the Nineteenth Cen-
     tury*, trans. C. Woodall (Cambridge 1997) pp. 98f. K. Lystra, *Searching the
     Heart. Women, Men, and Romantic Love in Nineteenth-Century Amer-
     ica* (New York 1989), e.g. pp. 159ff., concerns herself generally with a
     later period and different classes than I am concerned with, and with-

out regarding locus and social position; and D. S. Smith, "Parental power and marriage patterns: an analysis of historical trends in Hingham, Massachusetts," *Journal of Marriage and the Family* 35 (1973) pp. 422ff, is careful and specific but regards a milieu very different from upper-class New York. E. K. Rothman, *Hands and Hearts. A History of Courtship in America* (New York 1984) pp. 27, 30, sees the young as generally in control by the turn of the 19th century. In real life, among Woolsey's peers, I can instance only Pintard, recording an elopement without serious consequences, Barck 1 p. 172; his own consent casually mentioned, to his teen-ager daughter's marrying, 2 p. 150; strong condemnation of a minister who knowingly married an of-age woman against her father's wishes, 3 pp. 181f., where, however, the mother consented; and Scoville 1 p. 78 seeing the rigid affirmation of a father's rights as something very old-fashioned and English. It may be worth mentioning that Sarah at the age of seventeen saw her brother William engaged and reported to Theodore, FP 7/24/22, "This took place upon the condition of her parents' consent"; and in 1829 a young woman friend of hers baulked a suitor by yielding to her mother, and accompanying her to Europe—where he eventually pursued her, FP 10/19/29.

101. L-b 146, 160, in Sarah's view Carrington was prosperous enough to qualify by her father's own standard; and FP 7/8/32, Woolsey to Theodore, at the end of the letter, "to Sarah, nothing."

102. FP 7/9/34.

103. Charles Johnson's character was often remarked on: FP 9/26/27, Sarah noting his "awkward exterior"; an orphan, hard to read and buttoned-up, so, his cousin William to Theodore, 10/31/28; "surrounded by many friends he has always [been] in some measure an isolated being," Laura to Theodore, 6/15/29; and Sarah after marriage, to Martha, "we are both so disinclined to company," 1/21/35.

104. Dwight (cit., n. 2) 1 p. 250, death in 1870.

Index

MacMullen first pages   2000/11/21 12:57 v5.9a   p. 201   Windfall Software

A forgotten love affair emerges from a woman's letters. The story reads like a novel, anticipating Henry James' *Washington Square* (*The Heiress*): with the same charming young businessman, the same devoted fiancée, a very rich implacable father, and a setting in upper-class New York of the second quarter of the 19th century. The end of the affair, however, is very different, and unexpected.

Sarah Woolsey – called on to make the agonizing choice shown in the correspondence – belonged to the best of families: herself, sister of a president-to-be of Yale, niece of a Yale president, great-grand-daughter of Yale's first intellectual luminary, Jonathan Edwards. Beyond these names, so prominent in New Haven, her ties and acquaintances in New York were all of the same set. It is this world that she gently tests, and cannot much change, as a woman with a mind of her own.

Readers may enjoy a dramatic and touching story; but there is much more here. With a new and special vividness, the letters and rich surrounding sources provide a picture of older, more dominant values and some of the developing trends to be found in New York, New Haven, and other centers of the eastern upper classes in the early generations of the Republic.

Recent winner of a lifetime Award for Scholarly Distinction given by the American Historical Association, Ramsay MacMullen is the author of *Sisters of the Brush . . . 1797-1833* among other history books. He is Dunham Professor of History at Yale, emeritus.